mlr

MARXISTLEFTREVIEW.ORG   NO.19 $17

Marxist Left Review

Editor: Omar Hassan
Editorial team: Mick Armstrong, Sandra Bloodworth, Omar Hassan,
Louise O'Shea
© Social Research Institute

Published by Socialist Alternative
Melbourne, January 2020

PO Box 4354
Melbourne University, VIC 3052

www.marxistleftreview.org
email: MarxistLeftReview@gmail.com

Contributions to *Marxist Left Review* are peer reviewed.

ISSN 1838-2932
rrp. $17

Printed by IngramSpark.

Subediting and production by Tess Lee Ack; proofreading by Diane Fieldes.
Cover by James Plested.

CONTENTS

RESISTING BARBARISM: CONTOURS OF THE GLOBAL REBELLION

OMAR HASSAN

The last twelve months were defined by the dramatic return of sustained and militant protests. Around the world, workers and students poured onto the streets demanding fundamental social change. "Much of the world at this moment is a laboratory searching for the cure for capitalism, and the social scientists running the experiments are in the streets"[1] wrote veteran US socialist Dan La Botz. Jack Shenker writing in the *Guardian* identified the youth leading these revolts as "the children of the financial crisis – a generation that has come of age during the strange and febrile years after the collapse of a broken economic and political orthodoxy, and before its replacement has emerged".[2]

The causes of the rebellion have been widely discussed by a press corps disturbed by their insurrectionary verve. The *New York Times* has suddenly rediscovered the existence of workers and the poor,

---

Omar Hassan is an editor of *Marxist Left Review*. He has long been a leading activist in the Palestine solidarity movement and has written extensively on the Middle East.

[1]   Daniel La Botz, "The world up in arms against austerity and authoritarianism", *Solidarity,* 12 December 2019, www.solidarity-us.org/the-world-up-in-arms-against-austerity-and-authoritarianism/.

[2]   Jack Shenker, "This wave of global protest is being led by the children of the financial crash", *The Guardian,* 12 December 2019.

describing the protests as "a louder-than-usual howl against elites in countries where democracy is a source of disappointment, corruption is seen as brazen, and a tiny political class lives large while the younger generation struggles to get by".[3]

The revival of revolt should come as no surprise. The post-GFC era has seen the intensification of class war through low pay, high rates of youth unemployment, unaffordable housing and education and an ostentatiously wide gap between rich and poor. These factors combine to produce a generation pessimistic about their future and angry about their present.

The mass strikes that shook France at the end of 2019 are typical. Emmanuel Macron was elected as a centrist saviour – neither left nor right but modern. In reality his presidency sought to reboot the French economy through savage attacks on workers and their organisations, most recently with proposed cuts to pensions. Under pressure from the rank and file, unions have called a number of major general strikes, which have been strengthened by more localised but ongoing actions by railway workers, petrol workers, teachers and others. Actions continued throughout Christmas holidays, as activists refused to give Macron the present of social peace. At the time of writing, the strikes had been running for 29 days straight, the longest period of continuous strike action since 1968. The determination of the Yellow Vest protesters prepared the ground for this breakthrough, normalising widespread and militant opposition to Macron. These crucial events are a reminder that the West will not remain immune to the social eruptions being seen in Santiago, Baghdad and Hong Kong. By bringing the global revolt to the imperial centre, French strikers have made it possible to imagine the defeat of neoliberalism at the core of the capitalist system.

★★★★★★★★★★★★★★★

---

[3]   Declan Walsh and Max Fisher, "From Chile to Lebanon, protests flare over wallet issues", *New York Times,* 12 December 2019.

For those looking, the first signs of the coming storm were visible late in 2018. Following weeks of militant protests by the Yellow Vests in France, Algeria and Sudan exploded with revolutionary fervour. North Africa thrummed to the beat of rebellion as protesters packed squares, brought down tyrants in quick succession, and once again began to dream of a democratic and socially just society. The Sudanese movement was particularly notable, led as it was by the Sudanese Professionals Association. This organisation echoed the long traditions of working class politics in that country, and gave the movement much needed backbone in both an organisational and political sense. After months of recurring street protests and strikes, an uneasy compromise was negotiated with the military. Many rightly criticised the final deal as too much of a concession to the old regime. Yet as Gilbert Achcar argues in this journal, the ongoing strength of the SPA and broader mobilisations mean that, as in Tunisia post-2011, the space remains open for further struggles.

Just as these negotiations were coming to a close, news began to trickle in of sizeable protests in Hong Kong. Having long established itself as an investment hub linking the Chinese bourgeoisie with the giants of global capital, its reputation was that of a corporate paradise. Back in 2014, the Umbrella Movement had presented a very different view of the city-state; a place of enormous inequality, growing attacks on already limited democratic freedoms, and a population determined to resist encroaching dictatorship. Those protests were repressed and their leaders imprisoned, but the same issues brought demonstrators back to the streets in unprecedented numbers in 2019, triggered this time by the proposed extradition law. It was impossible to ignore the movement after 1 July, when thousands of activists stormed the Legislative Council complex and trashed the pseudo-parliament. Intriguingly, the aftermath of this aggressive action saw little in the way of denunciations, and popular support for the movement remained high. This was demonstrated on 18 August, when an estimated two million people flooded the streets.

This pattern held through the year. There have been ebbs and flows in the mobilisations, yet the mass of people still view protesters favourably. Even the front line fighters, who engage in serious street fighting with police on a daily basis, are viewed fondly. To the distant observer reliant on the mainstream media, it seemed that the dramatic battles around the occupied universities could be one step too far, isolating the militants and giving the state *carte blanche* to brutally repress them. Yet the experience showed once again, that when the cause is just, people will accept and even celebrate violent struggle.

The occupation of the Polytechnic, which should find a place among the most heroic of all time, confirms this prognosis. Daily dispatches from *Red Flag* editor Ben Hillier described the defiant mood:

> "If we burn, you burn with us." For days, hundreds of young women and men raced frantically to barricade every entrance and exit. In the canteen they stockpiled noodles, biscuits, muesli bars, and bottles of water. Along with their supporters, they took over the retail shops and turned them into 24-hour communal kitchens. They set up medical stations with boxes and boxes of supplies. They collected for distribution hundreds of gas masks, goggles, fresh clothes, towels and soap. They armed themselves with bins full of broken paving bricks and garden stones, baseball bats, hammers and metal bars pilfered from railings along the roadsides. And they built an arsenal of Molotov cocktails, gas bombs, flour bombs and dye bombs. By Saturday afternoon, there were hundreds of petrol bombs to feed the front lines – and for the next 36 hours, a group of about 30 young people worked tirelessly to keep production going as the war raged around them.[4]

The people of Hong Kong responded with mass solidarity to growing police attacks on the university, with thousands thronging to public spaces across the region to divide police forces and assist the besieged activists to make an escape. This experience, one of many, reflects the findings of research into popular attitudes. Polling done by the Chinese University of Hong Kong in October found that

---

[4]   Ben Hillier, "Hong Kong: Why 'generation catastrophe' is rising up", *Red Flag*, 12 December 2019, www.redflag.org.au/node/6958.

59 percent agreed that "when large-scale protests cannot force the government to respond, it is understandable that protesters would take radical actions".[5] An impressive 49 percent rated their trust of the police at 0 on a scale of 0–10, while less than 10 percent blamed protesters for the escalating violence.[6] All of this was shown, yet again, in big wins for pro-democracy candidates in the elections to the district council elections.

Aside from the movement's unashamed militancy and widespread popularity, its other remarkable feature has been its longevity. Protesters have so far faced down violent assaults by gangsters linked to pro-Beijing politicians, intense police repression and the constant threat of military intervention by China. The latter was signalled early on, when Beijing sent dozens of troop-carrying trucks to neighbouring Shenzhen province. Coming soon after the anniversary of the Tiananmen uprising, activists had every reason to take this not-so-subtle warning seriously. Yet they have persisted, winning their first demand, the withdrawal of the extradition bill, and popularising the demand for universal suffrage in electing the legislature and chief executive.[7] The enormous rally on New Year's Day, chanting "resist tyranny: join a union", will surely have sent shivers down the spine of tyrants in Beijing. There is no sign that the movement is exhausting itself.

While Hong Kong successfully captured the world's attention, it could be read as an anomaly. But mass protests in Puerto Rico, Catalunya, Ecuador, Chile, Haiti, Egypt, Iraq, Lebanon and others made the pattern clearer.

The return of revolutionary struggle to the Middle East and North Africa is perhaps the most inspiring aspect of the new wave of revolt.

---

[5]   Francis Lee, "Our research in Hong Kong reveals what people really think of the protesters – and the police", *The Independent,* 12 December 2019.

[6]   Verna Yu, "Support for Hong Kong's rebels wavers after most violent week yet", *The Guardian,* 12 December 2019.

[7]   Francis Lee, "Our research in Hong Kong reveals what people really think of the protesters – and the police", *The Independent,* 12 December 2019.

After the devastation wreaked on the Syrian people for daring to challenge tyranny, it seemed likely that decades would have to pass before a new outbreak of struggle. Not so. Moved by events in Sudan and Algeria, activists in Egypt, Iraq and Lebanon have had the courage to throw themselves at the mercy of history once again. Protesters in Iraq deserve special mention. It is breathtaking to think of the determination required to continually protest in a country so ravaged by local and international elites, where hundreds have been killed by a government prepared to use machine guns on unarmed civilians. It is also highly significant that the protests against the Iranian-backed, sectarian Shi'ite government started in the predominantly Shi'ite south. That this kind of anti-sectarian uprising could then overflow into Iran is momentous. It is an example of the terrible cynicism that has distorted large parts of the left that some have failed to recognise the uprising in Iran as part of the global rebellion against neoliberalism. The reality is that these embryonic developments, along with the protests in traditional Shi'ite areas in southern Lebanon and Baalbek, offer the possibility of constructing a new identity for Shi'ite activism, free from the counter-revolutionary influence of the ayatollahs.

The movements in Latin America, particularly in Chile, have been noteworthy for the relatively strong influence of the left. For some time, the crisis of reformist governments across the continent seemed to be creating the conditions for an inevitable expansion of the hard right, symbolised by the victory of Bolsonaro in Brazil. Yet the underlying social and economic polarisation continues to find expression on the left as well as right, meaning the right has faced considerable resistance.

The radicalism and breadth of protests in the last year have led some to describe it as a Latin American Spring. In Ecuador, an attempt to increase the cost of fuel was repulsed following militant demonstrations, while protests in Haiti and Honduras have spent months demanding the fall of their US-backed presidents. An attempted coup in Bolivia was met with a spontaneous uprising of overwhelmingly Indigenous workers and peasants, though Movement for Socialism (MAS) has subsequently agreed to wind it up and allow the coup leader to remain in power in exchange for a new election. Protests in Puerto Rico brought down a government, and a general strike in Colombia evolved into a broader rebellion against the right wing regime. Until now, Argentina has been pacified by the prospect of the incoming populist Peronist government. Yet the severe economic crisis engulfing the country, the neoliberal nature of the new administration and the relative strength of the revolutionary left means that struggle is likely. Much of this was prefigured by the welcome resurgence of women's organising in recent years, with huge protests and strikes on International Women's Day demanding abortion rights and an end to sexual violence among other things.

If the situation in Latin America deserves more attention, Chile demands it. Numerous protests have shaken Piñera's grip on power and the regime's links to Pinochet's neoliberal dictatorship have been exposed. These include a constitution from the Pinochet era that has barely been altered and a willingness to deploy the military to repress protesters. Piñera embodies much of this continuity; his elder brother served as a key minister under Pinochet, and Piñera is on the record as opposing Pinochet's 1998 arrest. The mass movement in opposition to this vicious government has combined mass street demonstrations with working class actions shaped by existing – though much weakened – left traditions. Strikes by sections of the working class have been important, and have helped make the Chilean protests the most political and explicitly left wing of the revolts. This is reflected in the fact that the demand for a constituent assembly, which for its all its faults is a slogan of the left, has captured the imagination of millions. It is too early to tell whether the constitutional process initiated by Piñera will be sufficient to appease the movement, but it will leave an impact regardless.

As with any such wave of rebellion, there are both universal and locally specific dynamics to the struggles. Economic inequality is an obvious common factor. Another is the central role played by women. A Chilean feminist collective's artistic denunciation of Piñera's regime has been replicated in mass actions around the world.

There have been strong mobilisations of women in Hong Kong, Sudan, France and Lebanon, with women leading protests as well as fighting police and reactionary thugs on the streets.

The fight to defend and extend democracy is another common factor in these struggles, just as it was back in 2011. Catalunya rose up after the supreme court handed down harsh sentences to politicians for the "crime" of organising a referendum. This flagrant act of suppression and the struggle it triggered shares some similarities with the protests in Hong Kong and to a lesser extent Scotland, being largely framed around democratic rights and freedoms. Protests in Sudan, Algeria, Egypt and Hong Kong also have had democratic aspirations at their core. As Lenin explained in 1903, "without political freedom, all forms of worker representation will remain pitiful frauds; the proletariat will remain as before in prison, without the light, air and space needed to conduct the struggle for its full liberation".[8]

The issues of democracy and inequality are fundamentally interrelated. In an article discussing the success of pro-democracy candidates in Hong Kong elections, the *South China Morning Post* explained that "inaction in land and housing production, plus the widening wealth gap, sowed the seeds of separatism and disaffection towards mainland China among young people, with growing doubts about their future in a rising China".[9] Many who have reported on Hong Kong insist on emphasising the democratic component, yet it is unlikely that broad support for the movement would be so high in a less dramatically unequal society.[10] These connections can also be found in Scotland and to a lesser extent Catalunya. In both cases

---

[8] Lih 2008, p199.

[9] Regina Ip, "Anti-government victory in Hong Kong's district council elections won't bring about peace", *South China Morning Post*, 12 December 2019.

[10] Shirley Zhao and Bruce Einhorn, "How Hong Kong's taxes spawned billionaires and bred inequality", *Bloomberg*, 12 December 2019, www.bloomberg.com/news/articles/2019-10-15/how-hong-kong-s-taxes-spawned-billionaires-and-bred-inequality.

independence is associated with a more progressive and inclusive welfare state.

Further, it is not just in dictatorships or struggles for self-determination that the question of democracy has emerged. Slogans for real democracy have been raised even in countries that already possess formal bourgeois parliaments, and where protests began with more strictly economic demands. The slogan from the M15 movement in the Spanish state, "All of them must go!", has spontaneously arisen in country after country, finding its most direct translation in Lebanon with the chant "All of them means all of them". Importantly, these grievances cannot be accommodated by a simple shuffling of the personalities in power. We have already noted the demands of protesters in Chile to abolish the Pinochet-era constitution. In Lebanon, hostility to the sectarian system introduced by the French and strengthened by the 1990 Taif accords is palpable, and similar sentiments are expressed across the globe, from Paris to Baghdad. This line of attack on the system isn't surprising, given the decades of bipartisan, or multipartisan in the case of Lebanon, neoliberal policies. In the absence of a substantial organised radical left, this fusion of economic and political demands via explosive and uncontrolled movements seems to be the new pattern of social struggle in the post-GFC era.

Challenges and opportunities

It would be naive not to see the many challenges that these new movements will face. Most have taken place in countries in the global South, and have faced a global ruling class more cynical than in 2011. Then, the media thronged to cover the heroic activists, with *Time* magazine awarding "the protester" person of the year. Media organisations sought to make a name for themselves by reporting with exhilarating immediacy from the Arab street, led by the newly launched Al Jazeera English. That coverage helped spread the rebellion from the Middle East to Europe and North America, in the form of the movement of the squares, and then Occupy. This time the corporate media have been far less inclined to provide revolutionary activists with a platform. Hong Kong is a partial exception, where activists have been battling it out with Xi Jinping's thugs. Still, the activists there have not enjoyed the unambiguous support of a Western ruling class, who now fear the democratic impulses of the masses far more than their geopolitical rivals. Their struggle is not front page news, nor has there been any meaningful assistance offered.

On a related point, protesters this time around have faced states more immediately ready to resort to repression. This is most vividly illustrated by the violence of the coup and anti-coup actions in Latin America, but also in the massacres seen in Iraq and Iran. Accompanying the preparedness to use force has been an unwillingness to make meaningful concessions. Even in Chile and Hong Kong, the sites of the most sustained struggles, little has been achieved in policy terms. In the heartland of supposedly advanced capitalism, the French police have used brutal tactics against unarmed protesters and strikers. In an extraordinary break with tradition, the bourgeois media have at times been forced to admit that "violence is sometimes the answer", aptly denouncing double standards of mainstream reporting:

> Calling for protesters to always remain nonviolent winds up normalizing further state violence as an acceptable response when protesters hit back. Even if protesters only resort to violence after attacks by security forces, it is painted as "both sides" being violent in "clashes", despite inequalities in firepower or protesters condemning violence within their ranks. The burden is placed on protesters to sacrifice themselves in the name of nonviolence, rather than putting the onus on better-armed and trained security forces to maintain their own nonviolent discipline. When even security forces in liberal democracies such as France use disproportionate violence against protesters, it is crucial not to deflect responsibility from state actors,

who are usually more organized and far more militarily powerful than protesters.[11]

Yet should the protests continue, they will face more sophisticated methods of counter-revolution. The betrayal of the Sudanese revolution by the Forces for Freedom and Change, and the vacillations of the bureaucratic leadership of the SPA, were an early taste of how immense radicalism can be led down a blind alley. A similar danger presents itself in Chile, where the Communist Party and the *Frente Amplio* (Broad Front) are desperately attempting to engineer a parliamentary solution to the social crisis. The government's decision to initiate months of wrangling around a constitutional referendum is an obvious trap. In Lebanon and Iraq sectarianism is entrenched in a host of institutions, not to mention social and geographical realities, and will not easily be overcome despite promising early signs. Elsewhere, imperial interventions, be they military or fiscal, make genuine social transformation difficult and provide ready excuses for hesitant reformers. In all these ways and more, history has repeatedly shown that spontaneous uprisings are not enough to overcome the many trenches and fortresses protecting the power of capital. Faced with an immovable state, a previously unstoppable movement can easily flip from supposedly leaderless autonomism into bureaucratic electoralism, as per Podemos.[12] The absence of a sizeable revolutionary left inevitably puts a political ceiling on the development and horizons of even the most heroic struggles.

The other limit of the struggles relates to their class character. While the majority of those mobilised are members of the urban working class understood in the Marxist sense, they are not mobilised as such. Rather, they act as individual citizens: as democrats, feminists, environmental activists, and so on. These kinds of popular

---

[11] Kai Thaler, "Violence is sometimes the answer", *Foreign Policy,* 12 December 2019, www.foreignpolicy.com/2019/12/05/hong-kong-protests-chile-bolivia-egypt-force-police-violence-is-sometimes-the-answer/.

[12] Hassan 2016.

movements can pressure governments in crucial ways, and provide rich experiences and much needed skills for those who participate. But in a time of widespread economic stagnation and instability, they are not enough to force the ruling class to implement substantial reforms. Without the unique leverage created by stopping the flow of profits at the point of production, protesters risk exhaustion, governmental repression or some combination of the two. This makes the strikes in France immensely significant, not only for their geopolitical location but their methods of combat. If the rank and file union groups can continue to organise independently of the moribund bureaucracy, if the strikes continue to grow through the summer, and if they can win wider support from students and others, there is a good chance that the movement could decisively defeat Macron for the first time. These are, of course, substantial ifs. But in such a scenario, the demonstrated effectiveness of working class power could inspire copycat actions around the world, as per the occupation of public squares in 2011.

Despite these many challenges, the experience of Hong Kong and to an even greater extent, Chile, offers real hope. Successive generations of activism in both countries have led to more radical and sustained protests than elsewhere. Chile has now seen three cycles of protests, each more radical than the last. Protests started among school students in 2006, before spreading to universities in 2012. In the latest round of strikes and protests, radicals trained by previous struggles have taken a leading role, including in strategic sectors such as the dock workers of Valparaiso. Yet Chile also shows how sustained periods of struggle can revitalise reformist forces – former student leader Camila Vallejo has helped rebuild the credibility of the Communist Party, while many of the leading cadres of the Broad Front were mask-wearing autonomists just a few years earlier.

Studying these rich experiences is vitally important. This is doubly the case for those with the misfortune of living in the English-speaking world, which suffers from historically weak levels of class struggle and a left that is for the most part trapped in the orbit of electoral celebrities. With the return of mass movements globally, it is useful to recall Lenin's backhanded defence of electoral work:

> The Bolsheviks regard direct struggle of the masses…as the highest form of the [socialist] movement, and parliamentary activity without the direct action of the masses as the lowest form of the movement.[13]

This is a particularly important argument to emphasise given Jeremy Corbyn's substantial defeat in the 2019 UK elections. There is much to unpack and critique from this experience: the two most obvious issues being the endless series of concessions he made to moderates in the party and the failure of the Labour left to organise and support class or social struggle. Yet these weaknesses are the product of Labour's strategy – Corbyn's as much as Tony Blair's – of prioritising the electoral victory of a broad-church party. Any organisation that contains figures such as Tom Watson and Margaret Hodge will not and cannot bring about any kind of radical transformation. Certainly not in the absence of substantial struggle. Corbyn's commitment to the unity of the Labour party led him to backflip on Britain's Trident nuclear program, on freedom of movement, on Palestinian liberation, self-determination for Scotland and more. Despite this bitter defeat, and notwithstanding the fact that many on the Labour left continue to focus on internal party affairs, the key factor shaping British politics in coming years will be whether unions and the left can generate grassroots resistance to the coming onslaught. With climate change, anti-migrant racism, economic inequality and the various national questions looming as issues, there is no shortage of openings to organise.

Climate crisis, climate rebellion

The issue of climate change has thus far proved to be the major flashpoint for political resistance in the global north. The Intergovernmental Panel on Climate Change report last year gave humanity twelve years to avoid catastrophic climate damage. The

---

[13] Lenin 1909.

prospect of a time limit has raised the stakes in climate organising. Yet, as Hannah Holleman points out in her useful research on the Dust Bowl crisis of the 1930s, warnings about climate destruction have been seen and ignored before.[14] What was decisive in this case was the decision made by a young woman from Sweden, Greta Thunberg, to skip class every Friday until something was done to address the coming climate disaster.

Led by Thunberg, the climate strikes have provided a focal point around which a broad coalition of high school activists and their supporters have coalesced. Thunberg herself is rightly revered for her incisive speeches that sheet home the blame for planetary destruction to the insatiable greed of a global elite. These arguments, and the movement that she has mobilised in her wake, have noticeably transformed the politics of the issue. While not explicitly rejecting ethical consumption, the new movement centres the need for a total social rebellion against the complicity and complacency of governments and corporations. The choice of the word strike is significant, and offers opportunities for class-based collaboration that have been realised in some places.

The likelihood that we may have already crossed a number of irreversible planetary boundaries that will now trigger runaway climate change is sobering, to say the least. Yet as Sarah Garnham writes in her survey of the state of the climate movement, this is no reason to give up. There is still much to fight for, both in limiting the scale of planetary destruction and in ameliorating the social impact of the enormous changes that are already guaranteed. A number of other articles in this edition attempt to engage seriously with arguments and issues raised by the new movement. Da Silva presents important research regarding the centrality of coal to the Australian economy, and draws out the revolutionary political implications. Garnham assesses the politics of the global climate movement and makes a cohesive argument for a mass, militant, anti-capitalist perspective. In

---

[14] Holleman 2018.

the midst of a multi-faceted climate movement that shows no sign of slowing, these arguments will be more important than ever.

Economic fragility

The poor state of the economy has returned as a political issue. As has been well documented by Marxist economists such as Michael Roberts and Joseph Choonara, the recovery that followed the global economic crisis of 2007-8 has been uneven and shallow. In many countries wages have stagnated or continued their decline, even as rates of unemployment reach new lows. Mainstream commentators have been surprised by this practical refutation of one of the core assumptions of bourgeois economic theory. Yet low rates of unionisation and strike action mean that workers continue to be vulnerable to ruling class attacks, even as their objective capacity for struggle has improved. This state of affairs is itself partially a function of the historically weak state of the radical and revolutionary left.

As Tom Bramble suggests later in this journal, the point of Marxist economics is not to predict precisely the moment at which the economy will crash. Rather it is to explore the tensions and contradictions which make capitalist crisis inevitable, which in turn shape political developments. That we are on the cusp of some kind of recession seems likely. Unlike the previous crisis, it seems that the trouble will begin in what are sometimes called emerging markets. A number of important countries in this category have experienced slow or negative growth at various points in the last twelve months, including Turkey, Mexico, Argentina, South Africa, Russia and Brazil. India's GDP growth declined rapidly in 2019, while China continues to grow but at the lowest rates seen in decades.

A new crisis would have huge implications. From a strictly economic perspective, the aftermath of the GFC saw central banks engage in significant monetary stimulus, in the form of quantitative easing and low (and sometimes negative) interest rates. This worked to stave off total collapse, but the inability to phase out this stimulus means that the same tools will not be available next time around.[15] While some hope for a new era of pro-working class stimulus measures, the current preference still seems to be for intensified attacks on workers via increasingly anti-democratic state institutions. As monetary policy has undeniably failed to end the crisis, there has been a growing openness towards Keynesian fiscal policies. It is important to see that this in no way reflects a left or welfarist turn among economic managers. Thus far, stimulus spending has overwhelmingly taken the form of subsidies and handouts to capital, with no sign of an uptick in investment in programs and services relied on by workers. Macron's massive pension cuts are typical; the decades-long attack on the welfare state continues.

The global imperial order has seen real changes in the past decade. China's remarkable rise now poses a threat to the United States' position as the sole global hegemon, though this possibility remains decades in the future. The recent trade skirmishes between the two countries have sent jitters through the global economy, and portend greater tensions yet to come. Similarly, growing US support for right wing attacks on centre-left governments in Latin America reflects at least in part a desire to undermine their close ties with the Chinese regime. At a bare minimum, a new economic crisis would encourage a new round of protectionism and beggar-thy-neighbour policies. Even without such a crisis, it is hard to see the situation unfolding without a dramatic escalation of tensions and possibly open conflict. The abrupt rise in anti-Chinese discourse in American and Australian politics is concerning, as is the total lack of any opposition from any political leaders, including from those like Bernie Sanders and Richard di Natale, who are generally perceived as on the left. Tensions with Iran also continue to escalate. Though both nations have more interest in diplomatic sparring than all-out war, the risk of a serious military conflict has grown substantially in the wake of criminal US airstrikes on important Iranian targets.

---

[15] Willem Buiter, "The Federal Reserve will have to be creative in the next recession", *Financial Times,* 12 December 2019.

These turbulent economic and geopolitical dynamics have fundamentally transformed the political landscape. We have seen how most of the semi-revolutionary uprisings of 2019 are the consequence of a decade of economic hardship: a new crash would mean further bitterness and new rounds of rebellion. Of less importance, though still portentous, has been the fracturing of a series of parties of the neoliberal centre, who have struggled to maintain their grip on a disaffected body politic. This has been manifested somewhat on the left, but more decisively on the right. In their cartoonish supervillainy, figures such as Bolsonaro, Trump and Johnson have appealed to an enraged middle class desperate to preserve its traditional privileges and reference points. Their impact on their respective countries is likely to last more than one electoral cycle. Across Europe the extreme right are on the march, most clearly on the eastern fringes of the continent, but now spreading elsewhere. In Italy, it is hard to see how the country will avoid a far right *Lega* government in the near future. In the Spanish state the far right is resurgent, having overtaken Podemos as the third-largest group in the national parliament. In Germany, the centre-right is now debating the possibility of forming a coalition government with the *Alternative für Deutschland*, which would put fascists in positions of power in that country for the first time since 1945. Though this rise is by no means irreversible, there is a clear and profoundly dangerous pattern. The necessity of building anti-fascist movements has never been clearer, and Italy's "sardines" movement proves that it is possible.

Turmoil on the left

The situation facing the revolutionary left is thus a complex one. Explosive mass struggles exist alongside an extreme right that seems daily more confident. Joyful movements of millions fighting to save the world break out one day, the reality of accelerating environmental devastation confronts us the next.

In this otherwise dynamic situation, the ongoing weakness of revolutionary organisations remains a frustrating constraint. The collapse of the International Socialist Organization in the US, the bitter split in the Committee for a Workers' International, and the more general stagnation of revolutionary forces both reflect and exacerbate this situation. This is not the place for a systematic accounting of these developments, although decades of low levels of class struggle in the advanced capitalist world is clearly a major factor.

In contrast to the difficulties of the revolutionary left, neo-reformist currents have grown in size and confidence. Reflecting this has been the return of Karl Kautsky to the centre of theoretical discussions on the left in recent years. Kautsky was an advocate of social democracy at a time when gradual, eternal growth seemed inevitable, when war seemed impossible, and the expansion of democratic rights seemed irresistible. World War One proved him disastrously wrong on every count, and his undying belief in the German constitution later paved the way for Hitler. The failed political perspectives of this tradition have nothing to offer a modern left. Indeed, in the face of the multiple crises discussed earlier, the inadequacies of fatalistic and gradualist social-democratic perspectives should be more obvious than ever. To put it bluntly: only a fool or a knave would bet on decades of cumulative reform in a world of falling profits and rising oceans.

Despite these difficulties, there has rarely been a time where the necessity of revolutionary socialist politics and organisation has been more evident. Marxism comes into its own in times of contradiction and conflict; a unique tool that can help orient the left to act in a world pregnant with crises and possibilities. In this context, we are pleased to publish an interview with Isabelle Garo that makes a clear philosophical defence of Marxism in opposition to theories of populism and horizontalism. If we return to La Botz's evocative description of the global revolts as mass social experiments, there is absolutely no need to start this research from scratch. The past can offer insights and opportunities for strategic reflection. Yet without a sizeable and interventionist revolutionary left, these lessons are buried, and struggles for social transformation proceed in a blind and unconscious way. Combined with the parlous state of the world economy, this makes even small victories harder to come by. Sandra

Bloodworth's reflection on the French Popular Front and Nick Everett's examination of the Jesse Jackson campaign are thus best read as attempts to draw from the rich history of the workers' movement to make sharp interventions into contemporary politics.

Hopefully Australian readers will excuse the overwhelmingly international focus of this editorial. Until recently, politics in Australia was as desolate as the charred remains of our precious forests, animals and homes. But even before the fires, forests in Queensland were being cleared at a rate of 1,500 football fields per day, mostly for beef production and other agribusiness.[16] In the face of broad public desire for climate action, the major parties have doubled down on their commitment to coal and extractive industries more broadly. Those who resist our slide into Armageddon are faced with new bipartisan laws that clamp down on the right to protest, particularly against fossil fuels. Anthony Albanese, formally of the Labor Left, has shifted the party further to the right, justifying his cynical support for the fossil fuel industry as a defence of the rights of mining workers. The unions remain weak, and rather than initiate new organising drives officials have prioritised campaigning for Labor and merging their meagre forces to create new bureaucratic monstrosities. Worse, following the failure of the Change the Rules campaign, they have plumbed shocking new depths. When faced with Morrison's vicious anti-union agenda, union leaders chose to collaborate with far right politicians rather than mobilising their members and supporters. Meanwhile the hapless Greens remain committed to the carbon tax and, at least for now, have been totally unable to make the most of a newfound environmental consciousness among broad layers of the population.[17]

The size and vigour of the climate strikes, which mobilised hundreds of thousands on 20 September 2019, has been a healthy

---

[16] Michael Slezak, "'Global deforestation hotspot': 3m hectares of Australian forest to be lost in 15 years", *The Guardian*, 12 December 2019; Lisa Cox, "Beef industry linked to 94% of land clearing in Great Barrier Reef catchments", *The Guardian,* 12 December 2019.

[17] "The Greens and CPRS", https://greens.org.au/cprs.

antidote to the malaise of official politics. Together with the respectable turnout to disruptive actions organised by Extinction Rebellion and the Blockade IMARC coalition, there has been a substantial uptick in organising around this issue. This movement stands out for its capacity to rebuild an activist and socialist culture on campuses, in trade unions, and across society.

This climate activism has taken on a new urgency following the unprecedented bushfires that have ravaged the country for months. The situation has been transformed by the scale of the horror. Amidst the devastation and the endless smog, the left has a responsibility to reach out and offer a political explanation and lead. It is already widely understood that these fires are a product of government policy: they are a product of the myriad changes produced by global warming that successive governments have done nothing to avoid; but also that they reflect the systematic and criminal underfunding of firefighting and land management services produced by decades of neoliberalism.

The Morrison government, trapped by its complete loyalty to the fossil fuel industries, has been completely incapable of responding to the rising anger produced by the catastrophic fires. Each of the prime minister's actions has only drawn more attention to his failure to comprehend the extent of the crisis and his callous indifference to the escalating human, social and environmental costs. Large demonstrations called by Uni Students for Climate Justice, including a 40,000 strong rally in Sydney in December, are a testament to the depth of anger in the broader community, as are the numerous and glorious scenes of people in affected areas sending righteous abuse his way. Morrison's belated decision to pay volunteer firefighters a pittance for their heroic efforts is a totally inadequate policy response, but indicates the government is feeling the heat.

It is terrifying to think that the fires will last all summer. Yet so too will the crisis they have provoked, an opportunity for the climate movement to sheet home the blame for this tragedy to the climate criminals in parliament and in the capitalist class more broadly. Even when the fires ease, the disgracefully low compensation program, which offers an insulting $1,000 per adult to those who have lost their homes, will become a new target of public anger, as will the failure to invest in firefighting services. Caught unprepared by these mounting challenges, the Liberal government is highly vulnerable, just months after winning a shock election. The task is now to build a movement capable of laying the basis to destroy them and the destructive forces they represent.

References

Hassan, Omar 2016, "Podemos and the myth of left populism", *Marxist Left Review*, 11, Summer.

Holleman, Hannah 2018, *Dust Bowls of Empire: Imperialism, Environmental Politics and the Injustices of "Green" Capitalism*, Yale University Press.

Lenin, Vladimir 1909, "The faction of supporters of otzovism and god-building", https://www.marxists.org/archive/lenin/works/1909/fsotzgod/i.htm.

Lih, Lars 2008, *Lenin rediscovered: What is to be done? in context,* Haymarket Books.

IS THE WORLD ECONOMY ON THE VERGE OF A NEW RECESSION?

TOM BRAMBLE

There is general agreement among capitalist economists that the world economy is now at risk of a recession, potentially as bad as the global financial crisis of 2008-09, the worst economic downturn since the Great Depression. In its November 2019 Economic Outlook, the Organisation of Economic Cooperation and Development (OECD) stated that:

> The global outlook is fragile, with increasing signs that the cyclical downturn is becoming entrenched. GDP growth remains weak, with a slowdown in almost all economies this year, and global trade is stagnating.[1]

The purpose of this article is to outline some of the main features of this downturn but to situate it in the context of Marx's theory of economic crisis. Capitalism, Marx argued, is a system wracked by recurrent booms and busts, a never-ending cycle of economic advance followed by sharp contraction.[2] During the booms, businesses prosper, hire more workers and invest more. During the busts, the

---

Tom Bramble has published widely on political economy and the labour movement in Australia and overseas and is a regular contributor to *Marxist Left Review*. His recent books include *Labor's Conflict: Big Business, Workers and the Politics of Class* (with Rick Kuhn) and *Introducing Marxism: A Theory of Social Change*.

[1]   OECD 2019a.

[2]   For an introduction to Marx's theory of economic crisis, see Harman 1984 and Bloodworth 2008.

whole system goes into reverse, investment dries up, and the bosses try to restore their fortunes by cutting wages and sacking workers. But, Marx contended, the dynamism of the entire capitalist system tends to weaken over time as a result of the long term tendency for the rate of profit to fall. This tendency can be offset for a period by a series of countervailing factors but inevitably reasserts itself at some point. Profits are the fuel that drives the capitalist economy. When the rate of profit is depressed, the economy starts to sputter and malfunction: the upturns in the economic cycle become weaker and the downturns more severe. It is these two factors – a downswing in the current phase of the economic cycle exacerbated by the long term weakening of the rate of profit – that explain the crisis in the world economy today.

Overview of the global economy

There is ample evidence of the current downswing in the global economy (Figure 1).

The situation varies from country to country, but the overall trend is uniform.[3] Growth in the Euro area, already feeble at 1.9 percent in 2018, is projected at just 1.2 percent for 2019. In Britain growth last year fell to 1 percent, and even that may be optimistic if Brexit hits hard in coming months. Japan is crawling along at 1 percent. The US is the relative outlier among the G7, but even here growth is down from 2.9 percent in 2018 to 2.3 percent in 2019: in 2020, the OECD is predicting US growth of just 2.0 percent.

Growth is also slowing outside the advanced economies. In China, growth in 2019 came in at 6.2 percent, the lowest since 1992, with the OECD forecasting growth of just 5.5 percent by 2021. Growth in India in 2019 was also down to 5.8 percent, from a peak of 9 percent in 2016. And then there are the real danger zones. Brazil, which suffered a severe contraction four years ago, saw its economy grow by less than 1 percent in 2019. In Mexico, the economy flatlined, as did Turkey's. Russia registered growth of less than 1 percent

---

[3]   All data in the following are from OECD 2019a unless otherwise stated.

Figure 1: Overview of the global economy[4]

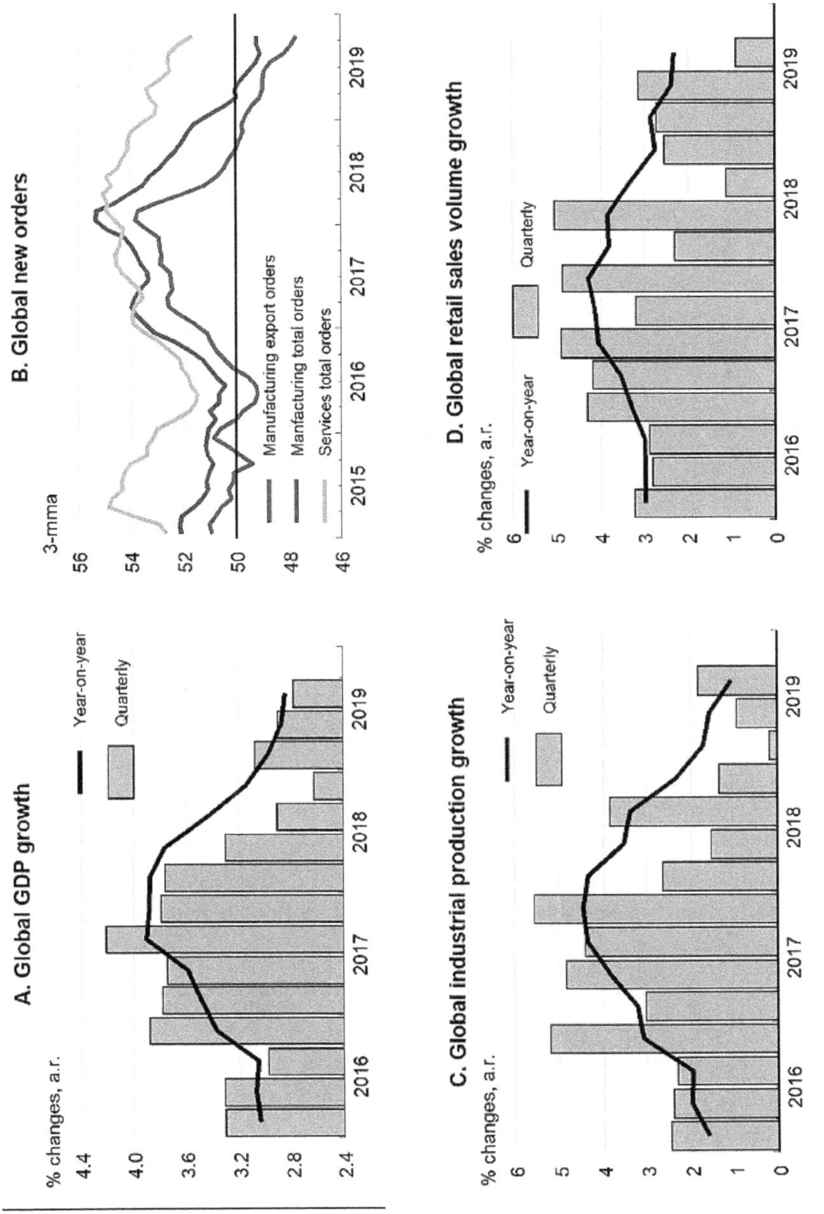

B. Global new orders

A. Global GDP growth

C. Global industrial production growth

D. Global retail sales volume growth

[4]   OECD 2019a.

last year, while the Argentinian economy has shrunk by 5.5 percent in the past two years. These are the so-called emerging economies which just a few years ago were held up as the bright spots in the world economy.

Several factors are responsible for the downswing. Global investment is forecast to rise by less than 1 percent in 2019, down from 5 percent at the start of 2018. World trade is anaemic and there is no sign that it will pick up soon. The only thing holding the US economy up is household spending, but with the effect of Trump's tax cuts beginning to wear off and with recession fears rising there is no guarantee this can be sustained. The OECD chief economist warns that unless action is taken "we run the risk of finding ourselves stuck in a long period of low growth".[5]

The downswing is not being felt evenly. The situation is worst in manufacturing. Industrial production in the advanced economies actually shrank in the first half of 2019 and future indicators are at their weakest for seven years. In the service sectors, things are not so grim. But the two sectors are intertwined and it's unlikely that services can remain buoyant with manufacturing in the doldrums.

And so, after three years of tentatively pushing up interest rates to try to damp down runaway increases in the price of shares and a surge in corporate borrowing, the Federal Reserve Bank is now dropping interest rates again to try to lift the US economy, while the European Central Bank (ECB) has set a cash rate of negative 0.5 percent for the 19 members of the Eurozone. All around the world, central banks are moving in the same direction.

Why the recessionary threat? Most accounts of the slowdown of the world economy point to the US-China trade war as an important factor. Average tariffs on trade between the two countries grew from low single figures in 2017 to 21 percent by the end of 2019.[6] Monthly trade between the two countries in 2019 was more than 10 percent lower than in the equivalent month in 2018. The uncertain state of trade negotiations between the US and China

---

[5]   Boone 2019.

[6]   Brown 2019.

means there can be no guarantees that higher tariffs will not be consolidated rather than wound back.[7] And while China is less able to inflict pain on the US with its tariffs, since it exports far more to the US than it imports, the Chinese government has allowed the renminbi to slide in the last 18 months to offset the effect of US tariffs.

Trade tensions are also blowing up with Europe, with the Trump administration threatening tariffs on European consumer goods in response to the EU's attempt to eliminate tax breaks for US IT companies and the World Trade Organization (WTO) finding that the EU continues to subsidise Airbus in its battle with Boeing. Trump is also mooting tariffs on Brazilian and Argentinian metals, accusing the two countries of currency manipulation. Within the EU, there remains the uncertain effect of Brexit, which will affect not just the British economy but trade relations across the bloc.

Why is this trade uncertainty important? It's not just the impact on flows of trade, but the wider effect of the breakdown in trade relations that matters: disruptions to trade are threatening cross-border investment plans and supply chains. Businesses are simply stalling their investments until they can be sure what the outcome with tariffs is going to be.

There is no doubt that the trade war between the US and its chief trading partners and the risk of a hard Brexit are having a dampening effect on the world economy and could be the trigger for a sharper economic slowdown. But the trade conflicts are just an indication of more profound underlying problems.

Growth in the Western economies since the recovery from the GFC has been feeble. The US, the most successful advanced economy, has grown at an annual rate of just 2.3 percent since 2010, far more slowly than in other previous recoveries. Across the OECD, we see weak investment and therefore slow productivity growth,

---

[7] James Politi, "Vague détente in US-China trade war hinges on tricky implementation", *Financial Times*, 15 December 2019.

what British economist Michael Roberts refers to as "the Long Depression".[8]

Why sluggish growth since the GFC?

In order to understand the slow recovery from the GFC, we have to go to the roots of the GFC itself.[9] Neoliberalism – a ruling class program to undermine the wages, living conditions and collective organisations of the working class and redistribute income and wealth to the capitalist class – was the capitalist response to the economic crisis of the 1970s. But it failed to solve the underlying problems that gave rise to that earlier crisis, in particular a low rate of profit. Corporate profitability in the US did rise in the 1980s and 1990s, peaking in 1997, but never recovered to the rates that undergirded the post-war boom, the longest sustained expansion of the world economy in history. In other advanced economies at this time, the rate of profit barely moved.[10] The fact that even in the middle of a sustained capitalist offensive against the working class, the capitalists could not fully restore the rate of profit confirmed Marx's argument about the long term tendency for the rate of profit to fall: Marx did not argue that the rate would fall year after year, only that over a period, which could extend over many years, the tendency would assert itself.

One of the reasons why neoliberalism did not spark off another boom on the lines of the post-war expansion can be found in the changing structure of capitalism itself. Marx argued that one of the most important ways in which the rate of profit could be restored for a period was through the working-out of crisis itself. Crises wiped out inefficient capitalists and devalued constant capital – the machinery, the factories, the railways, the raw materials. Those capitalists that survived the purging effect of the crisis could take advantage of the cheaper means of production now available and the reallocation of

---

[8]   Roberts 2016.
[9]   The explanation that follows draws on Harman 2009 and Carchedi and Roberts 2018. See also Bramble 2018.
[10]   Carchedi and Roberts 2018.

capital away from their more inefficient, now bankrupt, rivals. The rate of profit could revive for a period on that basis. However, as capitalism has aged, it has become more monopolistic, the blocs of capital have grown in size. In addition, the blocs have become more intertwined. Governments have been very reluctant to see their national champions go bust for fear of falling behind in imperialist competition and out of concern that the bankruptcy of one big company will have knock-on effects, causing multiple collapses. While bailouts avoided the kind of catastrophic business failures of the nineteenth century, by propping up inefficient businesses, governments have prevented the purging effect of crisis – what economists call "deleveraging" – from working its way through. The Western economies as a result remain weighed down by inefficient capitalists, preventing capital flowing into more dynamic sectors with higher rates of return.

The failure of the rate of profit in productive industry to lift significantly (or at all in many cases) during the neoliberal heyday led to increasing diversion of capital to the financial sector. One outcome was the increased frequency and severity of financial busts. The dotcom boom of the late 1990s collapsed in 1999 and it was only by slashing interest rates that the Federal Reserve Bank was able to prevent a sharp economic downturn in the US. But by doing so, the Fed only kicked the can down the road. Low interest rates sparked off the US housing boom in the early 2000s, but that only created more problems.

The GFC hit in 2008 when the accumulation of fictitious capital in the US, in particular in housing, was brought back into line with the production of real value which had lagged behind the growth of fictitious capital. The result was a sharp fall in house prices, the collapse of the enormous pyramid of mortgage-backed credit derivatives, bankruptcies in some of the world's biggest financial institutions and a stock market crash.

The austerity measures subsequently unleashed against the working class helped to depress wages. The bank bailouts prevented an avalanche of bankruptcies, while stimulus measures and the flooding of international markets with cheap money (quantitative easing) helped to put a floor under business.[11] The rapid recovery of growth in China after 2009, thanks to a massive stimulus package, pulled up many countries in Latin America, Europe, Africa and Asia, not least Australia. And so, starting in 2010, the recovery took hold.

The recovery had a particular character. Its benefits overwhelmingly went to the well-off, and this is most clear in the US where income inequality in 2018 reached the highest level since figures were first compiled in the 1960s. The share of wealth going to the top 10 percent of households rose to 75 percent, with the bottom half holding just 2 percent.[12] While employment grew by 20 million and unemployment more than halved after the GFC, as a share of the population, there are still fewer people in work or looking for work today in the US than there were on the eve of the GFC in 2007.[13] And while wages for private sector workers are now 11 percent higher than they were in the depths of the GFC, they are still lower than in the early 1970s. The huge expansion of the US economy over the past five decades has done nothing to lift working class living standards.[14]

---

[11] The Federal Reserve cut the cash rate, the basis for the whole structure of interest rates in the US economy, from 4.25 percent in December 2007 to zero 12 months later, where it remained until 2015. The European Central Bank first cut its rate to 1 percent and then in 2016 to zero (and in September 2019 to minus 0.5 percent).

[12] Taylor Telford, "Income inequality in America is the highest it's been since Census Bureau started tracking it, data shows", *Washington Post*, 27 September 2019; Kadhim Shubber, "Eight charts on inequality in the US", *Financial Times*, 4 January 2018.

[13] Federal Reserve Bank of St Louis, Economic Research, https://fred.stlouisfed.org/series/PAYEMS; Federal Reserve Bank of St Louis, Economic Research, https://fred.stlouisfed.org/series/EMRATIO.

[14] The index of real wages for private sector production workers and non-supervisory employees in the US in September 2019 stood at 105.6 as compared to 108.1 in January 1973 (January 1970 = 100), Federal Reserve Bank of St Louis, Economic Research, https://fredblog.stlouisfed.org/2016/09/wages-with-benefits/?utm_source=series_page&utm_medium=related_content&utm_term=related_resources&utm_campaign=fredblog.

Very significantly, the mass of corporate profits in the US has risen in the recovery since 2010 but still not by enough to drive up the rate of profit to the level where it would stimulate a new economic boom. Just as during the 1980s and 1990s, the deleveraging process, the bankrupting of inefficient capitalists and the liquidation of private and public debt, which in Marx's day would have lifted the rate of profit in the productive sector, has not occurred to the degree required to put a bounce back into the rate of profit; quite the opposite, as we shall see. The result is weak investment and slow productivity growth. Instead of investing in productive, value-creating industry, companies have simply borrowed money to buy their own shares in order to drive up their share price, to make them more attractive to investors: the S&P 500 stock market index more than tripled in value between January 2009 and December 2019. And it is not just the price of shares: the price of paper assets of all kinds has soared as a result of the decision by central banks to keep interest rates very low. This, like the dotcom boom of the late 1990s or the US housing bubble of the early 2000s, is not sustainable.

One new feature of the post-GFC recovery which distinguishes it from the preceding quarter century, is that it has not seen any resumption of globalisation. In the decades prior, world trade consistently outstripped economic growth as burgeoning trade in goods and services and international investments (cross border production chains; mergers and takeovers) helped to integrate national economies. During the GFC, however, world trade shrank dramatically, sending the process into reverse. This has had long term effects. In the decade since the GFC, trade has recovered but more slowly than GDP. The world economy is far more globally integrated than at the beginning of the neoliberal era but in the past few years international trade and investment have no longer been important drivers of growth. The current trade wars and the tendency towards decoupling of the US and Chinese information technology sectors will only exacerbate the slowdown.[15] About the only element of

---

[15] The editorial board, "The world should beware a technology cold war", *Financial Times*, 11 December 2019.

international capitalism that has accelerated in recent years has been the siphoning off of company profits to tax havens such as Luxembourg and the Cayman Islands.

The uneven recovery in the decade following the GFC, with the Chinese economy rising from one-third the size of the US's to two-thirds, is another indication of the reordering of the world economy.[16] China's growing economic power has had significant political effects which I will return to later.

Finally, the fact that the "solution" to the GFC involved bailing out the banks and shovelling money into the hands of the wealthy (those who hold the big majority of paper assets), while squeezing the working class through harsh austerity, only increased inequality in income and wealth in the G20. Resentment at this fact has had enormous political consequences, and I will also return to this later.

Recession then and now

Any new economic bust will not be a straight re-run of the GFC. For example, it is unlikely to be triggered by economic shocks in the US. Europe or China is more likely to be the source of problems. A housing downturn, which was the spark for multiple shocks in the financial system in 2008, is not set to be the catalyst this time around. Much more likely is the accumulation of corporate debt and government debt. Between 2007 and 2017, total global debt rose from $97 trillion to $169 trillion (in constant 2017 prices). Household debt rose by 11 percent to $43 trillion, but the biggest components were corporate debt, up by 29 percent to $66 trillion, and government debt, up by 31 percent to $60 trillion.[17]

Corporate debt takes two main forms: loans and bonds. Since the GFC, with banks having to rein in their commercial lending to meet tighter financial regulation, the biggest growth in corporate debt has been in the form of corporate bonds, in 2017 valued at $12 trillion. These bonds are booked as collateral or assets on the balance sheets of

---

[16] In US dollar terms. www.data.worldbank.org.
[17] All data on debt and bonds in this section are from McKinsey Global Institute 2018. For more on the significance of corporate debt, see Roberts 2019.

the banks and investment funds that buy them, attracted by the higher yields than they can get from buying government bonds. The problem is that a lot of the companies that issue these bonds have sub-standard credit ratings, just one step above junk bond status. This is particularly the case in the developing countries where bond issuance has been especially rapid in the last decade: 20-25 percent of corporate bonds in Brazil, China and India are at higher risk of default and in the event of financial or economic shocks, the figure could rise to 30-40 percent. The creditors holding these bonds could end up holding worthless pieces of paper, shredding the value of their booked assets, potentially bankrupting them or at least forcing them to call in loans, sparking off a broader financial crisis.

And then there is government debt. When governments stepped in to bail out failing companies during the GFC they simply transferred their bad debts onto government balance sheets. Stimulus programs also added to the columns of red ink. The result is that, relative to GDP, government debt in the biggest economies is twice as high as it was ten years ago and a record level in peacetime.[18]

Both corporate debt and government debt are vulnerable to any increase in interest rates: if rates rise, the debt burden weighing on businesses and governments could become unsustainable, potentially triggering off insolvencies, stock market falls and investor strikes. Obviously this is speculation, but these concerns are held by the IMF, OECD and World Bank.

The big international financial institutions prescribe three measures for governments and central banks to draw the world economy back from recession:

- Maintain low interest rates to encourage more business investment and consumer spending (monetary policy)
- More government borrowing to spend on infrastructure (fiscal policy)

---

[18] Tommy Stubbington, "Global debt at its highest level in peacetime", *Financial Times*, 26 September 2019.

- More deregulation of product and labour markets, more government funding of new industries, what the OECD calls "reforms to promote innovation".

These are unlikely to do much to restore growth.[19] In the US, the central bank rate was zero between 2008 and 2015 but this failed to spark significant investment in industry. All it did was fuel inflation in the price of financial assets. Why would low interest rates work to lift the real economy now? Capitalists invest in the expectation of making a return on their investments: if the rate of profit is insufficiently attractive, why borrow money to invest?[20] And with the Federal Reserve cash rate just 2 percent and the ECB's minus 0.5 percent, there is very little room for central banks to cut interest rates much further in the hope of stimulating investment and consumer spending. Low interest rates may prop up the price of financial assets for a while longer, but this will only make any market "correction" more destructive when it does take place.

As for public spending on infrastructure, the ruling class can certainly see the need to upgrade roads, ports, railways and internet services, but will they tolerate the increases in government debt or tax increases that will follow? This is relevant to Green New Deal proposals. Any serious effort to halt runaway global warming will cost billions of dollars in public spending. The large public sector infrastructure projects needed to ameliorate climate change might lift the economy and provide millions of new jobs. But if government debt is not to explode, business will have to pay more tax, something they steadfastly resist.

It is also not clear that big infrastructure projects will boost the economy much. They might stimulate growth in the businesses building the bridges, railways and 5G infrastructure but are unlikely to promote widespread recovery. The Japanese case is instructive. The government has run expansionary budgets for more than 20 years, boosting its government debt to 240 percent of GDP, the highest in the world, but the country has experienced low growth

---

[19] See Carchedi and Roberts 2018, pp22-28.
[20] Choonara 2019.

throughout that time. Again, the rate of profit is central. If the rate of return on capital is not sufficiently high, no amount of government demand management is going to prompt the capitalists to invest.

Last time around, Chinese growth helped to lift the world economy out of the GFC, but this is less likely this time. Even though it accounts for a much larger slice of the world economy, making it potentially an even more powerful locomotive, the Chinese government has been trying to shift the economy towards domestic consumption in recent years and away from heavy industry. While higher wages in China may boost overseas tourism and demand for European luxury goods, the move away from heavy industry and infrastructure spending cuts demand for German industrial machinery and Canadian, Brazilian and Australian coal, iron ore and gas. Further, the Chinese economy is awash with debt, with corporate bonds having grown from a standing start in 2010 to $2 trillion in 2017, and with the unregulated shadow banking system continuing to grow. China is more likely to be a bigger source of instability than stability during the next recession.

Political problems for the ruling classes

The crisis in the world economy interacts with and compounds imperialist tensions. Imperialist competition between the major powers is on the rise. During the GFC, two G20 summits resulted in member states, which dominate the world economy, putting in place a coordinated plan to implement stimulus programs and to avoid "beggar thy neighbour" currency wars or tariffs. In the event of a fresh crisis, there is less potential to do this this time around.

Even before the GFC, relations had become strained, in particular between the US and EU on the one hand and the big commodity exporters of the global South on the other, with the result that successive WTO forums ended in disagreement: there has not been a single multilateral WTO trade agreement since the 1990s.

Since the GFC, however, disruptions to the world trade system have only increased. With the rise of nationalist strongmen and the further discrediting of the "rules-based international financial order", conflict between the big powers is likely to grow in the event of a fresh crisis. Given Trump's tendency to see trade as a zero-sum game, it's likely that the US would be more inclined towards a mercantilist trade war than any commitment to find a common solution.[21]

But the problem is not just a matter of a few individual leaders. It's a systemic problem. The OECD, for example, understands that the old world order is gone. They know what is needed, but they know it's not going to happen. It urges a "collective effort to halt the build-up of trade-distorting tariffs and subsidies and to restore a transparent and predictable rules-based system that encourages business to invest" but laments:

> It is now evident that trade tensions are not a temporary side-show. The international framework which governed trade has been permanently impaired and the WTO as we know it will not come back.[22]

The OECD can only suggest a string of regional trade agreements that may end up only diverting trade from one country to another, complicating any attempt at a multilateral agreement at future G20 summits.

And how are the big powers meant to cooperate with each other when the two biggest are at each other's throats? During the G20 discussions in the midst of the GFC, relations between the US and China had not reached the pitch they have today. The pivot to Asia was still three years away. But today, the US political and military establishment is determined to confront China. What was only a developing contest has today become full blown competition. And relations between the US and EU have also become more vexed over the past decade.

Domestic considerations also weigh on ruling class strategists. Historically, the ruling classes have relied on the mainstream centre left and centre right parties to push through austerity measures when needed. Even though the share of the vote accounted for by the

---

[21] Edward Luce, "Trump is serious about US divorce from China", *Financial Times*, 19 September 2019.
[22] OECD 2019b; Boone 2019.

mainstream parties has been in decline since the 1980s, their loss of authority has snowballed since the GFC, with the collapse in support for many social democratic and conservative parties and the emergence, mostly, of parties of the hard right. These new parties have capitalised on the racism promoted by the old parties to deflect attention from their failings to drive things further to the right. Alternatively, as in Britain and America, "outsider" figures Johnson and Trump have taken control of the ruling class' preferred conservative parties and used them to promote projects to which many in the ruling class are quite opposed, Brexit in the case of Britain, Trump's erratic foreign policy (including support for Brexit among other things) in the case of the US.

Attempts by the ruling class to impose fresh rounds of austerity in the event of another financial crash might only create further political destabilisation. For some years, capitalist mouthpieces such as the *Financial Times* (FT) have been warning about the effect of rampant inequality on the social and political order. Leading FT columnist Philip Stephens for example, wrote in 2018:

> After a decade of stagnant incomes and fiscal austerity, no one can be surprised that those most hurt by the crash's economic consequences are supporting populist uprisings against elites. Across rich democracies, significant segments of the population have come to reject laissez-faire economics and the open frontiers of globalisation.[23]

Stephens' fellow FT columnist Martin Wolf, noting widespread dysfunction in the liberal order, argued in August 2019 that "the way our economic and political systems work must change, or they will perish".[24] Even the US Business Roundtable, representing the chief executives of 181 of the world's largest companies, has now begun to consider the limits of a "shareholder first" approach to capitalism,

---

[23] Philip Stephens, "Populism is the true legacy of the global financial crisis", *Financial Times*, 30 August 2018.

[24] Martin Wolf, "Why rigged capitalism is damaging liberal democracy", *Financial Times*, 18 September 2019.

with Roundtable chairman Jamie Dimon, CEO of JP Morgan Chase, warning last year that "The American dream is alive but fraying".[25]

The ruling classes can see the problems with continuing with the neoliberal prescriptions, but they have no alternative strategy. They could in theory support a program of Keynesian reflation and a boost to working class living standards in order to revive the "American dream", but none of them is prepared to act on it. None has an interest in doing so and none has the credibility to impose an alternative strategy to that which has been dominant since the 1980s. The ruling classes have two ways to restore the rate of profit: devalue constant capital or drive up the rate of surplus value. There are limits to the former, short of war, meaning that the latter remains their priority. The result is that governing parties, whether established or new, whether they emphasise globalisation or economic nationalism, are increasingly resorting to authoritarianism and racism to push their agenda in an environment of increasing cynicism towards politicians.

The main factor that the ruling classes in the West has going for them is the weak state of working class organisation and politics. Trade union organisation, industrial struggle, broader social struggle and the left are in a worse position than they were at the onset of the GFC in most countries, and some of the left projects that have arisen in response to decades of austerity – Rifondazione in Italy, SYRIZA in Greece, Die Linke in Germany, Podemos in Spain, the NPA and France Insoumise in France, Corbynism in Britain – have failed badly or are failing, demoralising their supporters who saw in them an alternative to the dead end of social liberalism. If the ruling classes of the advanced countries face political difficulties in coming years, the weakness of the left and working class may provide them with some respite.

---

[25]   Business Roundtable 2019.

How does Australia fit into all this?

Australia has escaped an economic recession for more than a quarter of a century. The economy has been propped up by a series of factors:

- household borrowing, which has fuelled consumer spending at a time of slow growth in income: household debt is now approaching double the level of household disposable incomes;[26]

- rising commodity prices and volumes exported, to China in particular, which drove record levels of investment in the resources industry and engineering for several years. Record exports of iron ore and LNG in 2018-19 have helped to return the balance of payments to surplus for the first time since 1975 and boosted government revenues;[27]

- strong demand from China for Australian services which generated billions of dollars for the universities and tourism industry: there are now 150,000 Chinese students enrolled at Australian universities and China has become Australia's largest tourism market. Both of these have stimulated the property, retail and hospitality sectors;[28]

- stability in the banking sector, combined with stimulus measures, which helped Australia weather the GFC better than other OECD member states;

- a boom in the property industry and construction in the period 2012-2017, when mining investments and commodity prices both dropped; and

- high immigration, which has contributed both to the labour force and demand for housing and consumer goods.

However, it's worth noting some limits to this growth. Once population growth is stripped out of the GDP figures, growth in Australia drops considerably in international comparisons. As the

---

[26] Reserve Bank of Australia 2019, p7.
[27] Martin Farrer, "Australia's mining exports hit $278bn – but bonanza at risk, says report", *The Guardian*, 29 March 2019; Angus Grigg and Angela Macdonald-Smith, "The trade war is making China more reliant on Australia", *Financial Review*, 15 August 2019; Reserve Bank of Australia 2019, p16.
[28] Department of Foreign Affairs and Trade 2019.

economic expansion aged, so it slowed: between 1997-98 and 2007-08, GDP per capita rose at an annual rate of 2.4 percent; since 2008 and the GFC the figure has fallen to just 0.8 percent.[29] Business investment as a share of GDP is now at its lowest level since 1994.[30]

As in the United States, the benefits have been uneven. The wages share of GDP is at its lowest level since the early 1960s and average household incomes are no higher than they were in 2012.[31] Australia has one of the developed world's highest rates of underemployment – those wanting more hours of work than they are currently working. While high house prices in Australia have boosted the wealth of home-owners, they have locked out many potential young house buyers who may never escape the private rental market. Along with the many concessions to those with housing and share investment portfolios and hefty superannuation balances, economic policy has significantly assisted older, usually Coalition-supporting, households at the expense of the young.

Young people are also faring badly in the job market. There are fewer 15-24 year olds in work as a share of their age cohort than there were a decade ago, while the participation rate has risen for all other age groups.[32] The underemployment rate has grown from 16 percent to 21 percent.[33]and while the number of young workers in jobs rose over the decade to 2019, the growth was entirely in part-time jobs (See Table 1).

Even university qualifications have not been enough to shield young workers from the deteriorating situation. On the eve of the GFC in 2008, 86 percent of graduates were in full-time work four months after graduating. The figure fell during the GFC as might be expected, but then kept falling in the years afterwards, bottoming out at 68 percent in 2014. The figure has since risen to 73 percent in

[29] Borland 2019.
[30] Reserve Bank of Australia 2019, p8.
[31] Greg Jericho, "Take it from me – a recession doesn't bear thinking about", *The Guardian*, 24 September 2019.
[32] Australian Bureau of Statistics 2019a.
[33] Australian Bureau of Statistics 2019b.

Table 1: Employed persons, by age and employment status, October 2009 to October 2019[34]

Age group	Total employed		Full Time		Part Time	
	15-24	15-64	15-24	15-64	15-24	15-64
Change in number employed	+80,000	+1,788,000	-83,000	+1,124,000	+164,000	+664,000
Percentage change	+4.3	+17.0	-9.7	+15.1	+18.0	+21.3

---

[34]   Australian Bureau of Statistics 2019a.

2018, but graduates are still positioned worse than they were a decade ago in finding full-time employment.[35]

Finally, government debt continues to rise long after the Rudd government's stimulus packages initially blew Peter Costello's surplus, making a mockery of the Coalition's boasts about its superior economic management. Net government debt has risen from $161 billion in 2013, when the Abbott government was elected, to $395 billion in October last year.[36]

Australia's 27 years without recession, a world record, therefore appears less impressive when viewed from this perspective.

And now Australia is experiencing the same rapid slow-down as other OECD members. Economic growth is forecast at just 1.7 percent for 2019, down from 2.7 percent in 2018. On a per capita basis, the Australian economy has contracted or failed to grow in three of the last five quarters. Even if the OECD's forecast of 2.3 percent growth in 2020 comes to pass, this will the slowest two year period of growth since the early 1990s.

Some other elements of the current slow-down:

- The Morrison government's income tax cuts have not stimulated consumer spending or investment, nor has the Reserve Bank's reduction in the cash rate to just 0.75 percent, the lowest level on record.[37]

- Business conditions and business confidence have fallen sharply and private demand is now lower than at the beginning of 2018.[38]

- Building approvals are down in response to the fall in property prices in Sydney and Melbourne in 2017-18. Construction is contracting. House prices are rising again, but it's not clear how long this will last given the broader economic situation.

---

[35] All figures on graduate employment from Quality Indicators for Learning and Teaching 2019.

[36] Department of Finance 2019.

[37] By comparison, the RBA cash rate on the eve of the GFC in August 2008 was 7.25 percent.

[38] Reserve Bank of Australia 2019, p9.

- Consumer confidence is sinking, likely to worsen ongoing problems in the retail sector, where empty shopfronts tell the story. New car sales have fallen every month for 18 months.
- Employment growth remains reasonable, but in the first ten months of 2019, half of the net increase in employment was in part-time jobs.[39]

The main bright spot for the capitalists is the depreciation of the Australian dollar since the beginning of 2018, helping to boost the competitiveness of exports and the returns to resource companies.[40] Nonetheless, with the Chinese economy slowing and with growth of Chinese imports of goods and services having fallen dramatically since 2016, the cheaper dollar may not help much.[41]

What of the political implications of the changing economic situation? Australia's relative economic stability in the past two decades has fed into relative political stability, with no significant breakthrough for minor parties or obvious political ruptures. That does not mean that the potential is not there for Australia to follow international trends at some point. The last two serious recessions in the early 1980s and early 1990s were severe, with unemployment rising to 11 percent. The first cost the Fraser government power, while the second nearly brought down the Keating government and did lead to defeat for several state governments. But we are not there yet and the political situation remains flat even if popular frustrations grow with the major parties.

The Morrison government is attempting to ride the commodity price boom to a budget surplus, but if it manages to achieve a surplus, this will be as much due to delaying spending on the NDIS as anything else. The government's budget predictions of significant

---

[39] Australian Bureau of Statistics 2019b.

[40] The prices of Australian resource exports are fixed in US dollars. A fall in the Australian dollar against the American means that resource companies get a higher Australian dollar return on the sale of a tonne of coal or iron ore on international markets.

[41] Chinese imports of goods and services from all sources were predicted to fall by nearly 2 percent in 2019 and for the next two years to rise by less than 2 percent annually. OECD 2019a.

surpluses in the early 2020s are predicated on GDP and wages growth projections that show no signs of being achieved. And the ruling class is hardly impressed with the government's surplus obsession. The attacks on welfare might help keep corporate taxes low, but Australian capitalism cannot prosper just by kicking Newstart recipients. In fact, business has been urging the government to raise Newstart. Of much more concern to the bosses is the fact that growth in labour productivity has halved since 2012 when compared to the preceding quarter century.[42]

The lack of economic dynamism explains why the Australian Industry Group and Reserve Bank are telling the government to start spending on infrastructure – to boost business orders for a year or two.

Conclusion

This article started by arguing that the current conjuncture can be best understood as the coming together of two processes that form the centrepiece of Marx's theory of economic crisis: a downswing in the business cycle of the type that has characterised capitalism since its birth and the corrosive effect of the long term tendency of the rate of profit to fall. It is the latter in particular that explains why the GFC occurred, why the subsequent recovery has been so feeble and why we are facing a return to economic slump today. Only by understanding the deep roots of the crisis can we see why the various strategies being proposed by organisations such as the OECD are incapable of fixing the problem at the heart of the system. Only by coming to grips with the fact that it is the rate of profit that drives all else, and that the rate of profit is under long term pressure, can we comprehend why the capitalists and their governments have no alternative but to attack the working class, regardless of the pain it causes. This is so despite the handwringing by the *Financial Times* and ruling class think-tanks about the social and political consequences of rising inequality and continued austerity.

---

[42] Reserve Bank of Australia 2019, p11; Borland 2019.

Only time will tell whether the world economy, or substantial parts of it, enter a new recession during 2020. There are plenty of unknowns, including oil prices, the impact of Brexit, the potential for trade tensions to worsen, the risk of a sharper slowdown in China or a financial crisis sparked by the overhang of corporate indebtedness. On the other hand, it's possible that trade tensions could ease, boosting business confidence. It's possible that the resumption of central bank interest rate cuts might prevent investment and consumer spending from sliding (even if this will simply delay the day of reckoning and ensure a deeper crisis when it finally arrives).

However, if we can't be definitive, we can certainly say that a recession is due soon. It is already the case that corporate profits in the US have fallen for three successive quarters. And we can also say that the long term pressure on the rate of profit will exacerbate the downswing in trade, investment, output and employment. Interacting with these economic tendencies are two important political factors: rising imperialist tensions between the world's biggest powers and increasing recourse to authoritarianism and racism by the governing parties. An economic slump will only exacerbate both.

The issue, then, is ultimately whether the working class is willing to bear the burden of capitalism's long term crisis. The eruption of protests against neoliberalism in the last few months of 2019, ranging from Ecuador to Chile, from Lebanon to Iraq, demonstrates that workers around the world have had enough of ruling class attacks. Whether these outbursts of popular struggle against inequality and austerity in what are predominantly countries at the periphery of the world system can find their way into the centres of world capitalism will determine the shape of world politics in the years to come. We can only hope that the general strike in France in early December, the biggest since 1995, is an augury of things to come. But to make the most of these outbreaks of struggle, we need revolutionary socialist organisations. Without the left rebuilding its forces, the right, whether in government or outside, can step in to capitalise on popular hostility to austerity and use it to target not those who are

46

responsible for it but its biggest victims: immigrants, refugees and oppressed religious and racial minorities.

References

Australian Bureau of Statistics 2019a, *Labour Force, Australia, Detailed Electronic Delivery*, Table 1, Catalogue Number 6291.0.55.001.

Australian Bureau of Statistics 2019b, *Labour Force, Australia*, Time Series, Catalogue Number 6202.0.

Bloodworth, Sandra 2008, *A Crime Beyond Denunciation: A Marxist Analysis of Capitalist Crisis*, Socialist Alternative.

Boone, Laurence 2019, "Growth is taking a dangerous downward turn", *OECD Ecoscope*, 19 September 2019.

Borland, Jeff 2019, *Labour market snapshot*, #52, December 2019, https://sites.google.com/site/borlandjum/labour-market-snapshots.

Bramble, Tom 2018, "The crisis in neoliberalism and its ramifications", *Marxist Left Review*, 16, Winter 2018.

Brown, Chad 2019, "US-China trade war tariffs: an up-to-date chart", Petersen Institute of International Economics, 13 December 2019, https://www.piie.com/research/piie-charts/us-china-trade-war-tariffs-date-chart.

Business Roundtable 2019, "Business Roundtable Redefines the Purpose of a Corporation to Promote 'An Economy That Serves All Americans'", 19 August 2019, https://www.businessroundtable.org/business-roundtable-redefines-the-purpose-of-a-corporation-to-promote-an-economy-that-serves-all-americans.

Carchedi, Gugliemo and Michael Roberts 2018, "The long roots of the present crisis: Keynesians, Austerians and Marx's law", in Gugliemo Carchedi and Michael Roberts (eds) 2018, *World in Crisis: A Global Analysis of Marx's Law of Profitability*, Haymarket Books.

Choonara, Joseph 2019, "Economic warnings", *Socialist Review* (UK), October 2019.

Department of Finance 2019, *Australian Government General Government Sector Monthly Financial Statements*, October 2019.

Department of Foreign Affairs and Trade 2019, Fact Sheet on China, August 2019, https://dfat.gov.au/trade/resources/Documents/chin.pdf.

Harman, Chris 1984, *Explaining the Crisis: A Marxist Reappraisal*, Bookmarks.

Harman, Chris 2009, *Zombie Capitalism: Global Crisis and the Relevance of Marx*, Bookmarks.

McKinsey Global Institute 2018, *Rising Corporate Debt: Peril or Promise?*, Discussion Paper, June 2018.

Organisation of Economic Cooperation and Development 2019a, *OECD Economic Outlook*, Volume 2019, Issue 2: Preliminary version, November 2019.

Organisation of Economic Cooperation and Development 2019b, *OECD Interim Economic Outlook*, 19 September 2019.

Quality Indicators for Learning and Teaching 2019, *Graduate Outcomes Survey 2018*.

Reserve Bank of Australia 2019, *The Australian Economy and Financial Markets*, Chart Pack, December 2019.

Roberts, Michael 2016, *The Long Depression*, Haymarket Books.

Roberts, Michael 2019, "Corporate debt, fiscal stimulus and the next recession", The Next Recession blog, 22 October 2019, https://thenextrecession.wordpress.com/2019/10/22/corporate-debt-fiscal-stimulus-and-the-next-recession/.

FROM REVOLUTIONARY POSSIBILITY TO FASCIST DEFEAT: THE FRENCH POPULAR FRONT OF 1936-38

SANDRA BLOODWORTH

[Marx's] theory is a summing up of experience, illuminated by a profound philosophical conception of the world and a rich knowledge of history.

Lenin, *The State and Revolution*[1]

The cumulative experience of working class struggles stretching over two and a half centuries has created a history rich in lessons for activists of each new generation of fighters. Marxists, reformists, academic historians and the bourgeois media draw on this history to strengthen political arguments. Today, in the context of new stirrings of support for socialism in the English-speaking world, debates about how to build a new radical, workers' movement, how to win reforms and even to challenge capitalism inevitably draw on past experience.

As Eric Hobsbawm argues in his book *On History*, history can tell us "what problem we will have to solve".[2] If your goal is the self-emancipation of the working class, the problems which need addressing when drawing conclusions about any particular struggle

---

Sandra Bloodworth has written extensively about Lenin and the 1917 Russian revolution, Marxist economics, women's and sexual oppression and pre-class societies.

[1] Lenin 1917.
[2] Hobsbawm 1997, p35.

include: did this struggle build working class unity, self-confidence and a class conscious view of themselves and their enemies? For instance, Rosa Luxemburg wrote of the mass strikes in the 1905 revolution in the Russian empire: "The most precious, lasting, thing in the rapid ebb and flow of the wave [of mass strikes] is its mental sediment: the intellectual, cultural growth of the proletariat, which proceeds by fits and starts, and which offers an inviolable guarantee of their further irresistible progress in the economic as in the political struggle".[3] On the other hand, historians who reject the goal of revolution and the destruction of the state in favour of a strategy of radical reforms assess historical struggles much differently – for instance, they're more likely to emphasise whether the movement brought a left wing government to power, rather than the development or not of class consciousness.

So it is not surprising that in the political battles between reformists and revolutionaries, interpretations of history play an important role. History can at least indicate what to expect – likely obstacles, what is necessary to win – even though, as Hobsbawm went on to add, it can't help us predict every contour of future struggles. This is not a straightforward question of formulaic answers to past, present or future problems; it is not a question of taking a template from the past to apply to today. No new situation is an exact repeat of something in the past. Questions of comparison and interpretation are not always easily settled, and new historical research can challenge old analysis and pose new questions. Facts are not self-evident markers. Which facts are more important than others? So for instance, Hobsbawm, in *On History*, proclaims that "historians are the memory bank of experience",[4] but how does he sum up the experience of the twentieth century in his *Age of Extremes*? He hardly mentions the factory workers or the soviets in his account of the Russian Revolution, some of the central actors in the overthrow of the monstrous tsarist regime and the creation of the first workers' state in history. And as Chris Harman says:

---

[3]   Luxemburg 1906.
[4]   Hobsbawm 1997, p24.

This is no isolated aberration. The working class is the great missing link throughout Hobsbawm's book. It hardly appears at all in the first half of the book, and finally makes its appearance towards the end to be discussed solely in terms of lifestyle... There are no references to such key expressions of working class power in the 20th century as the Spanish CNT, the American CIO, the French CGT, the Central Budapest Workers Council; the Polish Solidarnosc is mentioned once. From this history you would never imagine that the occupation of factories was a key turning point in post First World War Italian history or the sit-ins of June 1936 in 1930s French history. Even the huge concentrations of workers which characterised much of 20th century capitalism are missing: the River Rouge plant, Renault Billancourt, FIAT Mirafiori, the Lenin shipyard in Gdansk.[5]

Hobsbawm's book, widely used in universities, is promoted as a Marxist text, contributing to the marginalisation of Marxism as the theory and practice of the working class struggle for power. You can find no guidance there when assessing the French Popular Front of 1936. Rather than this work serving as a memory bank of the working class, it is one of forgetting. This is an extreme case. But reformist histories invariably manifest this type of amnesia, because struggles are assessed in terms of whether or not they contributed to or undermined attempts by politicians to achieve their goal of the "exercise of power" (i.e. winning parliamentary office), as Léon Blum, the Socialist Party leader of the French Popular Front government put it.

I will argue that reformists today rely on a very limited, and indeed, misleading interpretation of the Popular Front in France from 1934 to 1938 in order to bolster their arguments to back Democratic Party politicians such as Bernie Sanders. They are inspired by the election of the Socialist, Léon Blum, but pay little attention to understanding why a mass upsurge of strikes of revolutionary proportions was not sustained, and indeed, ended with fascism, so their arguments cannot contribute to building the kind of movement needed to fundamentally change society.

---

[5] Harman 1999.

Interpreting history today

We are witnessing the emergence of new support for socialism in the English-speaking world. And a new left reformist current, especially in the US, with *Jacobin* as its ideological centre, has put interpretations of history on the agenda. Their support for the Stalinist Communist Parties' popular front strategy of class collaboration in the 1930s poses a question which has divided Marxists from reformists since Marx's *Address of the Central Committee to the Communist League* in 1850. In that speech Marx argued that the key lesson of the 1848-49 revolutions in France and Germany was that workers, and in particular their leading party, must not for one minute doubt "the necessity of an independently organized party of the proletariat".[6]

The popular fronts broke with this tradition, established by Marx and carried forward by Lenin and the Bolsheviks into the early, revolutionary, Comintern. Until the 1930s, Marxists took it as a matter of principle that workers' organisations should not form alliances with bourgeois parties. Principles are not just abstractions, but are established through experience. And the tragic outcome of all of the popular fronts entered into by the Communist Parties in the 1930s confirm that this is a principle which should be upheld.

However, left reformists in the US today are attempting to rehabilitate the strategy of electoral class alliances to justify their own political strategy of campaigning for Democratic Party candidates. They either ignore or dismiss the principle of workers' independence from bourgeois parties as an abstract shibboleth. In their view, this relic of the past needs to be junked in order to relate to the newly emerging sympathy for socialism. The problem is they aren't replacing outdated principles or shibboleths with something new and creative. They're merely recycling the Stalinist approach of class collaboration. And the Popular Front government in France is the archetypal example proving that this strategy is a recipe for defeats and demoralisation.

---

[6]   Marx 1850.

To promote the popular front as a model for today, reformist writers focus on high points of popular struggle in which the CP participated while promoting cross-class alliances. But they have to brush over the ultimate outcomes which, rather than maximising the potential of such struggles, contributed to catastrophic disasters. For instance, the Spanish Popular Front ended with the establishment of the fascist dictatorship of Franco in 1939, just two years after workers' power had been on the agenda.

In 2016 Mitchell Abidor set the standard. In an article in *Jacobin* he declared that "[i]n French Popular Front leader Léon Blum we find both the grandeur and misery of interwar social democracy". The misery is dealt with by rightly criticising Blum's refusal to give support to the Spanish Popular Front government under threat of defeat by Franco's fascist troops. But Blum's failure is not explained as the predictable capitulation to bourgeois politics we should expect of reformist politicians, but simply Blum's individual failure. He concludes that Blum "opted for reasons of state over socialist solidarity and his moral sense". Abidor gives no critique of the predictable failure of the alliance with the bourgeois Radical Party, adding not to a store of necessary knowledge for any new workers' socialist movement, but to the conscious forgetting which permeates reformist histories.[7]

In an article in 2017, Joseph M. Schwartz, national vice-chair of the Democratic Socialists of America, and Bhaskar Sunkara, editor and publisher of *Jacobin*, claimed that the communist parties became "tribunes for socialism and the best organizers" by promoting the class collaboration of the popular front.[8] First, how could a party which held up Stalin's brutal dictatorship as their vision of Communism be a tribune for any vision of human liberation? Second, and factually, the outcome of the popular front strategy in the US, even within the framework of a reformist view, was disastrous for the American working class. As Charlie Post replied, "[t]he Communist Party's 1930s popular front strategy weakened the labor movement". All it

---

[7] Abidor 2016.
[8] Schwartz and Sunkara 2017.

did was empower the bourgeois Democratic Party, no friend of the working class, when there had been the possibility of significant and lasting reforms as well as the creation of a serious workers' organisation. Post concludes his critique of Schwartz and Sunkara: "I embrace their call for engaging in both socialist education and the hard work of building resistance to capital in workplaces and communities... The popular front strategy won't get us there, though".[9]

More recently, the British journalist Paul Mason has promoted the popular front as the way to ensure Jeremy Corbyn's defeat of Boris Johnson. He repeats the dishonest practice of ignoring the actual outcome of the popular fronts of the 1930s. His summary of why Corbyn should form a popular front is simply that the "'popular front' against fascism...paid off within six months. In Spain...the Popular Front took power in January 1936. In May that year the Popular Front won in France, giving the country its first socialist prime minister".

Further, in order to legitimise his argument with a left wing Labour readership, he also misrepresents the history of the British Labour Party: "Nye Bevan and Stafford Cripps, two key figures on the Labour left, advocated an electoral pact including Communists, Liberals and anti-fascist Tories... So the popular-front tactic is not some piece of niche, retro-leftist memorabilia. It is the property of the western democratic tradition; the only tactic that halted or delayed the march to fascism in the 1930s. And it was invented by the Corbynistas of their day".[10] Bevan and Cripps were not the first advocates of the popular front. They were part of a small minority won over by the Communist Party which had members working as entrists in the BLP. In 1938 Sir Stafford Cripps made no secret of what a popular front would mean, unlike the modern day *Guardian* writer. It was "worth the abandonment for the time being of the

---

[9]   Post 2017.
[10]   Paul Mason, "Labour's best tactic to beat Boris Johnson? A popular front", *The Guardian*, 3 August 2019.

hope of working class control"[11] and Bevan and Cripps were expelled for their efforts. As in Australia, the vast majority in the Labour Party rejected the popular front, opposing its class collaborationist orientation.

In a critique of the experience in the US in the 1930s, Post's conclusions are, as we will see, eerily similar to the lessons I will draw about the experience of the French Popular Front of 1936 to 1938:

> The allure of the popular front/realignment politics is quite powerful. It appears to be a *shortcut* to building a significant socialist left and winning concrete gains that will improve the lives of working and oppressed peoples. The hope is that forging alliances with "progressive" leaders of the labor and social movements and using the Democratic Party as a "bullhorn" we can change the relationship of forces, win reforms, and build radicalism. Unfortunately, this strategy has only produced failures and setbacks – ultimately because it is based on an unrealistic understanding of capitalism and working-class consciousness. The simple fact is that real gains for working people, people of color, women, LGBT, and immigrants are only won through *mass social disruption*—through strikes, demonstrations, occupations, and the like. These disruptive actions also build working-class consciousness, as working people have to forge bonds of solidarity in common organizations and struggles, confront their employers and the state, and experience their own power to change the world. A strategy that allies the socialist left to the labor officials and Democratic liberals undermines our ability to consistently advocate and build independent organization and militancy.[12]

In this article I will look at the experience of the Popular Front in France from January 1936 to June 1938 – an alliance between the Communist Party (PCF), the Socialist Party (SFIO) and the bourgeois centre party, the Radicals – to argue that the politics of the popular front were a disaster for the working class. Further, I will argue that reformists rely on a completely disingenuous reading of the events of 1936 similar to the misrepresentations of the New Deal popular front critiqued by Charlie Post. Sunkara argued in February 2019:

---

[11] Stafford Cripps writing in *Tribune*, 10 April 1938, quoted in Harman 1965.
[12] Post 2018.

[S]omething unexpected happened when the Blum government entered office – the ambitions of working people were unleashed. Not content with a resounding electoral victory for Popular Front parties, workers went on strike, occupying factories and paralyzing production.[13]

Sunkara concedes that this is not likely today in the US; in fact he admits "we're in an almost unprecedented state of weakness". But he blithely assures his readers that a Sanders presidency, with no mass base and no workers' organisations of any strength or militancy, can forge a path to reform "through confrontation with elites". How this is a strategy to win, when a militant, well organised working class could not, he admits, "is vague". Why the popular front is of interest is not even explained. The only purpose it serves is to legitimise class collaboration, and reduce what is a question of class struggle and organisation to the election of a president at the head of the Democratic Party representing, not organised workers and the oppressed, but the major imperialist bourgeoisie in the world.

As I will show, this massively understates what it took in 1936 in France to force the ruling class to offer reforms and presents no realistic assessment of why an impressive movement, far beyond anything even Sunkara thinks is possible today, could end in catastrophic defeat. Like others who sing the praises of the Popular Front government of Léon Blum, Sunkara ignores the consequences, including the minor detail that the Popular Front paved the way to fascism. And all he can offer as an explanation of the ultimate failure of Blum's government, is: "[i]t's difficult to keep workers mobilized once gains are made, and capital has the structural power to undermine those gains".[14]

If a genuinely socialist movement is to be rebuilt, the revolutionary left needs a keen sense of historical meaning, the relevance or not of any particular struggle for our time and an honest assessment of strategies tried in the past. Otherwise workers will be condemned to avoidable defeats and miss opportunities to win

---

13 Sunkara 2019.
14 ibid.

victories. With such a wealth of experience behind our movement, we need not rely only on our own experiences. If the sacrifices and achievements of past generations are not to be wasted, reformist misrepresentations of the lessons from their fight for a better world need to be vigorously combated. That is why understanding the popular front strategy matters.

Background to the Popular Front

On 6 February, 1934, fascist and monarchist armed gangs attacked the French parliament. The fighting with police left 15 dead and 1,435 wounded. The coup brought down the government headed by Édouard Daladier of the bourgeois Radical Party. To gleeful acclaim from the fascists, the new government was headed by the right winger Gaston Doumergue.

But at the grass roots it led to a new era of unity between the Stalinist PCF and the SFIO. It was also the catalyst for a rising tide of working class militancy, strikes, and occupations lasting until the end of 1938. Within a week, on 12 February, in response to a call by the Socialist Party and endorsement at the last moment by the reformist union, the CGT, the PCF and its smaller union federation, the CGT-U, four and a half million struck across the country. Two demonstrations in Paris, one led by the Socialists, the other by the Communists, made history by joining forces for the first time since the Communists split from the SFIO in 1920. It is said that a million marched, chanting "Unity! Unity!".

The threat of fascism and the need to respond to growing economic attacks from employers underpinned workers' desire for unity. The PCF since 1928 had denounced the Socialists as social fascists, refusing joint activities. Now this so-called "third period" sectarian idiocy was under enormous pressure from worker militants. At the same time, with Hitler rearming on a massive scale, Stalin began looking for allies among the Western powers, and sought to rebuild the CP's support, which had declined since 1928. This intersected with the growth of a radicalising left inside the Socialist Party.

There were PCF militants who had never fully endorsed the third period policy. So for instance, Jacques Doriot, based in Saint Denis, to the north of Paris, had been arguing since the increasing violence of the far right in 1933 for overtures to the Socialists. He refused to disband an anti-fascist committee of Communists, Socialists and other militants set up in response to the February riot, publicly challenging Stalin's policy. His expulsion in June could not stop the growing tide of support for unity.[15] In fact the very conference at which he was expelled voted for a united front with the SFIO. In spite of continuing resistance from the PCF leader Maurice Thorez, in July 1934 the PCF and SFIO signed a pact for a united front and held a massive joint rally on 14 July.

However, the PCF was under pressure from Moscow, which was anxious to form something of an alliance with Britain and France against Hitler. This was difficult if their parties in Western Europe were agitating for *class* rather than just popular struggle. And so the PCF argued to extend the new united front to include the Radicals, the party of the Republican bourgeoisie with an urban petty bourgeois and peasant voting base. Thus the term Popular Front, or *People*'s Front as it was called until later, was devised to highlight its cross-class nature. The Popular Front was formalised in January 1936 in preparation for a joint election campaign, which they would go on to win, making Léon Blum the first socialist President of France. The Socialist and Radical parties then formed government with the backing of the PCF.

A massive strike wave exploded following the election of Blum as prime minister. This is a fact. *Jacobin* writers create the illusion that if Sanders were elected president, there could be a similar response. Building on the fudging by Sunkara I referred to above, where he implied the comparison with 1936, Eric Blanc more openly suggests the election of Sanders could spark a mass strike wave. "Just by running for president in 2016, Bernie helped catalyze the deepest labor fight-back in decades. Imagine what could become possible by electing him 'organizer-in-chief' in 2020. Combine heightened

---

[15] Trotsky 1979, p25.

working-class expectations with a democratic-socialist White House, and you have the recipe for a potentially unprecedented strike upsurge."[16] But any comparison with France in 1936 is pure fantasy. There is nothing to compare between the US today and then.

The atmosphere when Blum became PM on 4 June 1936 was electric. But it was not generated just by the electoral victory. Actually the Popular Front had ridden on the back of the rising wave of working class radicalism. And there were not just a handful of individuals calling themselves socialists elected as candidates for a bourgeois party like the Democrats. Blum headed a genuinely mass Socialist Party with 202,000 members and a youth wing of over 50,000. Today, in the US with a population eight times the size, this would mean 1.6 million, with a 400,000-strong youth organisation. The PCF, looked to as the far left, had been growing rapidly – from 29,000 in 1933 to 90,000 by 1936 – and it would continue to grow to 298,000 by December 1936. The youth wing grew even more rapidly: from 25,000 in January 1936 to 100,000 by November. Today the equivalent in the US would be an organisation of 720,00-1.6 million, organised among the most radical working class militants and well organised in workplaces across the country, plus a youth movement of 5-600,000.

In the election, the main swing, of 21 percent, was to the SFIO, increasing its seats from 97 to 146; and the PCF, with a 15 percent swing, increasing its MPs by 10 seats to 72. So these two mass workers' parties held 218 of the 598 seats in parliament. The front with the Radicals actually helped shore up their vote because Popular Front parties agreed to support each other in the second round of voting. This took place in seats where no one won an outright majority in the first round, which is most seats. This meant in a range of seats the SFIO and PCF candidates stood down in the second round and the parties backed the Radicals. So while the Radical vote fell, the Popular Front helped prevent an even more precipitate decline, which should have been welcomed, not minimised, by the workers' parties.

---

[16]   Blanc 2019.

The strike wave

Yes, there was a strike wave; a quarter of the workforce were out on strike within weeks. That would mean about 40 million in the US today. The Communists had become the dominant force within the working class. Its power was not simply based on its numbers, but also its control over a reunited trade union movement combined with its radical image.

In the Renault factories alone, 35,000 workers went on strike on 28 May 1936, occupying the factories in Boulogne-Billancourt and in Flins. They were followed by all of the Paris metallurgy factories. Up to six million struck and occupations spread like wildfire, drawing in non-unionised workers, many of whom had never taken industrial action before, including department store employees, bank and insurance clerks. For instance, a socialist recorded how the workers in a small artisanal workshop where he lived approached him for help: "[n]aturally we are going to stop work like everyone else. Would you be able to help us draw up a list of demands?" In a department store in Paris, in June when other such stores had been on strike for days, workers felt too intimidated by management to speak to each other. Nevertheless, "something indefinable was in the air" and by the afternoon, notes saying things like "You can count on me" and "Do you want help?" had landed on the desk of the one employee known to be a CGT member.[17]

Bank workers and concierges joined the strike movement. There were general strikes in confectionery, woodwork and furniture, military clothing, apprentice hat-making, footwear, leather goods, car washing, water authorities, cinemas and publishing. In Paris, insurance company employees went on strike on 8 June, with pickets and occupations. A day later 50 companies were occupied. Danos and Gibelin, activists in the movement at the time, give an ironic sense of the atmosphere:

> The managers of these firms, used to the habitual docility of their employees, had never dreamed of a day when they would see their

---

[17] Jackson 1988, p93.

well-behaved staff camping on the pavement in front of their office doors, and at the very first meeting...they agreed to sign a deal.

The press reported a settlement agreed to by the union, only to print the next day that actually, it had only been a draft, and was still being considered. But other than one office, the strike continued, with workers pressing for more than the employers were inclined to give.[18]

The employers signed the Matignon Accords, which granted sweeping reforms, within days. They granted huge pay rises, the 40-hour week, paid holidays, union rights and unemployment insurance – all long term union demands, signifying a stunning advance in workers' conditions. But it didn't work, the militancy continued. In the regions, in industry after industry, union officials struggled to get workers back to work. They either wanted more than was guaranteed in the Accords or they didn't trust employers to implement them unless the agreement was more clearly binding. In one instance, the union, after coming back with an improved offer, could not convince 700 delegates to end their strikes. And employers couldn't now dismiss them as misled by troublemakers. The Popular Front leaders were anything but. In fact when one of them tried to address "his" workers in the absence of the strike committee, according to Danos and Gibelin he was driven out "before a forest of clenched fists, while all the workers chanted 'Out! Out! Out!', and his exit was crowned by a burst from the *Internationale*".[19]

But Sunkara intones: "Blum had neither the support or resolve for more radical measures". [20] Hah! Yes, the bourgeois Radicals predictably did not support him. But millions of workers were clamouring for more.

Marceau Pivert, the leader of the left wing of the SFIO, became famous for his declaration that "everything is possible". Over three-quarters of the strikes in June were occupations. A beautiful painting titled "The Strikes of June 1936", by a young left wing artist, Boris

---

[18] Danos and Gibelin 1986, pp88-98.
[19] ibid.
[20] Sunkara 2019.

Taslitzky, depicts the streets of the Parisian suburbs as a carnival of the oppressed. Julian Jackson, in his excellent book *The Popular Front in France*, records the words of Alexander Werth at the time:

> [B]uilding after building – small factories and large factories, even comparatively small workshops – were flying red, or red and tricolour flags – with pickets in front of the closed gates.

Later, in his trial by the pro-fascist Vichy regime, Blum would describe the situation as: "a social explosion" which "struck the government in the face" as soon as it was installed in power. Jackson paints a picture of a high level of class consciousness and confidence: "[t]he occupations were generally organized and disciplined...machinery and stocks were looked after with jealous care by the striking workers". And Blum would particularly remark that it was this "tranquillity, this sort of majesty" which inspired terror in the capitalists' breasts.[21]

Strikes were provoked by victimisations of militants, made easy by rising unemployment. Anyone could easily be replaced. Attacks on union rights went hand in hand with layoffs and attacks on conditions. So once the strikes took off, any attack by an employer was met with strike action if not an occupation. Workers with no experience sent delegations to union offices to ask how you went on strike. We don't know what to demand, they'd say, you will have to help us. Or workers in one factory would help less experienced draw up a log of claims so they could walk out, or even to justify an already accomplished walkout.

Just as in many other revolutionary situations recorded in history, workers got a taste of their power and, after over a decade of threatening far right militias and increasingly vicious employers, everyone just wanted to join in.

So let's turn to some explanation of the factors which resulted in this massive outpouring of working class self-activity.

---

[21] Jackson 1988, pp85–86.

Jackson looks at several reasons why the strikes took off in 1936. They did not just erupt because Blum was elected president.[22] The first impetus towards mass struggle was the fascist riot of February 1934, when managers had tried to prevent workers attending the counter-protest, something which was not forgotten in the succeeding years. Secondly, the unity between the Socialist and Communist parties contributed to the growth of the SFIO-controlled CGT from 785,000 in 1935 before unification with the much smaller PCF-controlled CGT-U to 4 million in the united union federation (CGTU) in 1937.

The PCF militants were leaders of hundreds of thousands of organised trade unionists. In the process of unification, the PCF had boosted its factory cells' activity in order to maintain and advance their influence, and turned towards an emphasis on organising around workers' concrete demands, beginning with a round of rolling stoppages. The strike wave had begun before the election, the second round of which was held on 3 May. A dock strike in Marseilles in December 1935 played a significant role in creating the momentum of 1936. It was called by the newly united union federation, over wage cuts which the former SFIO-controlled CGT had agreed to, and was closely followed by a one-day strike which again was over a proposed 10 percent wage cut. The 1 May strike by coal miners in 1936 was prepared over weeks before. Union membership in the mines had escalated from 26 percent in 1935 to 43 percent by March 1936.

The CGTU used the impetus of the expectations raised by the coming elections to get 85 percent of workers out on strike for 1 May. But the Renault strike which began on 28 May was not some spontaneous outpouring of enthusiasm for Blum or the election win. Surrounded by strikes over conditions in smaller plants, they received an appeal from the strike committee at neighbouring plants. The PCF-controlled artillery workshop went out in solidarity. Then after

---

[22]   The general argument and facts in the following paragraphs are from Jackson 1988, pp90-91 unless otherwise indicated.

the arrival of several leading Communist union officials, strikes spread through the plant.

The election win gave some impetus to an already rising level of struggle, but it was union militants, many of them PCF members, who were responsible for the massive strike wave, not simply the election of Blum.

Once the movement took off, many strikes and occupations were quite spontaneous and involved even non-unionised workers. Yet still the role of the PCF and CGTU officials and militants was crucial. The first factory occupation, on 29 May at Coder engineering, was "carefully prepared by the factory's Communist union activists in close collaboration with the party and the local Popular Front committee". The PCF had done long-term propaganda work there. Jackson argues that each subsequent outbreak was partly the result of local issues and emphasises the central role played by Communists both in preparing the ground by long-standing propaganda and in the timing and organisation of the strikes which broke out at the end of May. In fact, one official told the PCF Central Committee that the organisation of the strikes had occurred "on the basis of methods developed for fifteen years by the CGTU". "But often, where no union members existed, the strikes threw up their own leaders. The relationship between these new strike leaders, the mass of strikers and the official union leaders was far from easy: the workers wanted 'their' strike", but of course the union officials wanted to take control. Even where the PCF had a base, such as at Renault, a revolt by the rank and file delayed the end of the 28 May strike because some workers wanted more than the agreement the union signed.[23]

Clearly, the election of the Popular Front government made workers more ready to take action, assuming it would be more sympathetic to them than previous right wing-dominated governments. But this new sentiment was not generated by Blum particularly. Some local councils where the Popular Front had won elections in 1935 organised food supplies for factory occupations. The Communist Doriot's St Denis council produced 130,000 free meals in

---

[23] Jackson 1988, pp92-94.

15 days. And the election of one of their own, a former Renault worker, to the Boulogne-Billancourt seat in the first round of the national elections was a real boost to confidence.

But Jackson emphasises "the end of the fratricidal struggle between CGT and CGTU" as of fundamental importance. Apart from the growth in union membership, unification also reinvigorated the CGT and improved the authority of the Communist officials. And, after the defensive situation workers had been in during the Depression of the early 1930s, an improvement in the economy in 1935 gave a boost to confidence that gains could be won.[24]

Reformist misrepresentation

Today in the US, the far right is not staging attempted coups and marches of tens of thousands under arms; Sanders is not a leader of a mass workers' party of any kind; he's tied to one of the bourgeois parties which rules over the major imperialist state of the world. While it was reprehensible that the PCF pushed for the alliance with the bourgeois Radical Party, the SFIO was at least a mass working class party. There are no organisations in the US anything like the PCF or the SFIO, let alone one with over a million members, which even pretend they are anti-capitalist.

But the argument against the way the events of 1936 are depicted by modern day reformists doesn't stop there.

Reformists exaggerate the importance of Blum and other such politicians brought to power on the back of workers' struggles as a figurehead. To do that, they write out of history the importance of thousands of worker militants. They ignore or downplay the organising efforts of worker activists who laid the basis for the inspiring occupations, the discipline and solid stance which electrified other workers and intimidated their class oppressors. The idea that the upsurge of strikes and occupations in mid-1936 was largely "spontaneous", or that it was simply inspired by the election of Blum, who wasn't even on the left of the SFIO, seriously misrepresents the

---

[24] ibid., p92.

reality. It trivialises the effort which went into building strong working class organisations which made such radicalism possible. And it dishonestly creates illusions in parliamentary elections and the role of even not very radical politicians as the road to working class mass struggle.

Militants used an important victory at the electoral level to escalate what was already a mass movement of resistance. Nothing like them exists today in the US. So to maintain the fairy tale that a similar outburst could follow the election of Sanders, the mass of workers and their grassroots leaders have to be airbrushed out of the picture. In this reformist narrative, millions of workers are reduced to mere props for politicians and their electoral campaigns. However, Julian Jackson, an honest academic historian, sympathetically catalogues the workers' actions and draws interesting conclusions: "if they lacked political sophistication, they possessed intuition of the highest order: the chance might not come again".[25]

Think about that, "*intuition of the highest order*", a characteristic of workers' struggles which underpins the Marxist confidence in workers' ability to emancipate themselves and thereby humanity. Reformism depends on wiping from our collective memory the many talents and organisational genius which workers demonstrate when challenging the power of our oppressors. The effects of the struggle on workers' consciousness and confidence is of little consequence if the goal is to portray electoral victory as the all-important question.

At the time observers wrote descriptions of the impact of the strikes on workers' experience. Simone Weil, the intellectual of anarchist sympathies who had previously worked in a factory, describes what many observers did in the months of May and June: "joy", "smiling workers", music, dancing and laughter in the factories and streets. Photos from the time show striking café workers out in the streets with demonstrators, workers dancing, playing cards or just socialising in their occupied factories and in the streets. It truly *was* a festival of the oppressed, as the young artist portrayed it.

---

[25] ibid., p93.

But some commentators use these descriptions to argue that workers weren't really revolutionary, it was all just a bit of fun before they knew they'd have to go back to normal. Jackson argues that this is only one side of the events: there were always clenched fists and red flags. "As well as joy there was fear; as well as celebration there was struggle; as well as friends, enemies...grim faces as well as smiling ones."[26]

A photo of a mass meeting in the Renault Billancourt factory on 28 May 1936 is typical. The thousands of workers stand, smiling but determined, with clenched fists in the air voting for strike action. Even a photo of a group of middle class women, Popular Front supporters, shows them with raised fists. Once our focus is on these glimpses of both sides of working class self-activity, the fundamental difference between reform and revolution leaps out of these images. As Marx said in the *German Ideology*, a revolution is necessary, not just because there is no other way to overthrow the ruling class, but because it is only in the mass struggle that workers can change and become fit to rule over a new social order.

Wasn't the Popular Front worth the gamble?

But when workers are drawn into class collaboration the joy, the promise of liberation, the potential for their confidence to grow and develop is overridden by debilitating compromises. But before we discuss this constraint, it's worth noting that there were observers who recorded their misgivings at the time.

In France, Trotsky predicted confidently that it would end in disaster. Again and again, he warned that the aim of the popular front, initiated by the Communists, was to curtail the workers' militancy, to prevent the development of a revolutionary movement:

> [W]hen the masses are impatient and explosive, a more imposing brake is needed, with the participation of the "Communists". Joint meetings, parade processions, oaths, mixing the banner of the

---

[26] ibid., p97.

Commune and of Versailles, noise, bedlam, demagogy – all these serve a single aim: to curb and demoralise the mass movement.

He pointed out that Sarraut, leader of the Radical Party, openly

declared that his innocent concessions to the People's Front were nothing but the *safety valve* of the regime. Such frankness may have seemed imprudent. But it was rewarded by violent applause from the benches of the extreme left.

Trotsky firmly believed revolution was possible. And it was necessary, if the fascists were to be defeated. Yet with their meagre forces, the Trotskyists could not impact events.[27]

In Britain, Edgar Hardcastle, a member of the Socialist Party of Great Britain, wrote of the compromises already made by the Communist Party to enable this alliance:

They had to deny to the workers that "Socialism is the only hope" and independence the only method. On the contrary, they had to say that capitalism is not so bad after all, provided that its representatives are Liberals, not Conservatives... They had to help save the Radical party from being reduced heavily in size. Here are some statements from Communist sources about how they helped the Labourites [by which he means the Socialists] and Radicals...

[T]he *Daily Worker* quoted from the Russian Communist paper, *Izvestia*, the statement that the Radicals "have preserved their influence among the main mass of their voters. This was the direct result of the fact that they had joined the Anti-Fascist People's Front..."

This, it will be seen, proves that the Communists made and kept a bargain which was fair to the Radicals, but saving a capitalist Liberal Party from extinction is queer work for an alleged working-class party to be doing.

Some might dismiss his comments as typical rancour from a sectarian. But they were based on what was already being established in the public record:

---

27   Trotsky 1979, pp142-144.

At first the election results frightened the capitalist investors, but Mr. Blum soon made a "reassuring statement," and this "relieved the tension" on the stock exchange (*Daily Telegraph*, May 12th). Mr. Blum's assurance was that he would govern "within the present social regime" (*Times*, May 12th).

And Hardcastle's prediction of a likely outcome was tragically prophetic. He argued that the SFIO and PCF had entered a trap, and said of those who thought that "entering into pacts with capitalist parties" could solve the urgent questions they confronted:

> They forget that in taking on the administration of capitalism they do not gain strength, but lose it. They at once begin to earn the unpopularity and contempt which always centres on the Government which carries on capitalism. The effort to solve problems inside capitalism creates uncertainty, mistrust, apathy and despair among the workers who have cherished false hopes, and it correspondingly helps the Conservatives and Fascists later on.[28]

These contemporary observations, which proved to be tragically prophetic, must be the basis for thinking through strategies for today. Anyone who has lived through neoliberalism with Labour and Socialist parties imposing capitalist attacks can easily recognise the process. But the foresight of a socialist at the time, the devastating experience of experiments in cooperation between workers' parties and the capitalist class, find no empathy among those who reject the need to overthrow the system.

From revolutionary possibilities to disaster

> A consistent, resolute, progressive tactic on the part of the social democrats produces in the masses a feeling of security, self-confidence and desire for struggle; a vacillating weak tactic, based on an underestimation of the proletariat, has a crippling and confusing effect upon the masses.
>
> Rosa Luxemburg, 1906.[29]

---

[28] Hardcastle, 1936.
[29] Luxemburg 1906.

The narrative of the Popular Front does not end in June 1936. In the next two years Luxemburg's insight and Trotsky's warnings were borne out, with tragic results. Bhaskar Sunkara has argued on multiple occasions that the reforms contained the seeds of their undoing:

> The upsurges of May and June 1936 triggered a business counteroffensive over the implementation of the reforms. With political instability growing, Blum's middle-class coalition partners abandoned the fight. The leader had neither the support nor the resolve to pursue more radical measures. Blum was pushed out of power in little more than a year.[30]

Superficially this is a factual description of events. But it leaves out that workers had enormous expectations, and there was huge support to take on the right. And, by ignoring politics – the role of the parties in the Popular Front, what alternatives might have been considered – it offers no hint that there could be a different route available to workers in a similar situation. In his account, history marches on in an inevitable arc back to capitalist normality. Which in the conditions of France in the 1930s meant the triumph of fascism.

So let's deconstruct Sunkara's narrative. Much of the bourgeoisie, in response to France's economic woes and working class demands, were turning to support for the fascists. The Radical Party – the traditional party of the peasantry and the urban petty bourgeoisie – was also moving to the right; meanwhile the desperate, disillusioned middle classes were turning away from the moderate Radical Party. They were attracted to the fascists because they seemed to offer extreme solutions to an extreme crisis.

It was only by the working class becoming a revolutionary – i.e. extreme – alternative pole of attraction, that there could be any hope of winning them away from the far right. This made the idea of a bloc with the Radicals a disaster for the workers' movement. It was absolutely predictable that such a party would abandon the fight if it meant confronting the capitalists and their state. As Trotsky argued, in

---

[30] Sunkara 2019.

opposition to the PCF, the proletariat had to fight for their own interests.

In one of his first proclamations after being installed as prime minister, Blum, at the employers' behest to "shoulder his responsibilities, called on his supporters to 'submit to the law of the land'."[31] And this was before anything had been won! Hardly a basis on which to lead workers to achieve the most that was possible. In fact, the employers falsely create the image of Blum as the instigator of the negotiations which ended with the Matignon Accords in order to increase his prestige, all the better to use him to discipline an unruly working class. Only years later would Blum reveal his subordinate role: "[n]o doubt I would myself have attempted what is now called the Matignon agreement. But I am compelled by respect for the truth to say that the first initiative came from the employers' leaders."[32]

The Communist militants in particular had laid the basis over years of experience for the massive upsurge of June 1936. But once it became clear that workers were not satisfied with vague promises, that they didn't assume the Blum government would defend their conditions and were determined to keep fighting, the PCF sharply changed tack. They now discouraged any development of independent activity by workers. After all, they were under pressure not to alienate the Radicals for fear that they would walk out of their alliance. Strikes had multiplied during May, while waiting for the new government to take office. Employers complained in a communiqué from an assembly they convened, that "our impression is that the employees do not seem to see the solution to the conflicts in the same light as when negotiations were begun". On appeal from the government-in-waiting, the CGT issued statements calling on workers to preserve the movement's "calm, discipline, order, prudence and dignity" because they should remain "peaceful, controlled and correct". They should avoid "exaggeration, bouts of demagogy, and dangerous disorder". Soon after Blum's call for law

---

[31] Danos and Gibelin 1986, pp60-62.
[32] ibid., p72.

and order, the PCF issued a statement reassuring the press that they were "determined to retain the same discipline, and peaceful character which the movement had had since the beginning". By 11 June, the PCF was moving to end the occupations and strikes. Their attitude was summed up by Thorez, the Stalinist supremo, with his infamous phrase: "one needs to know when to end a strike". In reply to Pivert's exuberance, *L'Humanité*, the Communist paper, ran the headline "everything is not possible".

The assertion that Blum did not have support for more radical measures sits uncomfortably if anyone looks beyond the leaders of the unions and the popular front parties. The fact is, workers had occupied thousands of workplaces across the country, millions had joined a union, struck, and marched. But what is that to the reformist Sunkara? He assumes they didn't support anything more than one round of reforms. Yet strikes continued after June, at such a rate that one historian[33] has argued they represented a "revolt against work". Jackson summarises the situation at Renault: "workers' resistance took the form of absenteeism, lateness, production slowdowns and violence against non-union workers". A lot of the militancy was aimed at foremen, to the extent that at Renault in March 1937 the foremen went on strike against "union tyranny"! Strikes continued to be endemic, but were and are dismissed by historians. This ongoing economic struggle was the basis on which the movement could have been taken to higher levels of organisation and determination. Instead, strikes remained "wildcat" because the unions and the PCF spent all their time trying to prevent them, condemning them, and appealing to workers to honour appalling agreements they signed with management. The CGT's paper *L'Unité* repeatedly attacked such strikes, noting on one occasion:

> [a]n unusual number of absences on trivial or non-existent grounds...everyone should respect the work schedule set up by the management and accepted by us. We implore you to obey our

---

[33] Michael Seidman, "The Birth of the Weekend and the Revolts against Work: the workers of the Paris region during the Popular Front", *French Historical Studies*, 12 (2), Autumn 1981.

union's discipline, for in no way should we lay ourselves open to the enemy.[34]

According to this approach, the best way to defend themselves and the government against growing agitation from the far right was to capitulate to the bosses' offensive against the gains achieved in the June strike wave! From start to finish, the aim of keeping the Radical Party in the Popular Front government led to the PCF holding back the workers' movement from pushing further, or challenging for power.

Even Simone Weil, an anarchist, decried the militancy rather than arguing to build on it. After a visit to the Nord, in autumn 1936, she wrote:

> [B]efore June there was in the factories a certain order, a certain discipline founded on slavery. The slavery has largely disappeared; the order linked to the slavery has disappeared at the same time. One can only welcome this. But industry cannot survive without order.[35]

She went on to complain about the "arbitrary" control of production and the elemental nature of strikes organised by newly appointed delegates who had the temerity to act without consulting their officials. Jackson dismisses these cynical attacks: "It is too simple to stigmatize the delegates and workers for irresponsibility or abuse of power. There were serious issues at stake". In the coal mines of the Nord and Pas de Calais, the union argued for workers to work ever harder because "the precondition of the success of the Popular Front" depended on the maintenance of high productivity. At some places the CGT created vigilance committees to police their members. Unsurprisingly, "this productivist rhetoric fell on deaf ears"![36] The PCF condemned strikers who booed leaders like Johaux, the General Secretary of the CGT, and who wouldn't end a metal workers' strike in March 1938, as "Trotskyist provocateurs", arguing that if they made the strike official, Blum's government would fall. In the face of

---

[34] Jackson 1988, p106.
[35] ibid., p107.
[36] ibid., p107.

all this, it's not surprising that there developed "a difference of perceptions between the unions and the workers about the purposes of the strike movement of 1936".[37]

The attitude of the PCF was never a secret; it had to be openly stated in order for them to play the role that Stalin expected of them. In February 1938 Ambroise Croizat explained in the parliament why the Communists voted for new legislation designed to tie unions up in an arbitration bureaucracy:

> The working class wants order. For the workers, a strike is a weapon of last resort imposed by the employers' intransigence. The working class will be only too glad if we give them something to use instead of a strike.[38]

It would be one thing if Blum and the SFIO had stood to the left of the PCF and campaigned to take things beyond what suited Stalin's class collaborationist policies. But the SFIO didn't pretend to be revolutionary as the PCF did. They acted as reformists before and since, taking pride in being "loyal managers of capitalism", as Blum described himself. Blum was very much on the right of the SFIO; however, Marceau Pivert on the left did nothing to forestall the coming sell-outs. The eulogies in *Jacobin* to Blum do not inspire any confidence that those who subscribe to their politics will play a positive role in any future mass struggle by workers against the capitalist class.

At the end of 1936, the PCF called for a broadening of the Popular Front into a *French* Front by incorporating right wing conservatives who were anti-German on nationalist grounds. This, at the same time that the Blum government launched a major spending program on armaments which undercut workers' living standards. The PCF, thought of as the far left, refused to arm workers, refused to seriously organise and prepare for an offensive against the employers and the gun-toting far right. Stalin's alliance with their

---

[37] ibid., p108.

[38] Danos and Gibelin 1986, p212.

class enemy was totally counterposed to the class struggle their militants courageously led.

As Hardcastle, the British socialist quoted earlier argued, it is the logic of capitalism that no matter what reforms can be won, they will always be precarious. This was especially the case in the Depression of the 1930s. And 1937 saw a marked decline in workers' activity as the unions became tied up in the new arbitration system introduced as part of the Matignon Accords. This downturn in struggle encouraged bosses to take the offensive against the 40-hour week. Prices shot up, wiping out all the wage gains by May 1938.

The Popular Front government moved steadily to the right. In March 1937 Blum's police fired on workers protesting against a fascist meeting, killing six. On 22 June 1937, just one year after becoming prime minister, Blum resigned, when the right wing-controlled Senate refused to pass bills to deal with the growing economic crisis. Is it any wonder that the news of Blum's resignation was met with indifference by an increasingly disoriented working class on the defensive in the face of a ruling class counter-attack? They lacked any leadership which could inspire them to rise up and defeat the right once and for all. In fact their leaders were intent on the exact opposite: to accept whatever the bosses demanded and to defend a government which increasingly offered no defence against the onslaught. And so began a spiral of increasing attacks by the government and employers.

Blum was replaced by Camille Chautemps of the Radical Party, who would later propose they hand over power for Pétain to form a fascistic regime. The Popular Front would remain in government under the Radicals (with Blum returning for a month in 1938) until it was finally dissolved in June 1938.

In 1934 Trotsky had predicted that "if the united front [between the PCF and Socialists] enters upon an unworthy romance with the Radicals, ...apathy, the precursor of catastrophe, will make headway".[39] And events from late 1937 into 1938 were a ghastly vindication of his words. In spite of some heroic struggles, workers

---

[39]   Trotsky 1979, p59.

could not get on the front foot again, suffering more defeats than victories while their leaders preached order.

In December 1937 workers occupied the Goodrich tyre factory near Paris, the only photo of which survives because the Nazis used it on their propaganda poster, campaigning against the "threat" posed by a combative working class and left. On 23 December, the Minister of the Interior, wanting to make an example of this strike, sent 600 mobile guards to surround the factory. In response to blaring sirens, neighbouring workers mobilised, and by the end of the day Goodrich was encircled by 30,000 supporters, forcing the minister to call his attack dogs away. At Christmas public servants made history by striking against the Popular Front government. So on 29 December, Paris had no transport, gas or electricity. In March and April 1938, 150,000 workers in the metallurgical plants of Paris struck, the largest strike since June 1936.

The PCF and SFIO, rather than leap to the defence of their working class supporters and use their determination to push back against the growing attacks by the far right, warned workers that if they persisted the government would fall. When it did, the PCF let the strike escalate, trying not to be outflanked. But once they had got control of the strike, the Communist officials brought it to a quick end in spite of widespread protests by militants. In disgust, 80,000 left the metal workers' union in the next few months.

But even then the struggle was not over. In November 1938, wildcat strikes to defend the 40-hour week broke out across the country. In an attempt to rescue something of their reputation, the CGT called a general strike for 30 November, the event Jackson labels the "death knell". The miners responded and some factories were occupied, but without transport and other vital industries going out, the strike was a terrible defeat. At the Renault factory a bloody confrontation with police left 46 cops and 24 workers badly injured. And the workers were forced to walk through police lines as they ended their occupation, making the fascist salute and chanting "long live the police"!

This devastating defeat was the direct result of the craven attitude of the PCF and CGT. The unions declared that the general strike would be strictly limited to one day, and there were to be no occupations, demonstrations or meetings. That didn't stop the ruling class from mobilising. Over five days the government made requisitions, mobilised their forces, threatened civil servants and railwaymen, and stiffened the employers' resistance while using the public radio for propaganda. Danos and Gibelin comment: "[a] workers movement weakened by two years of capitulation could not resist such a mobilisation...by ten o'clock on the morning of the 30th the government was able to announce that 'the railways are working normally'". And other sectors soon followed. [40] They endorse a statement in *Syndicates* which drew what they describe as "the essential lesson". The strike was an attack on the government, "therefore necessarily took on the character of an insurrection... But an insurrection cannot declare in advance that it will act in accordance with the law. That, however, is just what the CGT did".[41]

In the wake of this humiliating defeat, hundreds of thousands were sacked and militants were victimised in the midst of widespread lockouts and repression. CGT membership plunged and by late 1939 all the gains except the paid holidays had been swept away.

Assessment

How do we know that the working class would have fought and won more? We don't, because it was never posed as an alternative by either of the organisations with sufficient strength to carry the struggle forward. So let's consider this issue by looking at another famous episode in history. If Lenin and the Bolsheviks had kow-towed to the Provisional Government in Russia after February in 1917, it would be accepted wisdom now that there was no support to go further, that the soviets could not have taken power.

---

[40] Danos and Gibelin 1986, p229.
[41] ibid., p230.

Leading organisations, and their leadership, have to *fight*, fight to explain why workers need to do x and not y. The determined leadership of Lenin and the broader Bolshevik party, their painstaking and persistent work on the ground, nurtured and built on every flicker of militancy. Their arguments for the soviets to take power increasingly made sense in light of the actions of the Provisional Government. This combination of objective circumstances and decisive leadership is what made the October revolution possible.

In France in 1936, it was vital that a party with some weight argued that the working class should fight tooth and nail to win the leadership of the middle classes; a party which recognised that this could only be done by posing the solution of revolution, of taking power from those who were funding and encouraging the fascists. The petty bourgeois masses, moving towards the fascists, could only be won by actions to combat the effects of the crisis and by pointing out who was responsible for the misery inflicted on everyone. In other words, to win the middle classes away from the fascists, workers had to offer a *revolutionary* alternative. Moderation did nothing to win the middle classes, instead it repelled them by seeming helpless in the face of social breakdown. In July 1936 Trotsky wrote: "If the 'middle Classes' in whose name the People's Front was expressly created are unable to find revolutionary audacity on the left, they will seek it on the right".[42] Tragically he was proven right.

The argument that there wasn't support for anything more radical is pure ideology and acts as a cover for reformist and Stalinist leaders who failed the test of events. We can't definitively prove they could have challenged for power, simply because that alternative was never posed, except by tiny handfuls of Trotskyists. As Danos and Gibelin conclude, we cannot guarantee that a serious struggle could have ended with socialism. "But there is one thing we can say – that such a struggle was not engaged because the leaders of the mass organisations took a deliberate decision that it should not be."[43] Sunkara and other reformists cannot face this issue because their agenda is to promote

---

[42]   Trotsky 1979, p171.
[43]   Danos and Gibelin 1986, p232.

the same class collaboration of the popular front. If a bourgeois party with its roots in the middle classes could pull socialists with a mass base among militant workers to preside over a crushing defeat of that base, how much more inevitable is it if socialists with no base in society, let alone one including militant workers, are elected in a party of the big bourgeoisie. Especially when in government they will be presiding over the major imperialist power in the world.

Interestingly, Jackson, in his detailed study, comments that by mid-1938, the small group of Trotsky's supporters were beginning to grow as workers drew lessons from the sell-outs and passivity of the reformist parties. But they were too small to turn the tide. Jackson sums up:

> It is far from the case that the Matignon Agreement was the only possible outcome to the labour conflict of June 1936. The strikers may not have always had a very clear notion of their objectives, but their movement was much more potentially menacing to the social order than many people have, for different reasons, been willing to admit.[44]

Conclusions

The Popular Front in France has terrible, but vital lessons for anyone who wants to see society fundamentally changed. Every revolutionary situation illustrates the incredible potential for self-emancipation of the mass of workers and oppressed. But such a situation becomes counter-revolutionary if the subjective factor does not develop in tandem with the objective. The policy of the popular front sapped the energy of the workers, and gave succour to the right. The PCF, under Stalin's directions, and determined to prove themselves to the Radicals as capable of keeping control over the working class, treated their followers as an army to be marched on and off the stage of history as it suited them. As a result, a mood of fatigue and despair took hold among masses of workers who had stood on the brink of revolution. In June 1936 Trotsky saw both potential and danger in the situation, writing prophetically: "[t]he

---

[44] Jackson 1988, p104.

struggle must now be consummated in the greatest of victories or it will end in the most ghastly of defeats".[45]

Tragically, the narrative does not just end with a return to capitalist democracy and the loss of hard-won gains. Far from stopping fascism, the class collaboration of the Popular Front paved the way for it. The Radicals preferred fascism to workers' power. The same Popular Front MPs who had been backed by the Communists and joined in government by the SFIO voted to ban the PCF in September 1939 and then in July 1940 supported the installation of the Pétain fascist-type regime which moved to Vichy to allow the Nazis to occupy most of France.

The black and white image of Pétain shaking hands with Hitler in October should be burned into our memories. It is the ultimate indictment of the popular front strategy.

In today's glowing accounts of the Popular Front, leaders or political parties are not apportioned any responsibility for this catastrophic defeat of the movement at the head of which they stood. As Danos and Gibelin conclude, "[t]he leaders emerged victorious; but they must take responsibility for the events which were to follow, the working class alone bears the honour for the success achieved. The conditions and the lessons of that success deserve to be remembered today".[46]

Those who hold up the popular front as a way to change society for the better need to be defeated today if the mistakes of the past are not to be repeated. As Trotsky said, nothing is more dangerous than "the sugared poison of false hopes".[47]

References

Abidor, Mitchell 2016, "Assessing Léon Blum", *Jacobin*, 26 September, https://www.jacobinmag.com/2016/09/leon-blum-popular-front-france-socialists-ps-fascism.

---

[45] Trotsky 1979, pp163-164.
[46] Danos and Gibelin 1986, p236.
[47] Trotsky 1979, p43.

Blanc, Eric 2019, "How Bernie helped spark the teachers' revolt", *Jacobin*, 30 October, https://www.jacobinmag.com/2019/10/bernie-sanders-teachers-strikes-movement-building.

Danos, Jacques and Marcel Gibelin 1986, *June '36: Class Struggle and the Popular Front in France*, Bookmarks.

Hardcastle, Edgar 1936, "The United Front in France", *The Socialist Standard*, June, https://www.marxists.org/archive/hardcastle/1936/united_front.htm.

Harman, Chris 1965, "Tribune of the People 1", *International Socialism* (first series), 21, Summer, https://www.marxists.org/archive/harman/1965/xx/tribune.htm#n26.

Harman, Chris 1999, "The 20th century: an age of extremes or an age of possibilities?", *International Socialism*, 85, Autumn, https://www.marxists.org/archive/harman/1999/xx/20thcentury.htm.

Hobsbawm, Eric 1997, *On History*, The New Press.

Jackson, Julian 1988, *The Popular Front in France: Defending Democracy 1934-38*, Cambridge University Press.

Lenin 1917, *The State and Revolution*, https://www.marxists.org/archive/lenin/works/1917/staterev/.

Luxemburg, Rosa 1906, *The Mass Strike, the Political Party and the Trade Unions,* https://www.marxists.org/archive/luxemburg/1906/mass-strike/.

Marx, Karl 1850, "Address of the Central Committee to the Communist League", https://www.marxists.org/archive/marx/works/1847/communist-league/1850-ad1.htm.

Post, Charlie 2017, "The Popular Front didn't work", *Jacobin*, 17 September, https://www.jacobinmag.com/2017/10/popular-front-communist-party-democrats.

Post, Charlie 2018, "The New Deal and the Popular Front. Models for contemporary socialists?", *International Socialist Review*, 108, 1 March, https://isreview.org/issue/108/new-deal-and-popular-front.

Schwartz, Joseph M. and Bhaskar Sunkara 2017, "What Should Socialists Do?", *Jacobin*, 1 August, https://jacobinmag.com/2017/08/socialist-left-democratic-socialists-america-dsa.

Sunkara, Bhaskar 2019, "The exercise of Power", *Jacobin*, 25 February, https://jacobinmag.com/2019/02/the-exercise-of-power.

Trotsky, Leon 1979 [1936], *On France*, Monad Press.

WE'VE BEEN DOWN THIS ROAD BEFORE: JESSE JACKSON, THE DEMOCRATS AND THE LEFT

NICK EVERETT

"With few exceptions, the Rainbow Coalition was just another name for keeping progressives in the Democratic Party." – Peter Camejo.[1]

"You don't change the system from within the Democratic Party. My own feeling is that the Democratic Party is ideologically bankrupt. We have to ask ourselves, 'Why should we work within the Democratic Party if we don't agree with anything the Democratic Party says?'" – Bernie Sanders, 1986[2]

When *Jacobin* editor Bhaskar Sunkara made his first pitch for Bernie Sanders' 2016 presidential run, he argued that "Sanders's candidacy could strengthen the Left in the long run" and "raise the possibility for the realignment of progressive forces on a totally different basis". This was however no fail-proof strategy, he conceded. Previous attempts "to grow social movements through

---

Nick Everett has been involved in radical politics since the late 1980s. He has been a union delegate with state and federal public sector unions and an activist in anti-war, Aboriginal, East Timor and Palestine solidarity movements. Nick is a regular contributor to *Red Flag* and has recently contributed a chapter to the second edition of *Radical Perth, Militant Fremantle.*

[1]   Camejo 2010, p181. This memoir was published posthumously: Camejo, a leader of the US Socialist Workers Party in the 1960s and 1970s, died in 2008.
[2]   Interview in *Vermont Affairs*, Summer 1986. Cited in Michael Kruse and Manu Raju, "Can Bernie Sanders Win the Love of a Party He Scorns?", *Politico*, August 2015.

outsider primary runs — like the 1980s Jackson campaigns — were dead-ends, and possibly even weakened independent political efforts", he wrote. Yet this time around, according to Sunkara, it would be different:

> Sanders's candidacy doesn't have to channel left forces into what will likely be a Clinton nomination. Instead, it could be a way for socialists to regroup, organize together, and articulate the kind of politics that speaks to the needs and aspirations of the vast majority of people. And it could begin to legitimate the word "socialist," and spark a conversation around it, even if Sanders's welfare-state socialism doesn't go far enough.[3]

Despite Sanders' endorsement of Clinton's 2016 presidential run — and the channelling of his supporters into a suicidal Clinton campaign that eased Trump into the White House — every issue of *Jacobin* over the last 12 months has championed Sanders' 2020 candidacy with great enthusiasm. *Jacobin* and the Bread and Roses caucus of the Democratic Socialists of America (DSA), with which it is associated, have been at the forefront of making the case to the 60,000-strong DSA that they should throw themselves into backing Sanders. Their arguments for endorsement are that Sanders' campaign will raise class consciousness, further divisions inside the Democrats and strengthen the DSA as a vehicle for advancing "independent socialist politics".[4] The mid-term elections of Alexandria Ocasio-Cortez (AOC) and Rashida Tlaib to Congress, and Julia Salazar to the New York State Legislature, are held up as evidence for the potential of this strategy.

The argument that the DSA's enthusiastic campaign for Sanders' nomination is advancing the cause of "independent socialist politics" has also been put forward by some former members of the now dissolved US International Socialist Organization (ISO). They argue for a "dirty break" strategy: by working alongside a leftward moving constituency of Sanders supporters inside the Democrats, they can supposedly be won over to supporting the construction of an

---

[3] Sunkara 2015.
[4] Meyer and B. 2018.

independent working class party.[5] This argument is also advanced by Reform and Revolution, a self-described "Marxist caucus" within the DSA:

> It would be a serious mistake for socialists to stand aside and argue against trying to make sure Bernie wins. Instead, our job is to help the left wing of Sanders' campaign be politically conscious of this conflict, get organized, and develop a program and strategy to defeat the Democratic establishment and establish a party that is 100% on the side of working people.[6]

However, neither *Jacobin* nor Reform and Revolution offer any serious critique of previous attempts to advance "independent socialist politics" by joining a campaign for the nomination of a liberal Democrat outsider. In 1968, much of the anti-war movement threw their support behind Senator Eugene McCarthy, who had promised to wind down the war in Vietnam. At the Chicago convention, the Democratic Party machine imposed their pro-war candidate, Lyndon Johnson's vice president Hubert Humphrey, as the nominee despite anti-war candidates having won the popular vote. While McCarthy's campaign served to disorient and derail liberals within the 1960s New Left milieu, it is Jesse Jackson's 1984 and 1988 Rainbow Coalition presidential runs that offer the most similar precedent to Sanders' campaign.

While never claiming to be a socialist, Jackson popularised the term "economic justice" in rebuttal of Democrat and Republican candidates' embrace of neoliberalism and "unfettered capitalism". In contrast to his Democrat rivals, Jackson opposed US intervention in Latin America and called for a redirection of US military spending to poverty alleviation. He advocated a New Deal-style infrastructure program, a single-payer health care system, a reversal of tax cuts for the rich and free college education. Jackson's campaigns were

[5] See Owen Hill, "What Kind of Break from the Democrats?", *Socialist Worker*, 17 July 2018; Eric Blanc, "Socialists, Democrats and the Dirty Break", *Socialist Worker*, 6 August 2018; Eric Blanc, "On History and the Dirty Break", *Socialist Worker*, 15 August 2018.
[6] "The Biggest Opportunity for Socialists in Decades", *Reform and Revolution*, April 2019.

remarkably successful in electoral terms. In 1984, Jackson garnered more than three million votes (20 percent of the primary, including 80 percent of the Black vote) and in 1988 increased his vote to nearly seven million. While the Black establishment within the party pilloried Jackson's 1984 bid, his 1988 campaign gained their endorsement. Nonetheless, Jackson left the 1988 party convention empty handed, with no policy concessions from presidential nominee Michael Dukakis. Jackson had faithfully served his party by strengthening the Democrats' appeal among liberal and progressive voters. Several far left and ex-Maoist organisations went into the Rainbow Coalition advocating an "inside out" strategy, based on the premise that they could work both inside and outside the Democrats to build the base of a future working class party. Some never re-emerged; others dissolved soon after, having failed in their mission.

This Rainbow Coalition experience serves as a historical example of the dangers of electoralism, opportunism and liquidation when socialists throw their support behind a candidate for the "B team" of the US ruling class. Like Sanders, Jackson was a liberal who advocated social democratic policies that promised much to working class voters, but were never likely to be enacted by a Democrat administration. Like Sanders, Jackson framed his proposals in the interests of the country as a whole; not on the premise that the working class needed to act independently, not only to win reforms, but to strengthen its own power. In his second run, Jackson, like Sanders, ran a much more mainstream campaign, shorn of much of his earlier radical rhetoric. Most significantly, Jackson, like Sanders today, was firmly wedded to the Democratic Party and fundamentally unwilling to break with it.

A groundswell of support for Jackson

The precursor to Jackson's presidential bid was Black Democrat Harold Washington's campaign for mayor of Chicago. A coalition of sections of the labour movement and the Latino and Black communities from the city's most impoverished neighbourhoods registered 100,000 new voters and secured Washington a stunning victory, in April 1983. Washington's defeat of two Democratic career politicians, including the incumbent mayor, added momentum to Jackson's proposal for a Black presidential candidate. A strong showing by Black socialist Mel King in the Boston mayoral contest a few months later offered inspiration for a "Rainbow Coalition" of communities of colour, white progressives and elements of the union movement. When on 27 August, 350,000 marched in Washington DC calling for "Jobs, Peace and Freedom", Jackson was cheered with chants of "Run, Jesse, run!" On 3 November 1983, Jesse Jackson announced his candidacy in front of an audience of nearly three thousand supporters, where he condemned president Ronald Reagan as "pro-rich, pro-aristocratic, pro-agribusiness, pro-military, and pro-big business". He criticised Democrat front runner Walter Mondale for remaining "too silent and too passive in the face of the Reagan administration's reduction of funds" for civil rights enforcement and his support for "repressive foreign governments".[7]

Jackson, with little funds and few endorsees, was an unlikely contender. To the Congressional Black Caucus he was an outsider; the Black political establishment was overwhelmingly hostile to his candidacy. Clarence Mitchell, president of the 357-member National Black Caucus of State Elected Officials, told the media that a Black candidacy could "be divisive and hurt local efforts to gain more influence".[8] Detroit's first African American mayor, Coleman Young, declared, "The major task of Black America today is to get rid of Ronald Reagan. We cannot afford to support a Black candidate who cannot win".[9]

The politicians described above formed part of an ascendant Black middle class, which had come to view Black Power as a means to advance political careers from within the Democrats, and in the process demobilise and demoralise the militant Black movement that

---

[7] Ronald Smothers, "Jackson Declares Formal Candidacy", *New York Times*, 4 November 1983.
[8] M. Carl Holman, "A Black for '84", *New York Times*, 22 April 1983.
[9] Ronald Smothers, "Black Caucus Weighs Candidacy by Jesse Jackson", *New York Times*, 26 September 1983.

had swept through the urban ghettoes in the late 1960s. In the years preceding the cry of "Black Power", a sustained mass civil rights movement had employed militant direct action tactics, such as boycotts, sit-ins and freedom rides, as well as mass action, like the 250,000-strong March on Washington in 1963, to force an end to the Jim Crow system of segregation and political disenfranchisement of Blacks in the South. Yet the passing of the 1964 Civil Rights Act and the 1965 Voting Rights Act did little to ease the economic discrimination faced by Blacks: *de facto* segregation in housing, employment and education remained a fact of life in the North, as well as the South.

The Johnson administration responded to the pressure coming from an increasingly militant Black movement by declaring a "war on poverty". The Great Society programs significantly increased spending on infrastructure and job creation in inner city ghettoes. For the Democrat establishment, the spending spree offered a means to blunt the rising militancy and co-opt the movement, channelling discontent through official channels. They had good reason to fear this militancy. By 1967, civil rights leaders such as Martin Luther King and Stokely Carmichael had come out clearly against the war in Vietnam, linking the US war machine to the impoverishment of Black communities. Following King's assassination, anger turned to rage as 115 cities burned. Radical Black caucuses emerged within trade unions, making their presence felt in industries such as Detroit's auto factories. Organisations like the Dodge Revolutionary Union Movement (DRUM) and the League of Revolutionary Black Workers, based inside the United Auto Workers, emboldened worker self-confidence in Black communities in a way not seen since the sit-down strikes of the UAW's early years, in the 1930s.

However, social spending soon petered out as the US economy went into recession in 1973. The limited economic gains won by Black workers as a consequence of their new found militancy were quickly eroded. Even before the economic slowdown, the Nixon administration had launched a war against Black militancy. The FBI's COINTELPRO (Counter Intelligence Program) made militant and left wing organisations, such as the Black Panthers, the targets of surveillance and infiltration. Within a few years, much of the radical Black leadership had been imprisoned or assassinated. The result was the consolidation of an increasingly moderate, middle class Black leadership that asserted a role for itself within the Democratic Party.

The strategy of advancing Black interests by seeking elected office via the Democrats displayed remarkable success on its own terms. In 1966, there were only 97 Black members of state legislatures, six Black members of Congress and no Black mayor in any US city. By 1985, there were 20 Blacks in Congress and 286 Black mayors, including newly elected Black mayors in Chicago, Philadelphia and Baltimore.[10] While African American politicians, organised within the Congressional Black Caucus, were making their presence known, the situation for African American workers and unemployed continued to worsen.

Jackson had long been estranged from Black radicals for his embrace of Black capitalism. In Chicago, Jackson established Operation Breadbasket, a project of the Southern Christian Leadership Conference, and later People United to Save Humanity (PUSH) to encourage business to hire Black workers and invest in the ghettoes. Jackson used the threat of consumer boycotts to pressure corporations to establish hiring and training programs for African Americans. While these efforts brought some jobs to the poor, they failed to address the root causes of Black impoverishment and inequality in capitalist America.

Jackson's campaign for the Democrat nomination, which articulated a platform radically opposed to Reagan's agenda, represented a shift to the left. Jackson argued:

> Blacks have their backs against the wall. They are increasingly distressed by the erosion of past gains and the rapidly deteriorating conditions within black and poor communities. As black leaders have attempted to remedy these problems through the Democratic Party – of which black voters have been the most loyal and disciplined followers – too often they have been ignored or treated with

---

[10] Misnik 1988.

disrespect. Mounting a serious presidential candidacy is one way of insisting that black leaders play significant roles and help to shape policy and programs for the party.[11]

Yet Jackson's leftward lurch ran counter to the direction of the Democrats and official US politics as a whole. The post-war economic boom had come to an end and the stagnation of the US economy in the mid-1970s necessitated a sharp offensive to drive down wages and living conditions in order to restore the rate of profit. This impacted Black workers in particular, who were concentrated in manufacturing industries, such as auto, which were hardest hit by the economic crisis. As Manning Marable observes:

> The intense socio-economic crisis of the 1980s within Black America created the social foundations for a Black revolt against the Democratic Party; but given the lack of a socialist alternative, that revolt occurred within the Democratic Party. Jackson, long the representative of the Black entrepreneurial elite, became the conduit of the Black social revolt.[12]

The Reagan Revolution

Reagan's election in 1980 ushered in a period of neoliberalism worldwide and sharply polarised American society. Cuts to public spending and attacks on living standards that had begun under the Carter administration were ratcheted up with zeal by Reagan. Reagan's fiscal policies accelerated downsizing, plant closures and relocating production to areas with cheaper labour. Between 1968 and 1981, the real standard of living for average US industrial workers and their families dropped by one-fifth for those still employed. By 1982, 34 million Americans – one out of every seven – were living below the official government poverty line.[13]

Determined to defeat any potential resistance to his big business agenda, Reagan launched a frontal assault on the trade union

---

[11] Jesse Jackson, "Hey, You Democrats: We'll All Benefit if a Black Runs for President", *The Washington Post*, 10 April 1983.
[12] Marable 1985, p43.
[13] Misnik 1988.

movement. When the Professional Air Traffic Controllers (PATCO) went on strike in August 1981, Reagan refused to negotiate, instead giving the strikers an ultimatum to return to work. All those who refused were fired, their jobs filled with permanent replacements. This move gave a green light to employer assaults on unions. Unionisation rates slumped from 25 percent in 1970 to 19 percent by 1984 and 16 percent at the end of the Reagan-Bush era in 1992.[14] The AFL-CIO trade union bureaucracy, which had been closely tied to the Democrats from the time of Roosevelt's New Deal, was incapable of mobilising any serious opposition to Reagan. As Mike Davis observes, in the 1984 Democratic Party nomination contest "it was Jackson, not Mondale, who insistently denounced plant closures, supported labour law reform, attacked the open shop and stood up for the organizational rights of undocumented workers".[15]

Black workers were hardest hit by the 1981-82 recession. Throughout 1982-83, official Black unemployment was 20 percent and Black youth unemployment rose above 80 percent in most urban areas of the North and Midwest.[16] High unemployment, combined with a right wing ideological offensive, fuelled a resurgent racism. Representing the vigilante wing of Reaganism, the Ku Klux Klan initiated white voter registration drives and ran openly for office in the South. Bombings, shotgun killings and cross burnings were revived to terrorise African American communities.

Ratcheting up Cold War tensions, Reagan declared war against Third World liberation movements, claiming they were proxies for the "Evil Empire" (the Soviet Union). A force of anti-communist mercenaries, known as the "Contras", was assembled to wage war against Nicaragua's popular Sandinista government. Reagan also backed South Africa's apartheid regime and its proxy forces in Angola, allegedly to defeat Soviet and Cuban-backed "terrorists". In

---

[14] Cohen 1992, p2.
[15] Davis 1986, p19.
[16] Marable 1985, p8.

an effort to bankrupt the Soviet Union, Reagan launched a new arms race, with military spending reaching a record $365 billion in 1986.[17]

In the face of Reagan's right wing offensive, the Democrats offered little opposition. Mondale, the front runner in the 1984 primary, adopted a corporatist policy, advocating for tripartite coordination between industrial capitalists, the federal government and the AFL-CIO to rescue the declining industrial base of the Northeast. His main opponent, Gary Hart, pursued a more openly neoliberal policy, arguing for market-based mechanisms to promote new tech industry in the Sun Belt (the South East and South West). Both accepted Reagan's rationale that social spending had to be sacrificed to fund a massive arms build-up. On foreign policy, there was little to distinguish them. While Hart advocated a more circumspect policy, opposing Reagan's "dirty war" in Central America, both Mondale and Hart supported Reagan's 1983 invasion of Grenada and the deployment of nuclear missiles in Europe. Both attempted to outbid Reagan in their enthusiastic support for Israel.[18]

The New Left and the Democratic Party

Following the youth radicalisation of the 1960s, much of the US New Left had adopted a hostile attitude to working within the Democrats, and with good reason. In 1964, the Mississippi Freedom Party demanded its delegates be seated at the Democrat Convention in place of the openly segregationist official Mississippi Democratic Party, which excluded Blacks (40 percent of Mississippi's population) from membership. The party's refusal to seat the MFP starkly illustrated that it was an instrument of Southern reaction that would not give up Jim Crow segregation without a fight. No longer were Democratic Party liberals seen as allies (even faint-hearted ones) in the struggle for racial justice. Malcom X's break with the Nation of Islam, and his trajectory towards a revolutionary internationalist politics

---

[17] Carl Conetta and Charles Knight, "Post-Cold War US Military Expenditure in the Context of World Spending Trends", Project on Defense Alternatives *Briefing Memo*, No. 10, January 1997.

[18] Davis 1986, pp18-20.

before his assassination in January 1965, also catalysed a leftward turn by youth within the civil rights movement. Student Nonviolent Coordinating Committee leader Stokely Carmichael famously coined the term "Black Power" to capture the mood of rebellion that gripped inner-city ghettoes.

The events of 1968 further radicalised the emerging New Left. The Viet Cong-led Tet offensive ended Washington's hopes of victory in Vietnam and with it President Lyndon Johnson's hopes of re-election. Martin Luther King's assassination spurred Black rebellions in more than one hundred cities that were put down by 70,000 troops. In May and June, the eruption of mass student protests and a general strike in Paris, demonstrated that revolution was possible in the West. And in August, the crushing of the Prague Spring by Moscow's tanks destroyed the standing of Moscow-aligned Stalinist parties, such as the US Communist Party.

For a wing of the anti-war and civil rights movements that had backed Democrat "dove" Eugene McCarthy in the primaries, the August 1968 Democrat Convention proved a bitter, but salutary lesson. Despite anti-war candidates winning the vote in the primaries, the Convention nominated Johnson's pro-war vice president Hubert Humphrey. Outside the Convention, in the streets of Chicago, police viciously beat anti-war demonstrators. In the subsequent presidential election, Humphrey narrowly lost to Republican Richard Nixon, who attempted to temper anti-war sentiment by withdrawing US troops under a policy of "Vietnamisation" of the war. At the same time, Nixon intensified the bombing of North Vietnam and widened the war by invading Cambodia. The result was an explosion of protest across US campuses. Students for a Democratic Society (SDS), which spearheaded many of the protests, expanded from 30,000 to more than 80,000, organised in more than 350 chapters in November 1968.[19]

Out of this period of intense anti-war organising emerged a New Left that began to shake off the shackles of McCarthyism and embrace radical and revolutionary politics. Various ideological currents

---

[19]   Elbaum 2002, p65.

emerged, some reviving the fortunes of the existing US left and others, inspired by international developments, constructed new revolutionary organisations. The Communist Party gained some youth, especially following the campaign to free African American activist Angela Davis (a CPUSA member framed on murder charges). The Socialist Workers Party – the standard bearer of US Trotskyism for decades – also attracted significant youth from its work on the campuses and in the anti-war movement. However, the fastest growing current within the New Left between 1968 and 1973, known as the New Communist Movement (NCM), embraced "Third World Marxism", taking their lead from the Vietnamese and Chinese Communist Parties, Amilcar Cabral and the liberation movements of Southern Africa, and Che, Fidel and the Cuban Revolution. While the NCM's influence lasted little more than a decade, its significance for our analysis here lies in its evolution from a rejection of Democratic Party electoralism in the early 1970s to enthusiastic engagement with Jackson's campaigns a decade later.

The New Communist Movement

In the late 1960s, Che Guevara's call for "two, three, many Vietnams" appealed to young radicals looking for a revolutionary internationalist and combative resistance to the violence of US imperialism. In contrast, the "Old Left" – descended from the radicalisation of the 1930s – was viewed as stale and impotent. The international flagship of "world communism", the Communist Party of the Soviet Union (CPSU), under Khrushchev's leadership, advocated a policy of "peaceful co-existence" between the Eastern bloc and the West. Since the late 1930s, the CPUSA – the CPSU's US acolyte – had pursued a "popular front" strategy, tail-ending the trade union bureaucracy that had long since made peace with the Democrats. The NCM rejected the "revisionist" trend of Stalinism, allegedly pioneered by Khrushchev (but in reality dating back to Stalin's "popular front" turn), instead orienting to Beijing and embracing Mao Zedong Thought. Claiming to be the inheritors of the "Marxist-Leninist" tradition in the US, NCM groups adopted a sectarian attitude to working with others on the left. While a plethora of NCM groups existed in the early 1970s, the largest and most influential were the Revolutionary Union (RU), the October League and the Communist League.

In 1973-74, at the height of its influence, the NCM "held the allegiance of roughly 10,000 core activists and influenced many thousands more", according to Max Elbaum, a New Left activist who went on to play an influential role within the movement.[20] Inside SDS, Maoists argued for a disciplined, revolutionary cadre organisation in contrast to the loose structures that predominated in the New Left. The Black Panther Party (BPP), founded in 1966, provided a model, explains Elbaum: "the BPP's character as a disciplined, centrally led, cadre party…was a watershed in legitimizing the notion of a tight revolutionary party among young radicals".[21] By 1973, the BPP was sharply divided: a faction led by Eldridge Cleaver – then in exile in Algeria – accused the Huey Newton-dominated leadership of reformism for its focus on community and education programs, and legal defence work. Cleaver argued instead for building an underground cadre organisation that could carry out armed actions. After a bitter dispute that saw shootouts between the warring factions, Cleaver's minority faction left or were expelled. The BPP's implosion marked the demise of radical Black Nationalism just as Maoism was reaching the peak of its influence within the New Left.

Throughout the 1970s, NCM groups played important roles in trade union, international solidarity and anti-racist campaigns. Despite their often hostile interrelationships, they shared a common focus on building grassroots struggles. While theoretically weak compared to the Trotskyist left, the NCM maintained a much larger audience. This was due in part to the efforts of the *Guardian* newspaper, which at its height in 1973 claimed 20,000 readers a week and drew thousands to public meetings.[22]

---

[20] ibid p4.
[21] ibid p67.
[22] ibid p111.

By the late 1970s, all of the NCM groups were in decline. Elbaum identifies their demise as resulting from a "misassessment of how ripe capitalism was for defeat" and a self-proclaimed vanguardism, whereby each group asserted that they were the guardians of "one and only one correct, revolutionary doctrine".[23] Zig-zags in Chinese Communist Party (CCP) economic and foreign policy spurred a series of crises within the NCM groups. Following Nixon's 1972 visit to China, relations between the US and China began to thaw. After Mao's death in 1976, Beijing moved more closely into Washington's orbit, siding with the US amid escalating Cold War tensions. China also became the main supporter of the genocidal Pol Pot regime in Cambodia. After Vietnamese troops ousted Pol Pot in 1978, China attempted an ill-fated military incursion into Vietnam. The CCP had now disowned the Cultural Revolution, and under Deng Xiaoping's leadership set China on a path towards capitalist restoration. These moves tarnished the CCP in the eyes of even the most fervent US Maoists.

While several NCM groups had already distanced themselves from Beijing and abandoned Mao Zedong Thought, all NCM groups entered a period of crisis between 1979 and 1981. Most directly affected was the Communist Party (Marxist-Leninist), which had been the CCP's most loyal US supporter. When Daniel Burstein, the CP(ML)'s key leader and editor of its publication *The Call*, began to question the tenets of Marxism-Leninism, the organisation went into terminal decline. A series of realignments, splits and fusions resulted in the launch of the League of Revolutionary Struggle (LRS) in 1978 and the Communist Workers Party (CWP) in 1979. The latter (the larger of the two groups with 400-500 members) was catapulted to nationwide prominence in November 1979, when five of its members were murdered at a rally opposing the Ku Klux Klan. While the massacre evoked widespread public sympathy, the CWP was also roundly criticised for its ultra-left posturing and failure to build a broad front against the Klan.

---

[23] ibid pp88-90.

When Ronald Reagan entered the Oval Office in 1981 his right wing agenda provoked a wave of protest. In May 1981, 100,000 protested US intervention in El Salvador, launching a mass campaign against US intervention in Central America. The following September, the AFL-CIO initiated a rare display of defiance against Reagan's anti-union assault, mobilising 400,000. In June 1982, a million marched for nuclear disarmament. Reagan's ascendency underscored the need for a revolutionary left that could offer a way forward. Yet the NCM lacked both the cadre and political clarity to do so.

Other far left groups also entered the 1980s in crisis. The US SWP faced a series of splits and convulsions, having pinned its hopes on an expectation of rising class struggle that failed to materialise. As a consequence, its membership halved from a peak of 1,690 in 1977 to 885 in 1984. [24] The International Socialists, representing "Third Camp" Trotskyism, abandoned their newspaper and suffered a split. Former members of both groups formed Solidarity in 1986. A Solidarity pamphlet published two years later reflects on why the New Left was unable to consolidate the 1960s rebellion outside the clutches of the Democrats:

> [T]he movements of the 1960s in and of themselves did not have the social power and coherence to institutionalise this rebellion and translate it into a permanent, organized and unified feature of the political landscape. The U.S. labor movement, with its 20 million members, was the force that *should* have been capable of providing a social anchor for such a development. But the AFL-CIO had been tamed by the decades of post-war prosperity. Its firmly entrenched bureaucracy was steeped in business unionism, conservatism and reliance on electing Democratic friends of labor.[25]

Into this void stepped the forces of social democracy, which had been temporarily pushed aside during the 1960s rebellion. At the forefront of this revival was the DSA, which formed in 1982 through

[24] ibid., p262. For a discussion of the causes of the SWP's collapse, see Lorimer 1997.
[25] Misnik 1988.

a merger between the Democratic Socialist Organising Committee (DSOC) and the New American Movement (NAM).

The Democratic Socialists of America

Today the DSA is by far the largest organisation on the US left. However, in the 1970s, this was not the case. In 1973, when the combined forces of the NCM could claim thousands of members and a readership of tens of thousands for their publications, the DSOC was just getting established with 300 members. The DSOC emerged as a split from the youth wing of the Socialist Party. A minority within the SP, led by Michael Harrington and Irving Howe, backed the McGovern campaign and favoured a "realignment" strategy within the Democrats. Harrington argued that the task of US socialists was "to build a new American majority for social change" by bringing together US labour and a "new politics" centred on the liberal, anti-war sentiments of students and middle class voters who had backed McGovern.[26]

By the late 1970s, the conditions had ripened for the resurgence of social democracy. The 1974-75 recession resulted in a significant slump in industrial militancy and the decline of both union membership and rank and file organising. Black Power had renounced the early militancy of the Black Panthers in favour of seeking electoral office, following the brutal repression of the Nixon years. And, as Mike Davis observes, "The bizarre implosion of the 'new communist movement', as the Maoist left moved from the factory floor to frenzied party building and street confrontations, reinforced, if only by harrowing negative example, the growing claim of the electoralists to represent the sole rational hope for a mass American left."[27]

Harrington and the DSOC attempted to forge a Democratic agenda committed to Keynesian reformism, the so-called "left wing of realism". Yet the "realism" that was gaining ascendency within the Democrats was neoliberalism. From 1978, the Carter administration

---

[26] Harrington 1973, p5.
[27] Davis 1986, p7.

adopted a right wing turn, abandoning health reform, job creation programs and labour law reform in favour of savage budget cuts. Significant sections of the ex-New Left now gravitated towards the DSOC's electoralist politics. Publications such as *Socialist Review* and *In These Times* abandoned their former calls for a new American Socialist Party in favour of pragmatic endorsements of liberal Democrats.

The merger between DSOC and NAM, a successor organisation of SDS, brought hundreds of former New Left activists into the DSA. However, as Mike Davis observes, during the unity talks any serious analysis of the rightward transformation of the Democrats was shunted to the sidelines. "'Unity against Reagan' and unqualified support for the AFL–CIO Executive became the twin motivating slogans for DSA's headlong rush, first to Edward Kennedy, and then to Walter Mondale."[28] At the time of DSA's 1982 launch it claimed 6,000 members.[29] While this was a largely passive, paper membership, the formation of DSA established social democracy as the dominant trend on the socialist left. Efforts by New Left currents to build a base in the working class through organising on the shop floor were now well and truly eclipsed by a perspective of trying to build influence among union officials and liberal Democrats.

In 1984, the DSA shunned Jackson in favour of Walter Mondale's campaign, blindly hoping to drag Mondale to the left. In 1988, with no Mondale-like centrist contesting the nomination, the DSA backed Jackson. For the DSA, the Rainbow Coalition was not a vehicle to build a new party, but rather a means to consolidate support for its coalition-building efforts within the Democrats. The combined impact of the retreat of the revolutionary left and the revival of social democracy under the DSA's banner contributed to pulling much of the far left into the Rainbow Coalition. As Davis observes:

---

[28]   ibid., p8.
[29]   Joseph M. Schwartz, *A History of Democratic Socialists of America 1971-2017: Bringing Socialism from the Margins to the Mainstream*, July 2017. https://www.dsausa.org/about-us/history/.

The principal object-lesson of the militant 1960s, reliance on independent mass politics outside of and against the national Democratic Party, was stood on its head. Participation in bourgeois electoral politics was redefined as the admission ticket to serious popular politics *tout court*.[30]

Not since the 1930s, when the Communist Party rushed headlong into the arms of Roosevelt's New Deal, had the US left been so wedded to working within the Democrats.

The Left and the Rainbow Coalition

In 1983, the allure of Jackson's Rainbow Coalition proved too tantalising for the beleaguered remnant organisations of the NCM to resist. They now made their way down a well-worn path: entering the *cul-de-sac* of the Democrats to campaign for a liberal candidate. The NCM organisations that entered the Rainbow Coalition included the LRS, the CWP, Line of March (formerly the Rectification Network), the North Star Network and the Freedom Road Socialist Organization. The latter two organisations were attempts to unify several ex-Maoist splinters. Only a handful of revolutionary socialist groups, including Solidarity and the International Socialist Organization, resisted the pressure to join Jackson's campaign.

Many sincere activists and anti-racists were drawn to Jackson's 1984 and 1988 presidential campaigns, perceiving them as a vehicle for pushing back Reagan's right wing agenda. Sheila Collins, author of *The Rainbow Challenge*, argued that the Rainbow Coalition offered a solution to the failure of the 1960s civil rights and Black Power movements to consolidate their gains because of "the separation of the social movements from electoral politics".[31] Others argued that the Rainbow Coalition could give voice to the disenfranchised in the electoral arena and push US politics to the left. Still others claimed that the Rainbow Coalition offered a way to reinvigorate the anti-war and anti-racist movements.

---

[30] Davis 1986, p8.
[31] Collins 1986, p105.

For the left within the Rainbow, Jackson and other Rainbow politicians' electoral ambitions were viewed as secondary to building "mass movements". They argued that activists could use Jackson's star media profile and left wing rhetoric to build grassroots campaigns. Shelly Ross, a leader of LRS, argued that the Jackson campaign demonstrated "the importance of electoral politics as a platform for progressive ideas". Ross claimed, "The Jackson campaign thrust to the forefront of U.S. politics the demands of the Black Liberation Movement and in the process showed how the electoral arena could be transformed into a vehicle for revolutionary, mass struggle".[32] Similarly, Elbaum, then a leader of Line of March, argues:

[T]he political program of the Jackson/Rainbow movement, while not revolutionary, went well beyond the parameters of mainstream politics. Yet by bringing this program into the Democratic primary contests, the Jackson campaign found a mechanism to present its message to tens of millions and mobilize a nationwide apparatus. This meant a direct confrontation with white supremacy – in the form of a white electoral backlash – as well as conflict with accommodationist Black leaders who were crucial to maintaining the hegemony of bourgeois politics in the African American community.[33]

In 1984, with the Black establishment rejecting the Rainbow, leaders and activists from NCM groups were able to step into a vacuum in Jackson's apparatus to assume leadership and organising roles within the Rainbow Coalition. Yet this only served to reinforce their illusions that the Rainbow Coalition could be turned into a vehicle for building struggles outside the electoral arena. As Misnik observed:

In reality, there are *two* Rainbow Coalitions, each with its own idea of the Rainbow's purpose. The "pragmatic" Jackson supporters are primarily interested in strengthening their faction inside the Democratic Party. The "radical" Rainbow forces are attempting to advance progressive social movements through the Jackson campaign,

---

[32] Ross 1985, p41.
[33] Elbaum 2002, p276.

with many hoping to provoke a fundamental realignment in U.S. politics.[34]

Illusions expressed by leftists such as Ross and Elbaum that the Rainbow Coalition could take on a more permanent character stemmed from the objective need of Jackson to build a beachhead within the Democrats between the 1984 and 1988 elections. At the 1984 party Convention, 465 Jackson delegates, with the support of more than three million Democrat voters, experienced the indignation of having platform demands steamrolled by the party machine. Jackson himself readily endorsed Mondale's campaign without winning any serious concessions. However, as soon as the 1984 election was over, Jackson launched his 1988 campaign by keeping himself in the national spotlight with public attendances at peace and anti-apartheid protests. The Rainbow Coalition conventions, held in April 1986 and October 1987, provided a means to maintain the momentum of his campaign by building the Rainbow independently alongside Democratic Party structures. The 1987 convention was attended by more than one thousand delegates, living up to Jackson's claim that he was assembling a "rainbow" of Black, Latino, Native American and Asian American activists, alongside progressive trade unionists and social movements. Yet, despite claims otherwise, this "unity" ultimately only served one purpose: to get Jackson elected in 1988.

Inside-outside strategy

For a sizeable section of the left, the Rainbow Coalition was seen as a means to precipitate a break from the Democrats in favour of establishing a new, anti-capitalist party. The National Committee for Independent Political Action (NCIPA) typified this "inside–outside" strategy. Like the left within the DSA today, the NCIPA held the position that the way to break from the Democratic Party is to join it. This perspective is fundamentally defeatist. It is premised on the assumption that electoral politics is the primary sphere in which a

---

[34] Misnik 1988.

contest of ideas can be waged to shape mass consciousness. Collins' assertion that "the election of Ronald Reagan in 1980 shocked many left activists into discovering the dialectical relationship between social movements and electoral institutions"[35] is a concession to the idea that the way to reach a mass audience is not through direct confrontation with the capitalist class by building mass movements outside the two-party system, but rather by working within the structures of a capitalist party.

Elbaum explains how NCM organisations each worked to bring different constituencies into the Rainbow. LRS and Line of March supplied key activists for labour organising efforts and LRS in particular gained positions of influence within the Rainbow. According to Elbaum, LRS cadre "worked to forge strong ties with Jackson's inner circle, local elected officials and labor and community leaders" and were "often more willing than most others on the left to subordinate building the Rainbow to the immediate needs of Jackson's campaign apparatus". In contrast, Line of March was more "willing to engage in open fights over policy with what it saw as more accommodationist forces" to ensure that the Rainbow "was not completely dependent on the appeal of its charismatic standard-bearer or susceptible to pressures from the Democratic Party high command".[36]

For Jackson to maintain his allure on the campaign trail, he needed to project the image of a fighter outside of traditional party politics. The left inside the Rainbow served Jackson's needs by providing foot soldiers for electioneering and a bridge to constituencies otherwise outside of his reach. Yet the internal machinations within the Rainbow had little impact on the political direction of the campaign. Despite the assertion of the Rainbow Left that is was building a vehicle for "independent politics", the Democrat machine weighed heavily on Jackson's public profile.

---

[35] Collins 1986, p105.
[36] Elbaum 2002, p280.

Jackson's 1988 campaign

In electoral terms, Jackson's 1988 campaign was a stunning success. On March 8, 1988 – "Super Tuesday" – Jackson achieved a second-place finish in 16 out of 21 primaries in southern states, where a large Black voter turnout made Jackson the front runner in the delegate count. Jackson followed with a victory in Michigan, securing 55 percent of the vote, and ended the race with seven million votes (around 30 percent of the total). This time around, Jackson was aided by much stronger support from Black Democrat officials who saw the campaign as a means to strengthen their own clout within the party.

However, Jackson's 1988 campaign was much more moderate than his 1984 run. Machine politicians such as Charles Rangel worked to undermine the influence the left had exercised in 1984. And Jackson himself tailored his speeches to be more palatable to the concerns of leading Democrats. For example, Jackson criticised Reagan's deployment of troops in the Gulf during the Iran-Iraq war for endangering "our boys" and backtracked on his previous support for Palestinian self-determination. At the 1987 Rainbow Convention Jackson told stunned delegates that racial violence was an issue of the past and had now been resolved.[37]

Jackson also pursued a much more conciliatory approach to working with Democrat powerbrokers. Whereas in 1984 Jackson had vehemently protested rules governing delegate selection for the party convention, in 1988 he made no such protest despite a 15 percent increase in the number of super-delegates (party leaders and elected officials getting an automatic convention vote). Once the convention was over, Jackson moved to bring the Rainbow under his control, dashing hopes that it could be retained as a vehicle independent of the party machine. Activist participation in the Rainbow evaporated. The coalition itself was transformed into Jackson's personal political vehicle, rather than a membership organisation.

Elbaum's assertion that "the Rainbow offered the prospect of a durable, mass-based and independent vehicle" that "revolutionaries

[37] Misnik 1988.

could loyally help build, while retaining the freedom to advocate their own point of view"[38] proved sorely misguided. His hope that "Jackson was willing to build a Rainbow Coalition that would undertake non-electoral as well as electoral activism and remain independent of official Democratic structures, and even distinct from his own campaign structures" proved a mirage.

The outcome reflected the balance of forces, both within the Rainbow and the Democrats. It also reflected the confusion within the Rainbow Left as to the purpose of their intervention. For Jackson and aspiring Black politicians, the Rainbow offered a bargaining chip to negotiate with Democratic Party power brokers. Once the party leadership had resolved to cut a deal with Jackson rather than lock him out, the Rainbow's independence could only be a hindrance to his ambitions. Some viewed the Rainbow as a caucus intended to realign Democratic Party politics, while others on the left believed it could build a base for a new anti-capitalist party: a means of achieving a "dirty break".

Whatever their motivation, the NCM groups that had entered the Rainbow in 1983 came out of the experience weaker and more disillusioned. The Communist Workers Party abandoned Marxism-Leninism, transforming itself into the New Democratic Movement and then dissolving before the Rainbow was wound up. The Line of March disbanded in 1989 and LRS followed suit a year later. The *Guardian* ceased publication in 1992. Freedom Road still exists and continues to orient to electoral work within the Democrats.

Peter Camejo, a former leader of the Socialist Workers Party, joined with ex-Maoists in the Bay Area Socialist Organising Committee to form the North Star Network in 1984. Reflecting on his time building the Rainbow Coalition, Camejo says:

> At the time the North Star Network was formed I made a major political mistake. A new sense of possibility had emerged when Jesse Jackson started the Rainbow Coalition and ran (as a Democrat) for president in 1984. Within the North Star there was a desire to get involved in supporting Jackson's organisation. While there were

---

[38] Elbaum 2002, p276.

various points of view, mine being clearly opposed to the Democratic Party, I let myself be influenced into seeing the Jackson movement as a possible beginning of a real reform movement…or an actual split with the Democrats.

This error on my part lasted until I came to my senses and realised that, with few exceptions, the Rainbow Coalition was just another name for keeping progressives in the Democratic Party. Jesse Jackson was a hard-core Democrat and remains so today.[39]

Conclusion

Jackson's 1984 presidential campaign was more radical than Sanders' 2016 campaign, despite Jackson himself being a more conservative figure who had long represented a Black entrepreneurial elite. Amidst a deep social crisis that afflicted US society and African Americans in particular, Jackson was catapulted to prominence by a powerful revolt against Reagan's pro-war, austerity policies. Jackson's radical rhetoric was augmented by a loyal band of followers. A large section of the left, principally Maoists and ex-Maoists with origins in the New Left, provided not only foot soldiers but skilled organisers with roots in Asian and Chicano communities, and in anti-racist, anti-war, and women's, lesbian and gay liberation movements. The Rainbow Coalition was a pole of attraction to a fragmented left that hoped to build a beachhead *inside* the Democrats and a base from which to organise *outside* the Democrats.

By 1989, this project was in disarray. The mass anti-war and anti-intervention rallies of the early 1980s were no more. Working class resistance to the Reagan offensive and employers' assault on living standards had dissipated. Groups such as the League of Revolutionary Socialists made peace with the Democrat machine and wound up any public profile. Others withdrew from the Rainbow, but, demoralised, lacked any capacity to rebuild a left on the outside.

The Jackson/Rainbow campaigns provide valuable lessons for those looking to Bernie Sanders today. Firstly, the claim that it was possible to build "independent politics" through the structures of the

---

[39] Camejo 2010, pp180-181.

Rainbow proved to be a myth. The Democratic Party will tolerate such efforts so long as they can enlist new voters in Democrat caucuses and expand the party's voter base. However, the rationale for the Rainbow was to secure Jackson's electoral victory in the primaries. So long as the Rainbow Left worked towards that end they were tolerated – even welcomed – within the Rainbow. Once the Rainbow Left had served its purpose, it was cast aside. Having been locked into the Democrats for five years, the Rainbow Left found itself locked out.

Secondly, the idea that the Rainbow could serve as a means to bring about a realignment in US politics, either inside or outside the Democrats, was mistaken. US politics was moving sharply to the right. Reagan was the front man for neoliberalism, but Democrats such as Walter Mondale and Gary Hart were willing accomplices. The Democrats' rightward lurch, which began before Reagan's ascendency and continued in the 1990s under Clinton, was driven by the declining profitability of US capitalism. Whereas Roosevelt's New Deal and Kennedy's Great Society programs implemented a reform package in response to the demands of the union and civil rights movements, the Democrats could no longer accede to such demands while simultaneously meeting the demands of big business. Moreover, the US ruling class had forged a consensus that to maintain its imperial hegemony, it needed to embark on a massive armaments program that could ensure its victory in the Cold War.

Thirdly, the strategy pursued by the Rainbow Left, despite protestations to the contrary, was fundamentally electoralist. While NCM groups shared an analysis that the Democratic Party was a capitalist party that couldn't be reformed, a consensus also emerged that their decade-long engagement with struggles of workers and the oppressed needed to be complemented by electoral work that could win a larger audience for socialist ideas. For some, electoral work came to be redefined as a form of "mass" work. However, for the vast majority of Democrats, whether politicians or volunteers, they are in it to win. They are not in it for mass organising or left propaganda. Nor are they in it to disseminate arguments for building a new party *outside* the Democrats.

A successful strategy for winning elections differs fundamentally from one that can win strikes or build militant mass actions. Whereas strikes and protest actions are directed at an opposing party and are manifestations of class struggle and conflict, elections are a means to winning a vote from the largest possible audience. The former involves taking risks, making sacrifices and challenging the economic and political establishment; the latter involves getting as many supporters as possible out to vote. Within the time frame of an election and the rules of the game, an election campaign by itself cannot transform mass consciousness. It can only relate to existing consciousness. Inevitably, this requires adapting your electoral platform to the prevailing mood of the electorate.

Roosevelt's New Deal and Kennedy's Great Society programs were not won by canvassing for votes. They were the product of an upsurge in mass struggle. In 1934, general strikes rocked Toledo, Minneapolis and San Francisco. In 1935 and 1936, the CIO defeated General Motors in mass sit-down strikes, building the United Auto Workers union in the process. These mass struggles forced Roosevelt to push through the Wagner and Social Security Acts. Once the shop floor fell quiet and the CIO leadership turned to a strategy of dependence upon the Democrats, the reform period was over. Similarly, it was the militant direct actions of the civil rights era and the mass rebellions in inner-city ghettoes that forced Kennedy to enact the Civil Rights Act and the War on Poverty program. Once the rebellion ended so did the period of reform.

In a period of working class retreat, an electoral strategy can appear attractive, especially when the contenders for election are adapting their rhetoric to champion "socialist" ideas. Jackson's 1980s campaigns, unlike Sanders' more recent campaigns, were not infused with talk of "democratic socialism". Jackson was campaigning in the last decade of the Cold War, when socialism was associated in the minds of most workers with the gulags of Stalinist Russia. Yet his championing of "economic justice" did strike a popular tone. For socialists on the election campaign trail working alongside other socialists and progressives from differing political traditions, it can seem that connections are being made with a much wider audience. Yet such connections are inevitably temporary (for the duration of an election campaign) and do not demand the argumentation and polemics that are required to win over an audience to a course of action that requires direct confrontation with the political establishment.

Today, as in the 1980s, US society is racked by sharp social and class divisions. Over the last decade, since the Global Financial Crisis, movements such as Occupy and Black Lives Matter have challenged corporate greed and exposed the barbarity of contemporary global capitalism. The emergence of a more confident and combative far right, and the complete intransigence of Trump and his allies in the face of the climate crisis, demonstrate now more than ever the need to build a revolutionary left that can lead a struggle for socialism. The pathway to building that left does not lead through the DSA nor along the path of campaigning for a Sanders' presidency. Instead we must build a new, revolutionary left in our workplaces, in our schools and campuses, and on the streets.

References

Camejo, Peter 2010, *North Star: A Memoir*, Haymarket Books, Chicago.

Cohen, David 1992, "Organizing: Lessons Learned on the Ground", *CrossRoads*, 24.

Collins, Sheila 1986, *The Rainbow Challenge: The Jackson Campaign and the Future of U.S. Politics*, New York University Press.

Davis, Mike 1986, "The Lesser Evil? The Left and the Democratic Party", *New Left Review,* 155, Jan/Feb, https://newleftreview.org/issues/I155/articles/mike-davis-the-lesser-evil-the-left-and-the-democratic-party.

Elbaum, Max 2002, *Revolution in the Air: Sixties Radicals Turn to Lenin, Mao and Che*, Verso.

Harrington, Michael 1973, "The Left Wing of Realism", *Democratic Left*, 1, (1), March, https://democraticleft.dsausa.org/issues/.

Lorimer Doug 1997, "The degeneration of the SWP", in *Building the Revolutionary Party: an introduction to James P. Cannon*, Resistance Books.

Marable, Manning 1985, "Jackson and the Rise of the Rainbow Coalition", *New Left Review,* 149, Jan/Feb, https://newleftreview.org/issues/I149/articles/manning-marable-jackson-and-the-rise-of-the-rainbow-coalition.

Meyer, Neal and Ben B. 2018, "The Case for Bernie 2020", *The Call,* 16 August, https://socialistcall.com/2018/08/16/bernie-2020/.

Misnik, Joanna 1988, *The Rainbow and the Democratic Party – New Politics or Old? A Socialist Perspective*, https://solidarity-us.org/rainbow1988/.

Ross, Shelly 1985, "Moving Toward Higher Ground: The Politics of Jesse Jackson and the Rainbow Coalition", *Forward*, 4, January, https://www.marxists.org/history/erol/ncm-7/lrs-rainbow.htm.

Sunkara, Bhaskar 2015, "Bernie for President", *Jacobin*, 1 May, https://www.jacobinmag.com/2015/05/bernie-sanders-president-vermont-socialist.

NEW MOVEMENT, NEW DEBATES: THE CONTESTED POLITICS OF CLIMATE CHANGE

SARAH GARNHAM

"A few weeks before the koala – nicknamed Lewis – was euthanized, the newly reelected prime minister took his advocacy for coal to a new level. He pledged to outlaw environmental demonstrations, calling the protests a 'new breed of radical activism' that is 'apocalyptic in tone.' One month later, a *Sydney Morning Herald* headline described conditions in Australia's most iconic city as 'apocalyptic,' as residents choked in a smoky haze from bush fires. A coalition of doctors and climate researchers declared it a public health emergency."

Washington Post[1]

Concern about climate change has been increasing for years; it has gradually moved up the ratings of issues people are most worried about. But over the course of 2019, it accelerated sharply. The Scanlon Foundation's Mapping Social Cohesion Survey of 2019 registers a doubling in the number of people who name climate change as the issue that most concerns them, the biggest jump for any issue since the survey began 12 years ago.[2] At the same time, we saw a surge of anti–climate change activism across Australia, and around

---

Sarah Garnham has been a socialist activist since 2008. She is a regular contributor to *Red Flag* and is the author of "Against reductionism: Marxism and Oppression" in *Marxist Left Review*, 16 (Winter 2018).

[1] Darryl Fears, "On land, Australia's rising heat is 'apocalyptic'. In the ocean, it's worse", *Washington Post*, 27 December 2019.

[2] Markus 2019.

the world. It is now widely accepted not only that climate change is real, but that we are in the midst of an emergency which demands a response. Nothing underscores this more than the fires which raged across Australia for months beginning in September 2019. Climate chaos is upon us.

Few still question that human intervention has led to this disaster. There is now a scientific consensus that the Holocene is over and that we are now living through a new epoch, the Anthropocene. Beginning between 1945 and 1950, the Anthropocene describes the qualitative altering of the Earth System as a result of human activity. More specifically, it is a product of capitalism. Marxist writer Ian Angus, author of *Facing the Anthropocene*, explains this process:

> Capitalism has driven the Earth System to a crisis point in the relationship between humanity and the rest of nature. If business as usual continues, the first full century of the Anthropocene will be marked by rapid deterioration of our physical, social, and economic environment. The decay of the biosphere will be most noticed as global warming and extreme weather, but we can also expect rising ocean levels leading to widespread flooding, the collapse of major fisheries, poisoned rivers, and more. Every planetary boundary is threatened, and a catastrophic convergence of multiple Earth System failures is possible. If that happens, the Anthropocene may be the shortest of all epochs, a transition period from the Holocene to something far worse.[3]

This is the situation facing humanity. Climate change represents a deep crisis not only for the planet, but also society. It has become a political issue that can no longer be ignored.

This article takes a brief look at three aspects of the response to the climate crisis. First and most importantly, it looks at the politics of the new climate movement that has mobilised millions globally and demands "system change". Second, it looks at the ruling class's response, which should be understood as calculated more than denialist. And finally it looks at the revolutionary anti-capitalist

---

[3] Angus 2016, p192.

response that is necessary. But before all that it is worth looking at the factors that brought this crisis into the mainstream.

Setting the scene

The Intergovernmental Panel on Climate Change (IPCC) 2018 report represented a turning point in popular consciousness regarding the climate crisis. It was just the latest in a series of similar scientific reports but it cut through because it graphically detailed the difference between warming of 1.5 and 2 degrees Celsius and stated that we only have 12 years to reduce global emissions by half. Scientifically the report was not ground-breaking. Its predictions were conservative even at the time of release and have become more out of date in subsequent months. It widely accepted that 1.5 degrees warming is inevitable (4-6 degrees warming within this century is a serious prospect), and that feedback processes and catastrophic nonlinearities (tipping points) make it impossible to predict exactly how bad things may become. Nevertheless, one of the key features of the report was its accessible iteration of the scientific consensus that there must be "rapid and far-reaching transitions in energy, land, urban and infrastructure (including transport and buildings), and industrial systems on a scale of which there is no documented historic precedent for".[4]

Another reason the IPCC report had such an impact is that the effects of climate change have become more noticeable. Australia's 2019 bushfire season began in winter, after the warmest decade on record. By November fires raged across Queensland, a mega-fire had developed in northern NSW and 5 million people in Sydney were being poisoned on a daily basis by toxic smoke. By the end of December significant fires had erupted in Victoria, South Australia and Western Australia. By New Years Eve the fires had spread to the outer suburbs of Melbourne and in NSW families had been evacuated to the water as beachside towns were threatened or burned. Social media was awash with stories of friends escaping fires and pictures of

---

[4]   Intergovernmental Panel on Climate Change 2018.

towering infernos, charred koalas and the sky turned black at 9am. At the end of the first month of summer dozens had been killed, thousands of homes destroyed and over 500 billion animals perished.

It is not just Australia that has experienced such scenes. Globally, wildfires are more unpredictable and intense and the length of the fire weather season has increased by more than 19 percent since 1979.[5]

But it is only now that the fires are widely understood not as a natural disaster but as a product of climate change, and by association, as a product of inept political leadership and neoliberalism. In Australia over the past decade, successive Labor and Liberal governments have cut tens of millions from state budgets for fire services. In NSW the 2019-20 budget saw almost $40 million stripped from fire services.[6] The situation is similar across the rest of the world. Budget cuts were blamed for worsening the wildfires in California in 2019. And the fact that equipment and firefighters are now shared between the US and Australia (a mutually beneficial scheme to skimp on public services) is going to become a serious issue as the respective fire seasons are beginning to overlap. Neoliberal policies also fuelled fires in the Amazon in Brazil and Ecuador, in Lebanon, and in Greece in 2018. In Lebanon, shiny new anti-protest tanks fitted out with water cannons were used to attempt to extinguish the wildfires in October, a graphic depiction of the spending priorities of states.

If world leaders have shown themselves incapable of dealing with the effects of climate change, their efforts to resolve its causes are even more pathetic. The very best of the ruling class's response amounts to little more than shifting the deckchairs on the Titanic. Nothing sums this up better than the trajectory and state of the Paris Agreement. It has progressed from tragedy to farce, and now to a state of suspended farcical tragedy. In 2015 when the agreement was proposed, it was already too late to be talking about gradual emissions reductions. The non-binding targets that countries set for themselves are based on net

---

[5] Climate Council 2015.

[6] Simone White, "Morrison parties while Sydney chokes" *Red Flag*, 9 December 2019.

zero, rather than real zero – meaning that they are essentially figures drawn up through creative accounting and offsetting schemes. This is why the agreement was lauded by some of the world's biggest fossil fuel giants, particularly those who wanted to use the cover of emissions targets to bolster natural gas. In the lead-up to the Paris conference, a joint letter by fossil fuel giants BP, Shell, Statoil and several others announced their commitment to reducing carbon emissions and urged the Paris conference to place a price on carbon emissions. On the day the Paris Agreement came into effect, they announced a $1 billion climate change fund – a fund which is almost entirely dedicated to the expansion of natural gas industries.[7] BP was explicit about this: "We welcome the direction provided by the historic agreement reached at the UN climate conference in Paris…we will continue to play our part through means including energy efficiency, renewable energy and increasing the share of natural gas in our portfolio".[8]

Moreover, in the years since the Paris Agreement was signed – much like in the years following the signing of the Kyoto Protocol – emissions in all of the key signatory countries have risen. Trump's withdrawal from the agreement, which will likely be followed by other far right leaders, rendered the whole thing a farce. As with nuclear disarmament, the biggest polluters are exempt from even the pretence of reducing emissions.

Into this scene enter Swedish teenage activist Greta Thunberg. Thunberg has played a crucial role in generating the new climate movement and encapsulates the widespread indignation towards the deckchair shifters. She has directly blamed the world's rulers for the crisis. As a political figure Thunberg strikes the right moral chords, combining anger with hope. She has helped mobilise millions onto the streets. In late 2018 she spoke at the UN climate conference and called on students everywhere to join the student strikes. In November 2018 there were large student strikes in several cities around the world. In Australia, a few thousand turned out in

---

[7]   Oil and Gas Climate Initiative 2016.
[8]   BP 2016.

Melbourne and Sydney, as well as hundreds in smaller cities and towns. In many countries, there were regular – sometimes even weekly – school strikes throughout 2019. But the highlights were the two all-out strikes called globally, in May and September, with the latter being the biggest global day of action for climate justice in decades. Across Europe, millions turned out, while in Australia 350,000 marched. One of the things that positively impacted the size was the fact that it pitched itself beyond high schoolers, as a general "global strike" for climate.

The size and reach of the climate strikes have created space for others to act. Extinction Rebellion (XR) is the other significant group that has emerged. Local environmental issues have also flared up and taken on new meaning as part of the new climate movement. In Australia the campaign to stop the Adani coal mine, for example, has become an important part of the new movement. And the October 2019 blockade against the International Mining Conference (IMARC) in Melbourne was made possible by the new wave of climate organising and the sense of urgency motivating it. Similarly, a mobilisation of 40,000 against government inaction on bushfires in Sydney in December 2019 cannot be understood outside of the context of the new climate movement.

Altogether there has been a marked shift in the politics of climate change over 2019. And now that the crisis is such an overt part of life it is difficult to imagine it vanishing as an issue. However, we should not view the politics of the climate crisis – whether expressed in popular opinion, by the ruling class or by climate activists – as completely original. New political situations do not automatically generate new ideologies. Instead, the climate crisis has become a prism through which traditional political ideologies are refracted and tested as new questions are thrown up. On the other hand, the objective realities of the climate crisis and the fact that people are searching for answers creates a more volatile political environment, and opens up new opportunities for the radical left.

The new climate movement: rupture and continuity

Environmental activism has a long history. From the mid-1800s, ecology became an important part of science and social theory. Marx and Engels took a keen interest in environmental questions, considering the potential consequences of the metabolic rift as well as many early predictions of resource depletion, soil poisoning and even global warming.[9] Throughout the twentieth century the environment became not just something to analyse but something to campaign about. By the 1970s environmental activism had become a mass issue, and one that was taken up by the left and the workers' movement. In the US the 1970 "Earth Hour" mobilised 20 million people and helped to establish the Environmental Protection Agency (EPA) and bring about other progressive reforms.[10] Around the same time in Australia, the Builders Labourers' Federation pioneered "green bans", a militant working class approach to winning environmental justice.[11] In the 1980s much of this activism receded, along with other social movements, as neoliberal policies were pummelling an ever more defensive workers' movement and consequently pulling society to the right and disorienting the left.

The 1990s saw new waves of environmental activism, particularly around the questions of greenhouse gas emissions and global warming. Over this period innumerable environmental campaign groups and NGOs emerged. There were many mass mobilisations and a steady – though subterranean – increase in environmental consciousness. The character of this activity suffered from the fact that it came to prominence at a time when the workers' movement and left were very weak. Though there were occasional flash points and significant campaigns, environmental activism heavily consisted of lobbying and electoralism. The transformation of Earth Hour, from

---

[9] Mike Davis provides an interesting account of the early history of discussions about global warming and their intersection with the socialist movement, with a particular focus on the work of Kropotkin in Davis 2018.

[10] Olivia B. Waxman, "Meet 'Mr. Earth Day,' the Man Who Helped Organize the Annual Observance", *Time*, April 2019, https://time.com/5570269/earth-day-origins/.

[11] See Burgmann and Burgmann, 2017.

something that emerged from the radicalisation of the 1960s to its reinvention in the 1990s as a corporate PR stunt, epitomises the broader shift.

Despite a proliferation of environmental NGOs, a ballooning of government environmental bureaucracies, the signing of the Kyoto Protocol and the initiation of several "green" market reforms, global emissions went up by 32 percent between 1990 and 2010. Frustrated by official inaction, many took up lifestylism throughout this period. This strategy reflected the atomised individualism of neoliberalism, while for a demoralised left, it fitted with their autonomist rejection of working class and mass politics. As well as being futile, lifestyle strategies to save the planet reinforce the dominant narrative that humans are collectively to blame for climate change.

The new climate movement is inevitably shaped by but also breaks away from this political heritage. It positively builds on the best elements of environmental awareness and activism over the last couple of decades. And it has broken through some of the existing political limitations and more conservative, NGO-moulded tactics, partly because the stakes seem so much higher now. The objective horrors of climate change and the fact that people are scared and angry can mean the politics and tactics of the movement will continue to shift and change, and can push beyond the current parameters. This is especially the case given that the movement is not organised around a central leadership or narrow set of demands. Instead there are a profusion of organisations, tactics, objectives and mobilisations, which will continue to develop as the struggle proceeds. But for now, there are a few key political features of the movement worth examining.

Mass mobilisation and disruption

One of the most important features of the new climate movement is that it has drawn millions of people into street protests. These protests are not just an addendum to lobbying nor intended as purely symbolic events. Rather they are key to the strategy of the new movement, intended to stop business as usual. The focus has been on mass demonstrations in major cities, involving huge numbers of students and workers. Another positive has been the commitment to disruptive action. Although often more sentiment than reality — the demonstrations in Australia have not been hugely disruptive — it is a welcome development given the longstanding division in the environmental movement between those who favour mass tactics and those who organise small disruptive stunts. The fact that the mass mobilisations are called strikes, and take place on weekdays with the explicit goal of shutting down the city, is a massive advance on the type of actions that characterised the environment movement in the recent past, for example the relatively sedate Walk Against Warming rallies.

This development creates the political space for an argument about mass disruption beyond the climate strikes. Unfortunately XR, the main force seen to be filling this space, is increasingly reticent to be either radical or disruptive. This varies between XR branches and from country to country, but one clear example of the contradiction between the radicalism of XR on paper and in practice is the pro-police etiquette that accompanies their tactical use of mass arrests.[12] It's not just XR that suffers from this cognitive dissonance. In general, given the urgency of the situation and the emphasis placed on it being a crisis, the mobilisations organised by the new movement have been large and vibrant, but for the most part not particularly angry or militant. The tone is markedly different to that of other street protest movements that emerged during 2019. Common to all is young people fighting for their futures, which are collectively seen to be in serious jeopardy. But the cry of "death or liberty" from the Hong Kongers or the confrontations between Chilean students and the police are a long way from the mood of the climate protests. Nevertheless, the fact that people are on the streets "not drowning

---

[12] On XR in relation to the police, see Sarah Garnham, "Resisting repression is inseparable from the struggle for climate justice" and for a more general critique of XR see James Plested, "Roger and Me — a socialist view on Extinction Rebellion", both in *Red Flag*, 4 November 2019. Also useful is Andrew Charles, "Extinction Rebellion: a short, critical guide", *Overland*, 24 October 2019, https://overland.org.au/2019/10/extinction-rebellion-a-short-critical-guide/.

but fighting" creates natural bridges between the climate movement and the other rebellions and creates the potential for more radical politics and practice in the future.

System change not climate change

One common thread between the climate movement and revolts elsewhere is the widespread conviction on the part of participants and those who sympathise with them that the system is to blame. For the climate movement, this is encapsulated in the slogan: "system change not climate change". This cuts sharply against the previously established trope of mass complicity and the political conclusions derived from that, summed up by the slogan "be the change you want to see". It is now popularly accepted that lifestyle choices will not be sufficient to address the climate catastrophe, and that those with real power must be held to account. Thunberg articulated this very clearly at the World Economic Forum in Davos in 2019:

> [S]omeone is to blame... Some people, some companies, some decision makers in particular know exactly what priceless values they have been sacrificing to continue making unimaginable amounts of money, and I think many of you here today belong to that group of people.[13]

The desire for system change is expressed to an extent in some of the popular slogans of the movement: 100 per cent renewables, no new coal and zero emissions. But while the achievement of these demands requires system change in a technical sense, this doesn't usually translate into corresponding political slogans: there are no calls for governments to be overthrown, for example. This reflects the dominant conception within the movement that those who currently run the world need to be convinced to run it differently. Overwhelmingly it is understood that this argument will be won by applying mass moral pressure on them. Thunberg's repeated appearances at global forums of the ruling class are an indication of

---

13   Heather Landy, "A 16-year-old tells Davos delegates that if the planet dies, she's blaming them", *Quartz*, 26 January 2019, https://qz.com/1533904/greta-thunberg-blames-davos-delegates-for-climate-change/.

this perspective. Though she is angry and impassioned, the implicit aim is to convince the ruling class to see reason and embark on a comprehensive set of new policies. There is as yet no widespread imagining of an anti-capitalist form of system change, even as capitalism is more frequently blamed. Despite these limits, the popularity of the call for system change represents an important breakthrough, and creates a healthy space for political discussion in the movement.

"We're all in it together"

One of the more problematic aspects of the new climate movement is the emphasis on the idea that "we're all in it together". This is a statement reiterated frequently by Thunberg and XR and is often seen on placards at demonstrations. It reflects the longstanding idea that environmental questions are beyond class and politics. At one level it is true that environmental changes, especially severe ones, impact everybody. But the impacts are crucially mediated by class, to such a degree that it makes talking about any collective impact almost meaningless. These sorts of appeals to common humanity and universal interests have long been popular with a section of the ruling class. Note how centrist neoliberal leaders like Macron and Trudeau constantly proclaim the importance of international summits and agreements, using the anti-globalisation right as a foil for why progressive change cannot be achieved faster. This invariably builds a case for class collaboration, which if accepted, will be disastrous for the movement.[14]

---

[14] One of the first proponents of the slogan "we are all in it together" was Gorbachev, who used it to describe his vision of building bridges and moving into a harmonious, booming period of capitalist development. He argued that the combination of globalisation and the threat of environmental catastrophe necessitated common cause between states and social movements to offer global solutions. The effect of this was to sow illusions in the UN as an instrument of progressive change, in opposition to Reagan who at the time was openly flouting its resolutions. The parallel with today is hard to miss. See Gorbachev's speeches, "What made me a crusader" and "Nature will not wait", https://www.gorby.ru/userfiles/file/gorbaghev_book_speeches_en.pdf.

Worse, this slogan serves to blunt any critique of the ruling class. It suggests that even if they shoulder most of the blame, now that the damage is done we can all, brought together by the sheer urgency of the situation, find a solution. It is certainly true that the prognosis for climate change is dire and that the need for action is urgent. But there are different ways of understanding this catastrophic phenomenon. Right now in the climate movement it is most commonly seen in a classless, final way; the catastrophe that is envisaged is akin to a meteor hitting earth, where apocalypse is imposed on us in an instant by some external force. This is not the case. Catastrophic climate change is a product of capitalism. It is worsened every day because of the drive for profit accumulation and is made socially disastrous because of the inequality, oppression and exploitation that sustain the system. In the face of this reality, appealing to the ruling class is a dead end. The climate crisis is not the first issue to be seen as a uniquely urgent and existential threat; similarly disastrous arguments were made regarding the threat of nuclear proliferation and the rise of fascism.

To point to problems with treating climate catastrophe as an undifferentiated, universal threat is not to diminish the objective threat it poses. Some on the left have argued that it is tantamount to denialism.[15] But a preoccupation with distinguishing ourselves from right wing climate denialism cannot be the starting point for our political approach and does not help to build a movement that can be effective. It is undoubtedly positive that the threat of environmental Armageddon has jolted people into action, and we certainly should not downplay the significance of the threat. But the way in which the effects of climate change are going to create political conflict cannot be adequately addressed by a political approach that emphasises a unity of interests across the class divide.

---

[15] Ian Angus has argued this for years; Angus 2017, pp141-158. See also a debate about this topic between Angus, Eddie Yuen and Sam Gindin: Climate and Capitalism, https://climateandcapitalism.com/2013/12/02/yuen-angus-debate-environmental-catastrophism/.

Climate justice

Existing uneasily alongside the previous slogan is the demand for climate justice. This increasingly popular concept acknowledges that the key crisis resulting from climate change is social and that the human suffering incurred from climate change is not distributed equally. Rather it is drastically uneven, both spatially and socially. It is the world's poorest countries that face the most devastation from earthquakes, droughts and other events. Several Pacific islands are currently under threat of total submersion and whole townships have eroded and disappeared.[16] There are currently 20 million climate refugees, not accounting for those internally displaced. The International Organization for Migration estimates that climate change will create 1.5 billion refugees over the next 30 years, mostly from poorer countries. The compounding impacts of imperialism, weak infrastructure and poverty leave these societies highly vulnerable to climate change. Climate refugees, like all refugees, face a brutal matrix of regimes perpetually competing with one another to strengthen their borders. The intersecting crises of global capitalism are being used to ratchet up racism in country after country and the climate crisis will inevitably be used in the same way. Already there are questions being raised within the movement about how to respond to this situation. The socialist left needs to make a strong case that as we fight to avoid the catastrophes that will create climate refugees, we must also fight to build a climate movement that is internationalist in outlook, and will defend their right to seek asylum.

Though the climate movement has been an overwhelmingly Western phenomenon, we can expect struggles in the global South to continue both against specific environmental vandalism and, increasingly, the social breakdown produced by extreme weather events. For several years in India there have been protests against

---

[16] Carly Cassella, "There's a Climate Threat Facing Pacific Islands That's More Dire Than Losing Land", Science Alert, Global #Climate Strike, 19 September 2019, https://www.sciencealert.com/pacific-islanders-are-in-a-climate-crisis-as-rising-sea-levels-threaten-water.

environmental destruction.[17] There is a similar dynamic in China, where there have been explosive struggles in response to chemical pollution and disasters.[18] Many have argued that the dramatic social and economic effects of a sustained drought were an important – though not isolated – factor that helped trigger the revolution in Syria in 2011.[19] This points to the fact that, regardless of whether there are strong existing movements about the general phenomenon of climate change, the effects of climate change itself will continue to spur resistance and activism. Where these effects are felt most acutely, it is likely to produce visceral and potentially radical responses.

Because of the very different social backdrop, the movement in the West is likely to remain mainly moral for a long time and not linked to acute class struggle or a battle for survival for most of its participants. Nevertheless, the Australian fires have organically raised class issues to do with health and safety, the funding of public services and workers' rights.

Another aspect of the focus on climate justice, at least in Australia, has been a recognition of the class impacts of the crisis. Within the movement there is broad agreement building that workers working in environmentally destructive jobs which will have to be phased out should be ensured a just transition. This cuts against the notion, cynically spread by right wing politicians, that environmentalists secretly hate ordinary people, particularly blue collar workers in

---

[17] The construction of this dam in India was stalled for several years by protests: BBC, "Megadams: Battle on the Brahmaputra", 20 March 2014, https://www.bbc.com/news/world-asia-india-26663820; and in 2019 protests erupted when water supplies ran out in Chennai: Amrit Dhillon, "Chennai in crisis as authorities blamed for dire water shortage", *The Guardian*, 19 June 2019.

[18] Samantha Hoffman and Jonathan Sullivan, "Environmental Protests Expose Weakness in China's Leadership", *Forbes*, 22 June 2015, https://www.forbes.com/sites/forbesasia/2015/06/22/environmental-protests-expose-weakness-in-chinas-leadership/#22d8b5e53241. On a mass movement against the construction of a petrochemical plant in Jinshan: see "Protest against proposed relocation of Gaoqiao paraxylene (PX) plant into Jinshan, Shanghai, China", Environmental Justice Atlas, 10 June 2017, https://ejatlas.org/conflict/protest-against-gaoqiao-paraxylene-px-plant-relocating-in-jinshan-shanghai-china.

[19] See Ababsa 2015.

mining and other fossil fuel-related jobs. This shift is partly due to the mainstreaming of concern over climate change. Though specific polling has not been done about the attitudes of workers, by way of the fact that they make up the majority of the population it is clear that there is widespread opposition to climate change. And as well as there being overwhelming support for action on climate change in a general sense there is also a majority support – including in Queensland – for the specific demand to phase out coal in Australia. Almost three quarters (73 percent) of Queenslanders prefer that Australia's coal-fired power stations are phased out either as soon as possible or gradually. Thirteen percent believe that coal does not need to be replaced by other power sources like wind or solar power (compared to the national average of 9 percent). [20] As well as individual workers, several unions have backed the climate movement, including some that have been more conservative in the past. The NUW put out a strong statement supporting the September 20 climate strike. More impressively, Fenner Dunlop workers covered by the NUW, who were on strike at the time, explicitly linked their struggle to the climate movement. One of the lead delegates spoke at the September 20 climate strike demonstration in Melbourne. But apart from small, isolated examples like this, the union movement has done very little beyond giving verbal support to the general movement. The union contingents to the Melbourne strikes overwhelmingly consisted of paid officials. A mass union mobilisation would have fundamentally changed the nature of the event, would have given the climate movement a new confidence and power and would have been a step towards rebuilding the strength of the union movement. Instead the limelight was taken by the bosses of banks, universities and other polluting corporations, who were applauded for allowing - or even encouraging - their workers to participate. [21]

[20] "Climate of the Nation" research report, 2019 https://www.tai.org.au/sites/default/files/Climate%20of%20the%20Nation%202019%20%5BWEB%5D.pdf.
[21] Jerome Small, "Climate activism in the workplace", *Red Flag*, 27 September 2019.

Ruling class response

For years climate denialism was a heaven-sent strategy for dealing with climate change. Those who claimed not to believe could openly court the fossil fuel companies, ride high on the profits they generated and castigate greenies for spoiling the fun. As Da Silva details elsewhere in this journal, this has been particularly important in Australia, which is heavily reliant on coal exports. For non-denialist politicians, climate denialism provided them with the perfect explanation for why nothing meaningful could be achieved; every attempt to put a price on carbon or pass strongly worded resolutions was thwarted by right wing, creationist Neanderthals. Those days are long gone. It's no longer credible to claim ignorance of or disagreement with the climate science. The vast bulk of the ruling class now understands the basic facts of climate change, and they are now being judged over what they do about it.

Having said that, there is still a sizeable and important minority of the international ruling class who ostentatiously hold up the banner of climate denialism because it is core to their image as rampaging tyrants. For this set – Trump, Bolsanaro, Morrison – it is not so much about pretending to not believe the science as it is about arguing openly that deliberate and reckless plunder in the pursuit of obscene wealth is preferable to saving the planet. Possibly this will be a difficult posture to maintain. Morrison's previous insistent denial of climate change and attacks on climate protests put him on the back foot during the fire crisis. Rather than assuming the role of leader pulling the nation through a tragedy, he became a hate figure.

But whatever divisions exist between the ruling class in terms of public positioning, on all of the underlying essentials there is a high level of agreement. They are out to save their skins and their system. At an individual level this looks like taking out "apocalypse insurance" in the form of luxury bunkers. It is estimated that half of Silicon Valley have invested in this latest fad. The bunkers, which are dug into the ground or are repurposed old silos or nuclear bunkers, are fitted out with every essential: spas, jacuzzis, home cinemas. And of course all come with their own private security. Cli-fi barely had time to become a recognisable genre before all of the best material was stolen by the real world.[22]

Beyond looking after themselves, the ruling class has adopted several political strategies in response to climate change. The most important of these are authoritarianism, imperialism and greenwashing, none of them mutually exclusive. The common link is that all of these are strategies, not to stop or ameliorate the effects of climate change, but to defend and expand capitalism. The defence and expansion of capitalism is in fact antithetical to climate action. The stronger and more successful the capitalist class, the less capacity there is to halt the current trajectory of climate change. It is against the economic and political interests of the capitalist class as a whole to dismantle the fossil fuel industry at the rate and extent necessary (i.e. immediately and completely). Even if they were prepared to go against their interests, the system itself could not survive if the transitions necessary to solving the climate crisis were carried out. For capitalism, fossil fuels are not an addiction, they are oxygen. The most acute and distressing aspects of the climate crisis are social and in this way are directly caused by capitalism, rather than some natural ecological process. Authoritarianism, imperialism and the macabre beast that is "green capitalism" are every bit as much manifestations of the climate crisis as are rising sea levels and temperatures.

Authoritarianism

States have seen climate change as a security threat for several decades. Since the cold war various governments have intermittently argued that they need to strengthen border controls, surveillance and general military operations in order to respond to the dangers it poses. In *Facing the Anthropocene* Angus sites a Pentagon report from 2003, commissioned and adopted during the presidency of famous climate denialist, George Bush. The report made recommendations about "an abrupt climate change scenario":

---

[22]   Bendix 2019.

The United States and Australia are likely to build defensive fortresses around their countries because they have the resources and reserves to achieve self-sufficiency. With diverse growing climates, wealth, technology, and abundant resources, the United States could likely survive shortened growing cycles and harsh weather conditions without catastrophic losses. Borders will be strengthened around the country to hold back unwanted starving immigrants from the Caribbean islands (an especially severe problem), Mexico, and South America.[23]

As Angus points out, the only thing that this report failed to account for was that states would feel compelled to take these measures well before any abrupt catastrophic events.

Over the past decade borders everywhere have militarised to an extreme degree. Climate change is not the sole reason for this but it is certainly a factor and has increasingly been identified as a "threat multiplier". All of the key military and security organisations have described climate change as a significant security threat for over a decade[24]. Australia's Official Statement to the 2017 Global Platform for Disaster Risk Reduction stated:

> Asia is the most exposed region to low elevation climatic impacts like flooding and displacement…and has more than 90 per cent of the world's exposure to tropical cyclones… The Indo-Pacific region has the world's fastest growing economic hubs, its most populated cities, and the majority of the world's poor. It also has the greatest vulnerability to climate-induced humanitarian and natural disasters such as severe storms, flooding and extreme heat, as well as the flow-on effects such as damage to economic and social infrastructure, disease outbreak, malnutrition and food and water shortages. This is a

---

[23] Angus 2017, pp182-183.
[24] Several reports and risk assessments are summarised here: Senate report to the Senate Foreign Affairs, Defence and Trade References Committee, "Climate change-related threats to national security", Parliament of Australia 14 June 2017, https://www.aph.gov.au/Parliamentary_Business/Committees/Senate/Foreign_Affairs_Defence_and_Trade/Nationalsecurity/Final%20Report/c02.

volatile mix of factors that heightens the security risk posed to Australia.[25]

One of its recommendations is for the government to consider a "dedicated climate security leadership position in Home Affairs to coordinate climate resilience issues". These euphemisms barely disguise the intention of states like Australia to allow millions of starving, desperate people to languish and die rather than let them into their country. Given these are the reports available to the public it is safe to assume that the internal reports and resolutions from the department of defence and other sections of the ruling class are several degrees more callous.

As well as authoritarianism in order to keep *out* refugees and safeguard natural resources, it is also being ramped up on the home front. Governments everywhere recognise that there has been a turning point in social attitudes about climate change, that the majority now understand that we are in a crisis and demand urgent, serious action. Further, they know that the effects of climate change will result in deeper levels of working class deprivation and animosity that can spark rebellions. These developments are added incentives for states to continue the push for more draconian internal regimes and specifically to criminalise climate protests. In Australia this has begun in quite a brazen way in response to the spate of climate activism in the second half of 2019. The federal government is proposing a series of anti-protest laws and two major state governments – both controlled by the Labor party – are clamping down on climate activism. The Victorian premier Daniel Andrews gushingly congratulated the police for the brutality that they meted out to climate activists protesting IMARC. In Queensland the state government have introduced wide ranging anti-protest laws that give police the power to stop and search suspected protesters. These harsh responses to what is, at this stage, a very liberal movement with considerable popular support is an indication of how desperately

---

[25]   Foreign Affairs, Defence and Trade References Committee 2018, chapter 2.

important it is for the Australian ruling class to defend the coal industry.

Imperialism

The authoritarian fortification of borders cannot be understood without looking to the dynamics and impact of imperialism. It is the competition between states that leads them to fiercely control borders. But as well as encouraging the hoarding and protection of resources, climate change creates opportunities to plunder new markets and project strength. Resources like water represent future investment opportunities and key commodities like oil will become more valuable. We are already seeing governments planning to secure access to crucial resources. As one *Monthly Review* article explained:

> The U.S. military, meanwhile, is preparing for a host of new vulnerabilities, related in particular to oil and water, and for interventions to secure U.S. global hegemony in these changing circumstances. Economic and military interests are working together to strategise means for securing global value and resource chains, so as both to strengthen Fortress America and secure its supply lines—working as well with its junior partners in the triad, Europe and Japan. This is the strategic repositioning of imperialism in the Anthropocene.[26]

Though it is certainly the case that the climate crisis will spark new imperialist hostilities and conflicts over resources, it is important to recognise that resource wars have always been a feature of capitalism, from the vicious wars over bird poo in the nineteenth century through to the invasion of Iraq in 2003.[27]

More intense imperialist conflict necessitates stronger states. One of the popular assumptions about the future of humanity on a hothouse earth is that states will diminish and even collapse as various climate crises unfold. While some minor states may collapse under the strain of climate change, the state system as a whole will not. In fact states will necessarily be strengthened, not only in order to protect the

26 Clarke et al, 2019.
27 Kandelaars 2016, p7.

elite from internal dissent as previously discussed, but in order to defend "national" corporations against their foreign competitors.[28]

A key lesson from all of this is that when we talk about ecological crises like climate change, biodiversity loss, water pollution and scarcity, and soil degradation, we are necessarily talking about systemic social problems with long and brutal histories under capitalist development. Hannah Holleman provides a Marxist account of this history in her book on the subject, *Dust Bowls of Empire*.[29] When scientists describe the increase of Dust Bowl-like conditions under climate change, they signal a particular kind of violent ecological and social change. The projected crises have violent consequences. But equally violent are the social forces, historical developments, policies, and practices that produce such massive socioecological crises in the first place.

Greenwashing

At the same time, we can expect more and more greenwashing and supposed "market solutions" from corporations and governments. There is lots of money to be made from going green and there is mounting consumer demand for it. Kanye West, always at the front of the pack, has just launched a new exclusive line of green shoes made of pond scum. On a larger and more malicious scale, "Green Resources" is a Norwegian company that sells forests to corporate clients to help them offset the carbon footprint of their businesses. In order to provide this service, Green Resources has forcibly demolished several villages in Uganda to make way for tree plantations. Green Resources was given the go ahead for this by prominent international certification bodies.[30]

The largest global "green" enterprise is green energy. Much of what is branded as green energy is environmentally destructive and

---

[28] For an excellent summary of this argument see Jonathan Neale, "Social collapse and climate breakdown", *Ecologist*, 8 May 2019, https://theecologist.org/2019/may/08/social-collapse-and-climate-breakdown.
[29] Holleman, 2018.
[30] Mousseau 2019.

involves processes that are reliant on fossil fuels.[31] Nuclear energy is also increasingly branded as green, despite being responsible for murdering millions, poisoning whole populations and the earth. In addition to the toll incurred by nuclear disaster, it is also a highly environmentally destructive industry, using enormous amounts of water to mine uranium and requiring vast quantities of concrete to construct and stabilise nuclear plants. The other related scam is the green branding of fossil fuel extraction, a PR trick that fossil fuel corporations and their defenders are becoming proficient at.[32]

Side by side all of this, the more legitimate renewable sector is positively booming. It has grown larger every year but, despite this, has not resulted in any decline of the fossil fuel industry. In fact fossil fuel production has expanded and remains the most profitable and dominant energy source. As James Plested wrote in *Red Flag*:

> Even if investment (of renewables) keeps growing rapidly in coming years, when you factor in the growth in overall demand for energy, renewables are still going to make up only a fraction of the supply for decades to come.
>
> Total annual energy investment is US$1.8 trillion, more than US$700 billion being spent on the oil and gas supply alone. Investment in fossil fuels may be declining as a proportion of total investment in global energy capacity, but in absolute terms the industry is still growing, and is projected to continue growing for decades to come. Which is why, despite record investment in renewables, global emissions are continuing to rise.[33]

Many of the countries with the most investment in renewables have some of the biggest levels of growth of fossil fuel usage and emissions. China for example has the highest investment of any country in renewable energy but it is also responsible for the biggest

---

[31] See for example Amit Katwala, "The spiralling environmental cost of our lithium battery addiction", *Wired*, 5 August 2018, https://www.wired.co.uk/article/lithium-batteries-environment-impact.

[32] Richard Milne, "Johan Sverdrup: Norway's big bet on a rosy future for oil", *Financial Times*, 1 January 2020.

[33] James Plested, "From rebellion to revolution: socialism and the environmental crisis", *Red Flag*, 5 August 2019.

number of new coal projects and net increases to emissions.[34] The Nordic countries are another example.[35] Both of these are examples of growing economies. Wherever there is capitalist economic growth there will be emissions increases, a point I will return to.

Spurred on by popular opinion, governments are also joining the greenwashing bandwagon. But the bar has been set very low. The fact that many in the movement still put energy into urging governments to declare a climate emergency is an example of this. At the time of writing 1,261 legislatures around the world have declared a climate emergency, including 75 in Australia.[36] Unsurprisingly, little action has followed, so this is now becoming recognised for the empty gesture that it is.

Resolutions and concrete targets appear to be more useful than such declarations but, in reality, they are just as superficial. A good case in point is the Zero Carbon Bill recently announced by New Zealand prime minister, Jacinda Ardern. The bill commits to reducing all greenhouse gases to zero by 2050 – except for methane, which will only be reduced by around 25 percent. Agriculture is New Zealand's biggest industry and produces tonnes of methane, a gas that is far more destructive than CO_2. Given this exemption, it is no surprise that the conservatives happily voted for the bill.[37] Like pretty much every green policy adopted over the last decade, the bill leaves the profits and industries of the rich essentially untouched. This is achieved by fiddling the books, allowing companies to "offset" or "trade" their carbon footprint. These offsetting schemes are only going to become more elaborate and creative as green growth initiatives become more popular.

---

[34] Leslie Hook, "Climate change: how China moved from leader to laggard", *Financial Times*, 25 November 2019.

[35] Malm 2016.

[36] "Climate emergency declarations in 1,261 jurisdictions and local governments cover 798 million citizens", Climate Emergency Declaration, posted 18 December 2019, https://climateemergencydeclaration.org/climate-emergency-declarations-cover-15-million-citizens/.

[37] Ben McKay, "'This is our nuclear moment': NZ passes climate change law", *Sydney Morning Herald*, 7 November 2019.

Green growth packages are an ever more popular greenwashing strategy being proposed by parties across the political spectrum. It is a strategy that puts governments on the front foot. Rather than making declarations and setting fake targets, green growth schemes aim to aggressively advance the interests of the capitalist class on the premise that economic growth can be paired with ecological sustainability. Whether green growth packages are put forward by the right or the left, they hinge on the idea that capitalism itself can solve the climate crisis. This is an important assumption to clarify.

Is a green capitalism possible?

Capitalism is inherently and unavoidably destructive. As Marx identified, the metabolic rift between human society and nature is built into the very nature of the relations of production and distribution.[38] The dynamic of capitalist production – to accumulate capital in competition with other capitals – requires the development and usage of techniques that are mass, cheap and quick. Sustainability is directly counterposed to the goal of capital accumulation. All capitalist industries are based on the endless depletion of finite resources, the utilisation of materials and methods with little concern for safety, all of which is done as cheaply, and therefore destructively, as possible. Even when it is in the long term interests of the capitalist system to protect the environment – in order to maintain stable and plentiful conditions for profit-making – it is extremely difficult for them to take any action which conflicts with the short term interests of individual companies or states. As Engels put it:

> As individual capitalists are engaged in production and exchange for the sake of the immediate profit, only the nearest, most immediate results must first be taken into account. As long as the individual manufacturer or merchant sells a manufactured or purchased commodity with the usual coveted profit, he is satisfied and does not concern himself with what afterwards becomes of the commodity and its purchasers. The same thing applies to the natural effects of the

---

[38] Marx's work on the metabolic rift is explained in a detailed and contemporary way in Kandelaars 2016.

same actions. What cared the Spanish planters in Cuba, who burned down forests on the slopes of the mountains and obtained from the ashes sufficient fertilisers for one generation of very highly profitable coffee trees – what cared they that the heavy tropical rainfall afterwards washed away the unprotected upper stratum of the soil, leaving behind only bare rock! In relation to nature, as to the immediate, the most tangible result; and then surprise is expressed that the more remote effects of actions directed to this end turn out to be quite different, are mostly quite the opposite in character.[39]

Though the system is inherently destructive of the environment, the current crisis has been brought on by the rampant use of fossil fuels. Andreas Malm provides a detailed look at how fossil fuels became the dominant energy method and how they are now unbreakably melded with the DNA of capitalism. Coal-fired steam was not initially the preferred energy source, but as production became larger scale and more capital and labor intensive, it became indispensable. Flowing water was not a commodity with an exchange value. It was not able to be reproduced nor stockpiled by private firms, making it far less compatible with the new capitalist mode of production. Coal on the other hand was easily able to be bought, extracted and sold. Coal was also spatially and temporally flexible in a way that was impossible for water. It allowed factories to be established near large labour sources in major cities and to be kept running regardless of weather, time of day or season. Very quickly, this energy source became a fundamentally unique commodity and one that is, under capitalism, intractable. Malm summarises it well: "The fossil fuel economy is the energy basis of bourgeois property relations". While other materials become physically embodied in specific commodities – leather in boots, raw cotton in textiles, and so on – coal, oil, and gas are "utilized across the spectrum of commodity production as the material that sets it in physical motion. Fossil fuels are the general lever for surplus-value production". This also means that any growth under capitalism involves the growth of the fossil fuel industry. This has been true since the early 1800s, hence Malm's

---

[39] Engels 1876.

suggested general law: "Where capital goes, emissions will immediately follow. The stronger global capital has become the more rampant the growth of CO_2 emissions".[40]

Given this, it is impossible for another commodity to replace fossil fuels by stealth. Their replacement as an energy source will require a deliberate and comprehensive conversion of a vast array of processes. Just to name a few: international shipping, aviation, plastics, fertilisers; and concrete production would have to be radically restructured or rendered obsolete to effectively phase out fossil fuels use.[41] Capitalists will never embark on such a mammoth shift willingly, the disruption would simply be too great. Additionally, the militaries of the major powers, which are responsible for substantial carbon emissions, could not be transitioned without a substantial weakening of their fighting capacity. In a society that constantly stokes imperial tensions, states will not be prepared to open themselves up in this way.

Green growth and the Green New Deal

In his excellent article "Origins and Delusions of Green Growth", Gareth Dale discusses the recent proliferation of green growth initiatives; comprehensive economic packages that aim to stimulate capitalist growth with new, green methods and industries. Dale describes how green growth has come to replace "sustainable development" projects and that this reflects a turn to a more rapacious and openly market-driven approach. The green element imbues these projects with a supposed social good while the growth element ensures that they are based firmly around the goal of capital accumulation. But rather than allowing market forces to operate freely, these projects revolve around state intervention, not primarily

[40] Malm 2016, pp52-53.
[41] Concrete is a good example of the hidden omnipresence of fossil fuels; despite not being derived from fossil fuels concrete production accounts for 4-8 percent of emissions globally. See Jonathon Watts, "Concrete: the most destructive material on earth", *The Guardian,* 25 February 2019.

by way of nationalising industry but by offering incentives in order to stimulate the economy.[42]

These projects became particularly popular after the GFC, a period in which the ruling class has been constantly scrambling for mechanisms to resuscitate economic growth. Because green growth initiatives are generally based on stimulating the productive side of the economy, they appear to represent an alternative to the strategy underlying quantitative easing and lowering interest rates. Instead of bosses being given handouts which they then refuse to invest, this form of stimulus flows directly into the real economy. In this way these projects can be described as green Keynesianism. There is nothing automatically supportable about Keynesian economic plans, and they do not have to be linked with any increases to welfare or the social position of workers. In fact many of the green growth packages proposed over the last ten years have had a distinct lack of socially progressive content. The South Korean green "five-year plan" that Dale discusses at length was put forward by an openly neoliberal government.

One of the most fashionable titles for green growth packages of late is the Green New Deal (GND) or just Green Deal. GND packages are being proposed from all over the political spectrum. As the *Financial Times* pointed out recently, "pretty much every sentence spoken by EU officials name checks the Green Deal".[43] The European Commission has launched a Green New Deal which is supported by parties from the left and the right.[44] The UN supports a Green New Deal and calls were made for one at the 2019 COP25 conference. The GND was first associated with progressive forces. The first proposal came out of a UK think tank headed by Larry Elliot and then taken up by the Green Party. Today it has been made

[42] Dale 2015.
[43] Alan Beattie, "Palm oil case is a cautionary tale for Brussels' Green Deal", *Financial Times*, 19 December 2019.
[44] Mariana Mazzucato, "Europe's Green Deal could be the most important in a generation", *Financial Times*, 11 December 2019.

famous by Alexandria Ocasio-Cortez and Bernie Sanders, who have both put forward policy packages under this name.

All versions of the GND claim that the dual purpose of the deal is to lower emissions and to provide a boost to the economy. It is pitched as a totalising reboot of society on a green basis. The versions of the GND put forward by Ocasio-Cortez and Ed Markey, Sanders, the British Labour Party under Corbyn, and several Green parties around the world contain a far more wide-reaching slate of policies, including many supportable welfare reforms. The versions offered by right wing and centrist forces are far more limited. The deal launched by the EU is essentially a glorified emissions trading scheme.

Nevertheless, despite the impression often given by their defenders, the packages which have captured the imagination of many on the left rest on the same basic premise as all green growth schemes. Like the original New Deal in the US, GND packages hope to revive the economy after a period of sluggishness, and to do so in a way that is both environmentally and socially transformative. But as was the case with the original New Deal, the left can support specific progressive policies that are bundled into it, without lending support to the scheme as a whole. Further, the claim that the scheme as a whole can use capitalist growth to advance social justice and radically reduce carbon emissions needs to be firmly rejected as both misguided and utopian.

Fighting for workers' rights and just transitions should not be tied to incentivisation schemes for capitalists. It is dangerous to blur the lines between what is good for industry and what is good for workers. It opens the door to arguments like that made by Tony Burke, after Labor's election loss in Australia in 2019, that demands for reducing emissions need to be downscaled because keeping coal profitable is essential to defending workers.[45] This kind of argument is the flipside of the trend towards the new climate movement taking up workers' rights under the banner of climate justice. It is about pitting workers against the movement, and even if it isn't posed in such a way, the

---

[45] Katharine Murphy, "Tony Burke floats Green New Deal-style approach to Labor's Climate Policy, *The Guardian*, 23 May 2019.

focus on GND policy obscures the way forward for workers' rights in relation to the climate. There will need to be serious struggle, incorporated into the climate movement, to ensure justice as industry and wider social conditions change as a result of climate change. An electoral approach to policy reform is not going to cut it.

More problematic is the claim by proponents of the GND that it is a strategy capable of driving down emissions and arresting the climate crisis. The scale of profit-sacrifice and inter-capitalist cooperation that would be required to achieve this is unimaginable. In addition to cooperation within countries, serious advocates for the GND acknowledge that it would be impossible for policies, even far reaching ones, to have a meaningful impact on the environment unless they are linked in to similar changes made on an international scale. But there is no prospect for the kind of international cooperation that would be necessary to achieve this. With almost no shred of irony, the go to example used to prove that such international cooperation is possible is World War II! The fact that governments were prepared to nationalise industry (and that capitalists were prepared to let them) was so that they could build up the military strength against rivals in order to secure profits for the future. It is precisely this rivalry that makes any international turn away from fossil fuels impossible. Green capitalism may on first glance look like the only viable way out of the climate crisis, but as Dale argues:

> The vision offered by green growth is beguiling: a lush, eco-balanced affluence engineered through ethical enterprise and smart markets. It is also a smokescreen. It is a red herring, a pink elephant, a delusion; it is a strategic mirage, a pied-piper panacea that seduces even critical spirits into complicity with capitalistic hegemonic projects that do little or nothing to repair humankind's relationship with the environment.[46]

In this context it is problematic for the GND to be popularised on the left at precisely the time when millions of people have begun to demand system change and are searching around for what that may

---

[46] Dale 2015.

look like. The proposals for a GND rest on a propagandistic argument that the totalising solution people are searching for can be achieved within the existing system. It is fanciful and counterproductive. Some on the left argue that the GND is a transitional demand. But it is more clarifying to see it as the anti-transitional answer. To the extent that there are transitional demands being raised by the movement – though it is dubious to classify them as such outside a revolutionary movement – they are things like 100 percent renewables, no new coal and zero emissions. These demands cannot be granted under capitalism, but the role of the GND is to argue that they can, that it is unnecessary and undesirable to transition away from capitalism because markets and governments can get it done. As a totalising political framework, the GND should be rejected by the revolutionary left in the same way that we reject the ideas that wage theft or imperialism can be overcome within capitalism. This does not mean that we should oppose individual policies or dismiss struggles for reforms that are conceived within the framework of the GND. Struggles for reforms are essential and are not the same as the ideological reformist response to the climate crisis.

The revolutionary socialist response

The only way to stop temperatures rising further and to mitigate both the environmental and social effects of climate change is to completely overhaul production as we know it. Emissions need to be taken to zero as soon as possible. This will require a radical remodelling of every major industry and service. Many machines, plants and factories will be unusable, others will require huge technical transformation. This will make it necessary to dedicate enormous resources to technological and scientific research to find new methods of production. Similar resources will also need to be poured into damage control. We need mass sequestration of atmospheric carbon dioxide, that will include reforestation among other techniques. In addition to all of this there needs to be a huge injection into housing, infrastructure and healthcare all around the world, in order to ensure that people can be safeguarded against the impacts of climate change now and into the future.

Unlike some issues – for example global poverty or inequality – proposing such a sweeping vision of transformation is not unfamiliar or confrontational to people outside the radical left. There is an overwhelming consensus among scientists for action on this scale. The demands of the new climate movement are also a reflection of this consensus; for example 100 percent renewables, no new coal and zero emissions. To get even close to fulfilling any of these would require an unprecedented transformation of production and the majority of social institutions and norms. To call it unprecedented is a major understatement. In fact, under capitalism it is impossible. Economically and politically capitalism could neither permit nor survive such changes. Instead we need to fight for a social system that can accommodate these changes. A socialist society, where production is collectively controlled by the whole of society, would be able to replace the profit motive with the human need motive. A society without private ownership of production and capital renders accumulation for accumulation's sake redundant. Decisions by the majority who collectively control and run production can only be made democratically. And there can be no doubt that the majority will decide to run things rationally, sustainably and justly. Such a society can only be built by overthrowing the current system through a mass upheaval of the poor and oppressed majority, led by the working class, not just in one country but as part of an international revolutionary process.

There are currently neither the organised forces nor the political consciousness required to carry out such a process. Yet the situation we face is urgent. But contrary to the catastrophist narrative that the end of days will be a single apocalyptic event, the climate crisis will unfold in various ways into the indefinite future. The situation is certainly urgent, but by a matter of degrees rather than absolutes. Tipping points will be reached at different times and will have different impacts depending on how society responds. The longer capitalism survives, the harsher the impacts of the crisis will be.

Humanity is not simply hostage to "runaway climate change". As has been the case for centuries, humans have the capacity to shape our environment – to impact weather patterns and soil conditions for example. This remains the case within the Anthropocene. The Anthropocene is the result of environmental destruction set in play by the dynamics of capital accumulation. But the parameters of the Anthropocene are yet to be determined.

The sooner we get to socialism, the sooner we can make the conditions of the Anthropocene habitable. The task is urgent because the damage to the planet is accelerating and because the social toll will be increasingly horrific. But whatever world we inherit for socialism, we will be able to make it compatible with a democratic and egalitarian society. There is no point getting too specific about the ways that we will organise housing, food, transport and so on, except to say that managing a hothouse climate and developing long-term sustainable production practices will be a priority for a socialist society. This means that some specific conceptions of post-capitalist paradise might have to be discarded (like for example the idea that everyone can eat steak for three meals a day or fly around in a jet at whim) but it does not mean that we have to look forward to a spartan existence on starvation rations. The outlook for socialism has not been fundamentally altered by the climate crisis. Socialism will still be built on the basis of abundance and incredible technological advancement. We already have the capacity to qualitatively transform production to run sustainably. Our capacity for this would dramatically increase under socialism, when society is reorganised on the basis of human need, and when the capacity and creativity of science is fully unleashed.

The logic of socialism is the logic of ecological sustainability and, for that reason, it is not necessary to put forward a specifically "eco-socialist" vision. To insist that socialism must be made "eco" is to suggest that the foundations of socialism are not naturally ecologically sound, that we will need to make a series of adjustments to socialism in order to make it green. The result of this is to draw a false separation between the democratic content of socialism and the environmentally friendly content of eco-socialism. Socialism – a society based on the principle of "from each according to their ability, to each according to their needs" – is automatically compatible with climate sustainability. If society was ruled democratically by the majority of ordinary people, why would they not want to organise production in a sustainable way? Similarly we should not draw a distinction between the aspects of socialism that are about making the planet more habitable and those that are about eradicating oppression and exploitation. It is only under conditions of human liberation that the planet can be saved. And the fight to save the planet is necessary for human liberation.

None of this is to say that time is irrelevant. Time is clearly working against us. But this just adds another item to the list of reasons to overthrow capitalism. Every day that this system survives is a disaster and a tragedy for millions of people. But unfortunately there are no shortcuts to overthrowing it. The socialist left needs to seriously build up our forces over the coming decades.

This means building socialist organisations, intervening into movements and weighing into the ideological debates of our time. There is a diffuse yet growing anti-capitalist sentiment within the new climate movement and within layers of young people around the world more broadly, growing up in the context of converging crises of capitalism. And there is a natural opening for socialist politics created by almost every slogan and demand of the movement. But there is not as yet a sizeable current who understand the fight against the climate crisis to be the fight for socialism. There is a gulf between what people know needs to be done and their strategic understanding of how to do it. This is understandable given the weakness of the revolutionary left and the left as a whole. But solutions that rest on the compliance of the capitalists or their system are not only futile but also harmful. For example the catastrophist prediction that everyone will open their eyes and act as one is a recipe for running headlong into the catastrophe with our eyes shut. The class battle at the heart of the climate crisis will become more acute and bitter, and the ruling class is already several moves ahead.

This will lead to several struggles. Short of socialism, there are many reforms that are worth fighting for in response to the climate crisis. Not because it's possible for it to be reformed away, but because struggle strengthens our side and because we can fight to alter the social impact of climate change. Small victories can be won against fossil fuel companies, and these can give people inside and outside the movement confidence in the purpose of struggle. In Australia the campaign to stop the Adani coal mine has played a useful role within the movement; it is a tangible immediate objective that can be fought for alongside fighting for the overall eradication of fossil fuels. Though Adani has not been stopped, there have been a series of small wins as phases of the construction have been held up. It has also been a key concrete example of the united front that the ruling class has when it comes to defending coal.

The other key reforms to fight for are those that respond to the social impacts of climate change. Policies featured in GND packages, like the expansion of public housing, explicitly address class inequality. But while these are worthy policies, struggles are most likely to develop when demands emerge organically from the climate crisis. The fires across Australia raised a series of immediate demands: housing protection, government compensation for victims, healthcare and protection from smoke, including the right to not work in an unsafe environment such as that created by a pall of smoke hanging over the city. By far the most persistent demand is for the fire service to be adequately funded and for hundreds of thousands of additional firefighters to be paid. As the crisis unfolds and people take stock of the damage a demand to tax the fossil fuel companies in order to pay for the rebuilding has begun to be normalised. Such is the public pressure that Morrison has agreed to compensate volunteer firefighters for their efforts. Given that there were approximately 70,000 volunteer firefighters assisting in NSW alone, it's easy to see how this promise could become a major problem for the government. Introducing decent payments to volunteers and exponentially expanding the number of full time paid firefighters directly cuts against the neoliberal organisation of the state. As the crisis plays out this will be an increasingly obvious obstacle to responding humanely and rationally to disasters. Consequently, "climate" politics and activism will very likely become more about social justice issues. That said, it is unlikely that the popular political understanding of the climate crisis that has been built up recently will dissipate. All the coverage and debate about the fires speaks to this. As well as demands for practical assistance, there is also huge anger at the government for its love of the coal industry and reckless approach to CO_2 emissions.

Ultimately struggles for climate justice, and struggles against the capitalist class more broadly, are the only way to build the foundations required for the overthrow of capitalism. As Lenin argued: "only struggle discloses to [the exploited class] the magnitude of its own power, widens its horizon, enhances its abilities, clarifies its mind, forges its will".[47] It is an extremely positive development that a new movement has broken through over the last 12 months, and that it is demanding system change. In a practical sense the movement is also a huge breakthrough and one that should be welcomed by everyone on the left. Millions of predominantly young people are now engaged in a fight against the most powerful and uncompromising forces of capitalism.

The fossil fuel industry will not simply relinquish its powerful position in the face of our struggle and neither will the governments who defend them. This creates the basis for serious struggles that will be very difficult to shut down now that there is such broad consensus about the stakes of the situation. As well as the new climate movement with its generalised demands about climate change, we are going to see an increase in struggles against the effects of climate change, which are likely to interact with struggles against the consequences of neoliberalism that we are witnessing around the world. These two aspects of mass struggle can strengthen each other and become one mass challenge to the system. These will potentially be bitter and protracted fights, shaped at least in part by the response of the existing left.

---

[47] Lenin 1917, p241.

The old socialist slogan "we have a world to win" has never been more apt. Anything less than that will be a disaster for the planet and the whole of humankind.

References

Ababsa, Myriam 2015, "The End of the World: Drought and Agrarian Transformation in Northeast Syria (2007-2010)" in Raymond Hinnebusch and Tina Zintl (eds), *Syria: from Reform to Revolt*, 1, Syracuse University Press.

Angus, Ian 2016, *Facing the Anthropocene*, Monthly Review Press.

Angus, Ian 2017, *A Redder Shade of Green*, Monthly Review Press.

Bendix, Aria 2019, "45 unreal photos of billionaire 'bunkers' that could shelter the super rich during an apocalypse", *Business Insider*, 11 June, https://www.businessinsider.com/billionaire-bunkers-shelter-wealthy-during-apocalypse-2019-6.

BP 2016, "The Paris Climate Agreement and the Future of Fossil Fuels", 19 April, https://www.bp.com/en/global/corporate/news-and-insights/speeches/the-paris-climate-agreement-and-the-future-of-fossil-fuels.html.

Burgmann, Meredith and Verity Burgmann, *Green Bans, Red Union: The Saving of a City*, New South Press, 2017.

Clark, Brett, John Bellamy Foster and Hannah Holleman 2019, "Imperialism in the Anthropocene", *Monthly Review*, 1 July, https://monthlyreview.org/2019/07/01/imperialism-in-the-anthropocene/.

Climate Council 2015, "The Burning Issue: Climate Change and the Australian Bushfire Threat", *Climate Council*, 2 December, https://www.climatecouncil.org.au/resources/burningissuereport2015/.

Dale, Gareth 2015, "Origins and Delusions of Green Growth" *International Socialist Review*, 97, Summer, https://isreview.org/issue/97/origins-and-delusions-green-growth.

Davis, Mike 2018, *Old Gods, New Enigmas. Marx's Lost Theory*, Verso.

Engels, Frederick 1876, *The Part played by Labour in the Transition from Ape to Man*, https://www.marxists.org/archive/marx/works/1876/part-played-labour/index.htm.

Foreign Affairs, Defence and Trade References Committee 2018, "Implications of climate change for Australia's national security", 17 May, https://www.aph.gov.au/Parliamentary_Business/Committees/Senate/Foreign_Affairs_Defence_and_Trade/Nationalsecurity/Final_Report.

Holleman, Hannah 2018, *Dust Bowls of Empire*, Yale University Press.

Intergovernmental Panel on Climate Change (86 authors) 2018, "Special Report: Global Warming of 1.5°C", *Intergovernmental Panel on Climate Change*, October, https://www.ipcc.ch/sr15/.

Kandelaars, Michael 2016, "Marxism and the natural world", *Marxist Left Review*, 11, Summer.

Lenin 1917, "Lecture on the 1905 Revolution", *Lenin's Collected Works*, 23, Progress Publishers.

Malm, Andreas 2016, *Fossil Capital: The Rise of Steam Power and the Roots of Global Warming*, Verso.

Markus, Andrew 2019, Mapping Social Cohesion Survey, Scanlon Institute, Monash University, https://scanlonfoundation.org.au/archived-research/mapping-social-cohesion-survey-2019/.

Mousseau, Frederic 2019, *Evicted for Carbon Credits: Norway, Sweden, and Finland Displace Ugandan Farmers for Carbon Trading*, The Oakland Institute.

Oil and Gas Climate Initiative 2016, "Taking Action. Accelerating a low emissions future", http://www.oilandgasclimateinitiative.com/news/2016-report-taking-action-accelerating-a-low-emissions-future.

FUELLED BY COAL: PIERCING THE MIRAGE OF A SUSTAINABLE CAPITALIST AUSTRALIA

CATARINA DA SILVA

The second decade of the twenty-first century ended with catastrophic bushfires across the Australian continent. In some states the bushfires began in September, well before the onset of summer. As early as 12 November 2019 a catastrophic bushfire warning was in place across most of NSW including greater Sydney. In an ominous start to the bushfire season, on this day fire threatened Sydney suburbs, and in some suburbs residents were told to leave or stay at their own peril. Almost 600 schools were closed. Those at risk from fire were told by NSW Rural Fire Service: "If you are threatened by fire, you need to take action to protect yourself...there are simply not enough fire trucks for every house. If you call for help, you may not get it. Do not expect a firetruck". A thick cloud of toxic smoke descended on Sydney, Canberra and Melbourne, and travelled even as far as New Zealand, resulting in poor visibility and burning eyes and lungs for any who dared to venture outside.

For many, New Year's Eve was a terrifying ordeal, such as the four thousand people fleeing an out of control fire in Mallacoota in Victoria's East Gippsland region, who were forced on to the beach to escape the flames. With all roads out of the area closed, the sea

Catarina Da Silva has been a socialist for many years and is a workplace delegate with the Community and Public Sector Union. Special thanks to Omar Hassan, Jack Crawford, Kate Doherty and Clara da Coasta-Reidel, who provided input and feedback on the ideas in this article.

offered the only refuge available to terrified residents and holiday makers who crowded into the water while the skies turned bright red and smoke closed in on them. It took the government over a week to fully evacuate the town. Victorian ALP premier Daniel Andrews invented a new category to declare Victoria in a State of Disaster, while days into 2020 NSW was declared in a State of Emergency. Deaths were rising, scores of people were missing and many thousands needed evacuating, while whole towns turned to ash. Emergency services chiefs warned that the crisis could go on for months, with fires expanding, creating their own weather patterns, and joining up to create "mega blazes" – far surpassing the damage caused by the Amazon fires that had created international outrage in 2019.

This came on top of an already significant environmental crisis. At the decade's close over 99 percent of New South Wales was in a drought category, with nearly 44 percent of the state in intense drought.[1] Large portions of NSW faced the potential of a serious water shortage crisis in the near future, the result of major multi-year droughts compounded by political neglect. Dubbo, a regional centre of nearly forty thousand people, faced the possibility of running out of water in the summer of 2020.[2] Early in 2019, a mass fish die-off in the town of Menindee sparked heated discussion about drought, climate change and farming practices.[3]

Meanwhile, the NSW Liberal-National Party coalition government has been trying to pass a bill that would curtail the power of planning authorities to consider climate pollution in its approvals

---

[1]   NSW Department of Primary Industries, "NSW State Seasonal Update – October 2019", October 2019, https://www.dpi.nsw.gov.au/climate-and-emergencies/seasonal-conditions/ssu/october-2019; NSW Department of Primary Industries, "Latest NSW Drought maps", 27 November 2019, https://edis.dpi.nsw.gov.au/.

[2]   Anne Davies, "NSW towns including Dubbo and Tamworth face water emergency within months", *The Guardian*, 24 May 2019.

[3]   Dennis Normille, "Massive fish die-off sparks outcry in Australia", *Science*, 22 January 2019, https://www.sciencemag.org/news/2019/01/massive-fish-die-sparks-outcry-australia; Anne Davies, Lisa Martin and AAP, "Menindee fish kill: another mass death on Darling River 'worse than last time'", *The Guardian*, 28 January 2019.

process for new coal and gas projects. The deputy premier of NSW, John Barilaro, said that it was a "bloody disgrace" to link climate change with the dramatic early start to the fire season.[4] As late as November 2019, Liberal prime minister Scott Morrison chastised those who tried to use the fires to discuss climate change, and claimed that there was no "credible scientific evidence" to link the fires to carbon emissions.[5] To add insult to injury, in the 2019-20 financial year the Berejiklian government cut $28.5 million dollars – or 35 percent – from the capital expenditure budget for Fire and Rescue.[6] In response, one family travelled from the mid-north coast to dump the charred remains of their home on the steps of the NSW Parliament, declaring, "When's the time to talk about climate change then, if I'm standing in the wreckage of my own house?"[7] There was plenty that's political in these fires.

Indeed, the contempt shown towards NSW residents has a simple commodity at its heart: coal. Coal is a central feature of Australian capitalism and, as I will argue in this article, its importance to the economy means that the interests of the coal industry take precedence over other considerations, regardless of the party of government. In order to understand this dynamic I will discuss the history of the industry with a focus on NSW and Queensland, as well as exploring some of the dynamics around the development of Australia's domestic energy supply. I will then move on to discuss what I consider the key driving factor of the Australian coal industry: the vastly profitable export market, which saw the Australian extraction industry expand faster than any other country's between 2000 and 2017.[8] Finally, I

---

[4]   Alexandra Smith and David Crowe, "Deputy Premier says climate change talk amid fire crisis a 'disgrace'", *Sydney Morning Herald*, 11 November 2019.
[5]   "Scott Morrison urges politicians arguing about bushfires to 'take it down a few notches'", SBS News, 13 November 2019; Paul Karp, "Scott Morrison says no evidence links Australia's carbon emissions to bushfires", *The Guardian*, 21 November 2019.
[6]   Tarric Brooker, "Gladys Berejiklian slashes fire service budgets while NSW burns", *Independent Australia*, 13 November 2019.
[7]   Tom McIlroy, "Now is the time to talk about climate, say bushfire victims", *Australian Financial Review*, 12 November 2019.
[8]   Katharina Buchholz, "Where Mining is Thriving", *Statista*, 4 November 2019, https://www.statista.com/chart/19824/biggest-mining-output-continents/.

will consider the influence the coal industry wields in the sphere of parliamentary politics, as well as providing a critique of the politics of several ideas that dominate the climate justice movement in Australia. The crucial underlying argument I make is that any serious attempt to challenge the coal industry will by necessity need to challenge Australian capitalism as a whole.

Australian coal: a black history

Andreas Malm's book *Fossil Capital* exposes some of the dynamics of capitalism's dependency on fossil fuels. Much of this dependence is historically embedded: Malm explains how coal became the energy source of choice in the industrial revolution, in particular displacing water mills in the early nineteenth century. Coal offered the emerging industrial capitalist class a number of advantages over water, in spite of water's plentiful supply and relative efficiency. Coal-powered steam provided an uninterrupted and relatively mobile energy supply, allowing factories to set up in areas where they could access a more disciplined and reliable working class. Malm's fascinating history explores a variety of factors that came together in the 1830s and 1840s to ensure that the industrial revolution was fuelled by coal, unleashing a path of development with fossil fuels very much at its centre.[9]

Fossil fuel dependence continues to shape the global economy to this very day. Through pressures of economic and military competition, coal quickly came to dominate energy supply around the world. Today coal supplies around a third of all energy used worldwide and makes up around 38 percent of global electricity generation. It also plays a crucial role in heavy industry such as iron and steel production, as well as other industrial applications such as cement and alumina refining.[10]

Coal has been a central factor in the development of capitalism in Australia, and in part this explains the industry's political weight. To capture this reality, I will sketch a historical overview of the

[9]   Malm 2016.
[10]   IEA 2018.

development of the Australian coal industry, with a focus on NSW and Queensland as the main producers of export grade black coal.

Unbeknownst to the colonial invaders, the eastern seaboard of what is now Australia happens to have several mammoth coal deposits. The fact that Sydney was founded on top of one of Australia's largest deposits of black coal would fundamentally shape the development of NSW. Coal was discovered very early in the process of colonisation, reflecting its bountiful supply: as early as 1791 coal was discovered in a creek near Newcastle by convict escapees. Coal littered the Sydney Basin, and accidental coal discoveries seem to have been frequent in the early period of invasion. In the late 1790s coal was discovered at what later became the town of Coalcliff, near Wollongong, and by 1798 it was evident to the colonial authorities that there were significant deposits of coal around Sydney from Newcastle in the north, the Blue Mountains in the west, and down to the Illawarra/Shoalhaven in the south. Exploration and excavation began in earnest in the early nineteenth century, with all mining interests owned by the crown.[11]

Early coal mining was brutal and conducted in poor conditions, and relied on convict labour. In both NSW and Tasmania, coal mining was used as a form of punishment meted out to the insolent and insubordinate. While rations and work hours may not have been substantially different to other work areas, coal mining involved harsh conditions and excessive punishment. Convicts forced to work in the mines were exposed to dangerous coal dust and damp conditions that left them vulnerable to diseases.[12]

In the 1820s private enterprise entered coal mining in Newcastle, and in 1826 privately owned coal mining was established in Wollongong. This latter development came with its own dedicated military unit to keep order among convict labourers. By 1860 Newcastle mines were supplying NSW as well as the other colonies with coal, and were exporting to Europe. Well before the gold rushes that were so important to other colonies, NSW had developed a

---

[11]   Martin and Hargraves 1993, pp2-25.
[12]   ibid., p7.

major extractive industry that reaped substantial export profits. Coal also drove infrastructural development. Wollongong harbour was developed in the 1860s to service mining needs, and the first shipment of coking coal sailed from there in 1868. Across NSW, shipping and rail often developed along with coal extraction. Similarly, technological imports and innovations were often in the service of coal extraction.[13] Thus from very early on, coal was a major part of the NSW economy.

The NSW deposits had the economic advantage of being located close to urban centres and were comparatively accessible for transport. In Sydney as late as the 1940s there was still a colliery operating in what is now the upmarket inner city suburb of Balmain: it was considered "favourably located logistically" and was only shut down because of an explosion that killed two people and threatened surrounding working class housing.[14] The logistically advantageous locations of both Newcastle and Wollongong, positioned close to sea access points, also drove early development there. For most of the twentieth century NSW dominated coal production and exports.

Coal was substantially more significant to NSW than other Australian colonies, although deposits of some significance would later be discovered in every colony or later, state. NSW was and is different to all these discoveries with the exception of Queensland, which I discuss below. NSW coal is largely high quality bituminous and thermal coal, or black coal as it is commonly known. Black coal is generally used in electricity generation or to produce coke for iron and steelmaking. It can also be used in other industrial applications such as cement and alumina refining. The high quality and large size of NSW coal deposits drove development beyond federation and continues to drive a significant portion of the economy. In 2012 47 percent of total raw black coal and saleable black coal production came from NSW.[15] Only Queensland has deposits of similar significance, whereas most other coal deposits discovered in Australia

---

[13]   ibid., pp2–63.
[14]   ibid., p75.
[15]   Geoscience Australia 2013.

are either low grade brown (lignite) coal or have not been large enough to be of such significance to the economy (see map on next page).

To give a sense of the significance of NSW deposits, in 2012 Australia was estimated to have 9.2 percent of world black coal deposits, making it fifth-ranked in the world. Twenty-four percent of these deposits are in NSW, and when assessed in terms of *recoverable* resource deposits NSW has 37 percent of Australian black coal. The Sydney Basin coal deposit is just marginally short of a third of all recoverable coal in Australia (31 percent), and is equal to the size of recoverable coal in the Queensland Bowen Basin.[16] According to the NSW Department of Industry, in the 2015-16 financial year coal was worth around $13.2 billion to the state in exports, larger than the value of tourism and education combined, making it easily the state's largest export earner. In 2015-16 the NSW coal industry produced 246.8 million tonnes of raw coal, yielding 191 million tonnes of saleable coal, worth nearly $14.6 billion – approximately 80 percent of total value of NSW mineral production.[17]

While coal production has generally been a stable part of the NSW economy, its development has varied depending on global factors. The Great Depression saw the shrinking of the global economy, which flowed through to extractive industries including coal. Similarly demand increased with the massive expansion of heavy industry during the Second World War. This drove expansion of coal in both NSW and Queensland.[18] The ebbs and flows of the global economy have generally impacted on the growth and contraction of the industry, reflecting its position as an export driven industry, the dynamics of which I discuss further below.

The experience in Queensland illustrates this process. Unlike in NSW, the growth of the Queensland coal industry was initially quite slow, due to the remote locations of many deposits.[19] Queensland

---

[16] ibid.
[17] NSW Department of Industry, "Coal in NSW", https://www.industry.nsw.gov.au/development/industry-opportunities/mining-and-resources/coal/coal-in-nsw.
[18] Martin and Hargraves 1993.
[19] ibid.

accounts for approximately 62 percent of all Australian black coal and 59 percent of recoverable black coal. The Bowen Basin alone accounts for 31 percent of recoverable black coal, while the Surat Basin accounts for 13 percent and the Galilee Basin 10 percent.[20]

Image 1: Major non-renewable energy resources in Australia

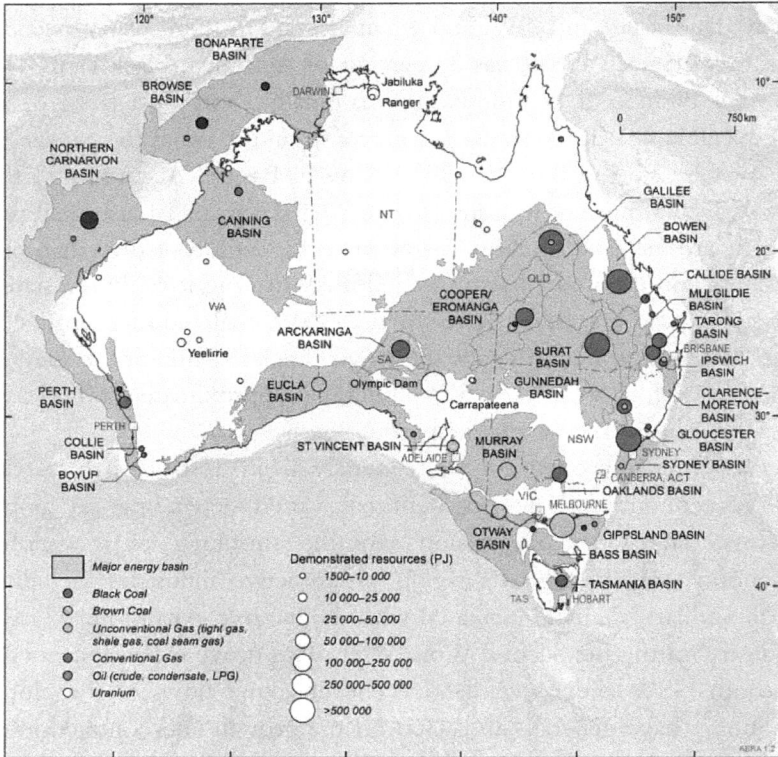

Source: Geoscience Australia, *Australian Energy Resources Assessment*, 2019.https://aera.ga.gov.au/.

The remote location of these deposits was historically compounded by Queensland's tropical climate, which resulted in frequent flooding that prevented efficient excavation. There was a significant coal discovery at Callide in the early 1900s but it wasn't developed until the 1940s; similarly there was limited mining around

---

[20] Geoscience Australia 2013.

Ipswich until the 1940s, in spite of known resources. The Second World War was part of the impetus that led to the development of these resources.[21]

The other major factor that drove the development of coal mining in Queensland was the rehabilitation of the Japanese economy after the Second World War. As the Japanese economy grew, it needed black coal for heavy industry and it lacked domestic coal deposits. Due in part to geographical proximity, Japan had a keen interest in Australian coal and coking coal in particular. Japanese hunger for Australian coal drove expansion in Queensland. In particular widespread exploration of the Bowen Basin revealed the extent of the deposit, although much of it was too deep for the colliery and long wall mining methods that dominated in NSW. The development of mining in the Bowen Basin led to the widespread expansion of open-cut mining, first established by the US owned Utah Development Company, which created the Blackwater open cut in 1967. This sparked rapid expansion of open cut mining in Queensland, so much so that by 1991 "the open cuts on the northern Bowen Basin stretch[ed] for an aggregate of 40 kilometres along the outcrop, dotted with massive equipment as large as any in the world".[22] By 1990 Queensland had surpassed NSW as the highest coal-producing state, largely due to open cut mining.

Coal and electricity supply

Outside of NSW and Queensland coal has been less central to state economies. While there are coal deposits in all Australian states, only in NSW and Queensland are they so great as to play such a significant role in export industries. However the fact of coal abundance has shaped domestic energy supply across the continent. And as a Gillard government report into energy supply noted, the energy sector plays an important role in Australia's economy, accounting for around 5 percent of industry gross value added.[23]

---

[21] Martin and Hargraves 1993.
[22] ibid., p97.
[23] Department of Resources, Energy and Tourism and Geoscience Australia 2010.

Australia has a unique history of coal-fired power stations being captive to local coal mines – that is coal power stations being attached to specific mines.[24] In South Australia, for example, the Playford B and Northern coal-fired power stations in Port Augusta were linked to the Telford Cut brown coal mine in Leigh Creek. Both plants were decommissioned in 2016, coinciding with a ceasing of production at the Telford Cut.[25] The Gillard government's report into energy resources admitted that Australia is disproportionately dependent on coal for energy supply compared to the global energy market.[26] Around three-quarters of Australia's electricity supply comes from coal, compared to 38 percent of global electricity supply.[27] The Gillard government attributed this to the "large, low-cost resources located near demand centres and close to the eastern seaboard".[28]

The development of brown coal power stations in Victoria serves as an instructive case in point for how the Australian energy supply has developed this reliance on coal. In the nineteenth century the Victorian colony was dependent on black coal imports for its power supply, mostly from NSW. However industrial action in NSW proved a regular disruption to coal supply, particularly in 1909, causing concern about the stability of Victoria's energy supply. This was further compounded by the electrification of the Melbourne and Bendigo tram networks, creating a further reliance on electricity generation. The Victorian government therefore embarked on a mission to discover and develop its own local coal deposits. Initially black coal was mined at Wonthaggi, but these deposits were comparatively small and the town was soon marked by the industrial radicalism the government had hoped to bypass. In the face of this challenge, the Victorian government chose to focus its attention on the vast brown coal supplies in the La Trobe Valley.[29]

[24] Martin and Hargraves 1993, p52.
[25] Luke Griffiths, "Alinta to close Port Augusta power stations, Leigh Creek coal mine a year early", *Advertiser,* 30 July 2015.
[26] Department of Resources, Energy and Tourism and Geoscience Australia 2010, p4.
[27] IEA 2018.
[28] Department of Resources, Energy and Tourism and Geoscience Australia 2010, p9.
[29] Martin and Hargraves 1993, pp183-91.

This points to an important factor identified by Andreas Malm regarding the relationship between power supply and social power: that energy supply is at least partially a question of class rule.[30] The development of Victorian brown coal electricity supply was designed to circumvent the disruption caused by the union activity of workers in the coal industry in NSW, and industrial unrest in Wonthaggi contributed to the decision to cease production there. Establishing coal in the La Trobe Valley was also in part intended by the government to circumvent this local industrial radicalism.[31] The coal industry – both extraction and electricity generation – has long been a site of intensive class struggle due to its centrality to the operation of Australian capitalism. There are numerous other examples one could point to, such as the use of the army by the Chifley government to break the coal miners' strike in 1949.[32]

The utility of brown coal in the La Trobe Valley had two intimately related parts: one was to establish a local energy supply, and the second was a means of reaffirming capitalist class power. It should be noted that brown coal is of significantly lower grade than black coal; it does not burn hot enough for use in heavy industry, and it creates significantly higher emissions. It's also less efficient: it can take up to four times as much brown coal to produce the same energy output as black coal.[33] The brown coal in the La Trobe Valley also has a high water content, meaning equipment and techniques for dredging and briquettes had to be imported from Germany to make the coal usable for energy supply.[34]

Yet the significant size of the deposit made the investment worthwhile, ensuring Victoria had a stable energy supply from locally-mined brown coal. In 1921 the first temporary brown coal-fired power station was established in the La Trobe Valley. It was replaced by the first permanent brown coal-fired power station at

---

[30] Malm 2016, especially Chapter 9.
[31] Martin and Hargraves 1993, pp183-91.
[32] Deery 1995.
[33] "Fact check: Does Australia export cleaner coal than many other countries?" ABC News, 27 November 2015.
[34] Martin and Hargraves 1993, pp183-91.

Yallourn in 1924. Yallourn B was established in 1927. By 1931 6.5 million tonnes of brown coal had been extracted at Yallourn for Victoria's power supply. The success of the Yallourn power stations laid the basis for the establishment of further brown coal-fired power stations in the La Trobe Valley, which carries on to this day.[35] It is estimated that the brown coal deposits in the La Trobe Valley could service current electricity needs for somewhere in the vicinity of 500 years.[36]

The interdependence between coal mines and their captive power stations means that today more than half of Australia's energy mix comes from coal, and three-quarters of Australian electricity supply. Around 20 percent of the total energy supply in Australia comes from brown coal.[37] Not only does this mean the Australian landscape is dotted with dirty coal power plants, many of them operating for years beyond their original intended retirement date, but it has also had a significant impact on the infrastructure that has been developed to support the distribution of energy supply and electricity supply in particular.

Australia has five electricity systems, the largest and most significant of which is the National Energy Market (NEM), followed by the south-west and north-west interconnected systems (SWIS and NWIS). The NEM allows electricity to flow across the Australian Capital Territory, NSW, Victoria, Queensland, SA and Tasmania. This interconnected electricity grid is the world's longest power system, stretching nearly 5,000 kilometres from Port Douglas in Queensland to Port Lincoln in SA. It also features the world's largest direct current seabed cable, which runs from Loy Yang in Victoria to Bell Bay in Tasmania. In this complex electricity system, "Exchange between electricity producers and electricity consumers is facilitated through a pool where the output from all generators is aggregated and

---

[35] ibid.
[36] Hughes 2018.
[37] ibid.

scheduled to meet demand through the use of information technology systems".[38]

NEM, SWIS and NWIS have all been developed largely around coal-fired power stations, with some later allowances being made for limited hydro and wind electricity supply. The electricity grid relies on specific coal-fired power stations as fuel sources, especially around major coal resources and to a lesser extent gas supply infrastructure on the eastern seaboard.[39] It also relies on a steady 24-hour supply of energy to the grid from these specific fuel sources (i.e. coal-fired power stations), and it is principally designed to *deliver* power rather than to receive power inputs.[40] This means that electricity supply is quite literally built around coal supply, and a significant expansion and redevelopment of Australia's energy infrastructure would be required for any substantial shift away from coal energy supply in Australia, because some of the most plentiful areas for geothermal, solar and wind electricity supply are far from the existing nodes for electricity fuel supply located along the eastern seaboard.[41]

This is compounded by other issues with renewable power supplies. While much has been made of the recent surge in household rooftop solar panels, the Australian energy grid is not designed to accept inputs from this source. The irregular flow of solar, which is generated in peaks and troughs, as well as the dispersed inputs from household rooftop solar, means that vast quantities of solar-generated electricity is simply wasted.[42] The Gillard government argued that major impediments to shifting to renewables included "higher costs

---

[38] Department of Resources, Energy and Tourism and Geoscience Australia 2010, pp23-4.
[39] ibid.
[40] Needham 2008; Lucy Hobday, "Electricity distributors warn excess solar power in network could cause blackouts, damage infrastructure", ABC News, 12 October 2018; Eryk Bagshaw and Rob Harris, "'Tipping point': Energy regulator says electricity grid won't cope with more solar", *Sydney Morning Herald*, 25 September 2019.
[41] Department of Resources, Energy and Tourism and Geoscience Australia 2010, p11.
[42] Needham 2008; Bagshaw and Harris, "'Tipping point': Energy regulator says electricity grid won't cope with more solar", *Sydney Morning Herald*, 25 September 2019. In addition household rooftop solar panels are creating a potential toxic waste problem: Rodney Stewart, Hengky Salim and Oz Sahin, "There's a looming waste crisis from Australia's solar energy boom", *The Conversation,* 17 June 2019.

relative to other energy sources, their often remote location from markets and infrastructure, and the relative immaturity...of many renewable technologies".[43] For there to be a shift in energy generation towards renewable energy supply, it would require a massive investment in energy infrastructure that is inconceivable in the current political context. In any case the political impetus is not towards renewables: early in 2019 it was revealed that the rate of investment into large scale renewable projects has declined significantly since 2016.[44]

A most valuable export

The real value of coal, however lies not in power generation but rather in exports. As mentioned previously, Australia accounts for 9.2 percent of global black coal deposits. However it is the largest coal exporter with roughly a third of global exports. Around 75 percent of all black coal extracted here is exported. Most trade occurs in the Asia region, with Japan the main receiver (45 percent) followed by China (16 percent) and South Korea (15 percent).

Some academics have contended that the mineral export industry is less significant than it is popularly perceived. Pearse, for example, argues that there is a broad popular perception that greatly magnifies the size of mineral exports compared to their actual size as a proportion of all foreign trade. Further, he points out that the proportion of the working class employed in mining is quite small: by his calculations in 2009, a mere 1.3 percent.[45] Counting dependent industries, mining is still only responsible for slightly less than 4 percent of workers employed in Australia.[46] Pearse argues this misconception is the result of a concerted campaign by mining interests to inflate the importance of both coal and mining more

---

[43]   Department of Resources, Energy and Tourism and Geoscience Australia 2010, p11.
[44]   Katharine Murphy, "Clean energy investment falls back to 2016 levels amid policy uncertainty", *The Guardian*, 11 September 2019.
[45]   Pearse 2009, p12.
[46]   Goodman and Worth 2008, p206.

broadly, so that the interests of mining companies are broadly perceived as being of utmost importance to the nation.[47]

Certainly Pearse makes a valid point with this last claim. He presents compelling evidence that popular opinion perceives mining as being a much more significant proportion of exports than it is.[48] However looking at these figures alone can be somewhat misleading. Australia is anomalous in its dependence on extractive industry exports; proportionally comparable only to Canada and Norway among developed nations, with more than 30 percent of merchandise exports coming from fuels and minerals.[49] As others have noted, Australia's reliance on extractive industry exports has more in common with underdeveloped nations than modern industrialised economies.[50]

Coal exports are disproportionately important to export profits. In 2018-19 coal overtook iron ore as the most valuable commodity export, worth approximately $67 billion.[51] Both metallurgical and thermal coals are exported but metallurgical coal is especially important because it is of a high grade and used in heavy industry, whereas thermal coal is principally used for electricity generation. While renewable energy sources are comparable to coal in their efficiency for energy generation, this is not true for heavy industry.[52] There is no efficient substitute for the use of metallurgical coal in heavy industry, and it is therefore a crucial part of world imperialist dynamics: it is impossible to imagine the global arms industry without coal. This is particularly the case during a period of sharpening inter-imperialist rivalry such as we are currently living through. While prices for metallurgical coal have been more volatile over the last decade, exports continue to grow (see Graph 1, next page).

---

[47] Pearse 2009.
[48] ibid.
[49] Goodman and Worth 2008, p206.
[50] Cleary 2011.
[51] Cole Latimer, "Coal is Australia's most valuable export in 2018", *Sydney Morning Herald*, 21 December 2018.
[52] Cunningham, Van Uffelen and Chambers 2019.

Graph 1: Metallurgical coal export volumes and values

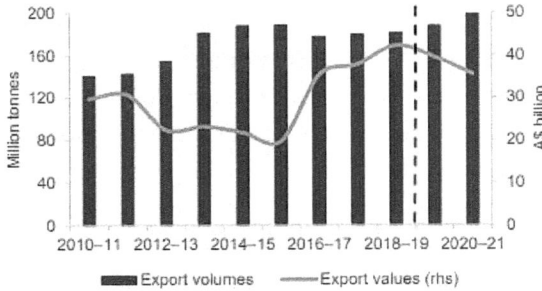

Source: ABS (2019) International Trade, Australia 5368.0; Department of Industry, Innovation and Science (2019)

Source: Resources and Energy Quarterly, June 2019.
https://publications.industry.gov.au/publications/resourcesandenergyquarterlyjune20
19/documents/Resources-and-Energy-Quarterly-June-2019-Met-Coal.pdf

Over the last 25 years Australia has experienced a fairly consistent boom in black coal exports. While domestic coal consumption has remained fairly steady, the export of black coal and particularly metallurgical coal has surged (see Graph 2).

Graph 2: Australian Coal Production and Exports

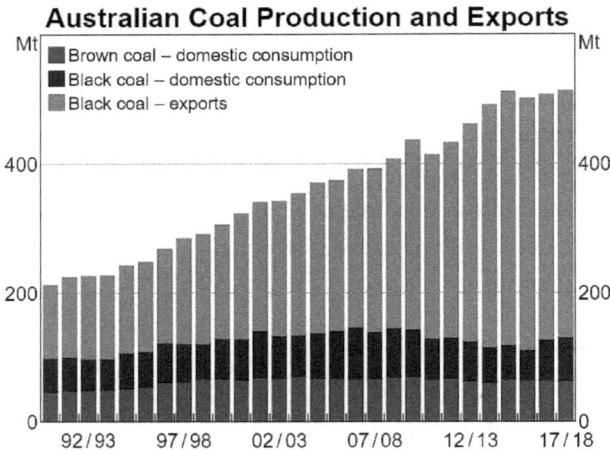

Sources: ABS; DOIIS; RBA

Source: Cunningham, Van Uffelen and Chambers 2019.

Black coal export volumes have more than doubled since the early 1990s, driving the rapid and massive expansion of coal extraction.[53] The unpopular Adani Carmichael mega-mine in the Galilee Basin is but one example of this. The mine is planned to contain six open cut pits and five underground mines, and will cover around 447 square kilometres. Adani expects the Carmichael mine will produce around 2.3 billion tonnes of coal over 60 years of production, an average of 40 million tonnes per year. This will make it easily the largest coal mine in Australia and one of the largest in the world.[54] It will also be entirely export-oriented. There are a number of other mining licenses granted to further open up the Galilee Basin in the near future. In NSW coal production has also boomed: in the Newcastle and Hunter regions production grew by around 33 percent between 1999 and 2008.[55] The never-ending thirst for ever greater access to coal reserves reflects the vast export wealth that lies below the surface: in a global economy reliant on coal for energy supply and in particular for heavy industry, there are enormous profits to be made from plundering what lies beneath the soil.

Coal is also linked to other highly profitable extractive industries, such as shale oil, shale gas and coal seam gas. It is worth diverging a moment to discuss the development of the coal seam gas (CSG) and shale gas extraction in Australia because it has expanded rapidly in recent years. CSG and shale gas are principally methane, caused by the decay of organic matter over millions of years. CSG is held within the coal seam by water pressure, while shale gas is held within sedimentary rocks at depths greater than 1,500 metres.[56] All known CSG reserves are in NSW and Queensland, although large shale gas reserves exist in the Northern Territory, WA and SA. Shale gas can only be extracted by hydraulic fracturing (fracking), whereas CSG can be extracted by fracking or by drilling a vertical well down to the coal

---

[53] ibid.
[54] Queensland Department of State Development, Infrastructure and Planning 2014.
[55] Cleary 2012, p41.
[56] "Factbox: CSG in Australia", SBS News, 3 September 2013.

seam and pumping out water.[57] This process, known as creating a CSG well, reduces pressure in the seam and allows the gas to be released. CSG is mostly extracted through wells in Australia, although it should be noted that this also carries with it substantial environmental impacts.[58] Collectively, CSG and shale gas are often referred to as unconventional gas (along with another form of gas called tight gas).

In 2013 CSG accounted for approximately 23 percent of Australian gas reserves, and 78 percent of gas reserves in the eastern states (Queensland, NSW, Victoria, Tasmania and SA). It is projected to supply at least 30 percent of the domestic gas market by 2030.[59] In recent years there has been a vast expansion of CSG wells, particularly in Queensland. In December 2018 official data suggested there were nearly six and a half thousand CSG wells in Queensland. Paul Cleary estimates that each well generates about one kilometre of roads, so projected well development could result in 40,000 kilometres of pipelines and access roads.[60] He argues that current well production is potentially only a tenth of the likely number of wells to be drilled by mid-century, including three huge projects worth $70 billion. He claims the combined total of Queensland's CSG projects is "arguably the biggest engineering feat since the Snowy Mountains Scheme".[61] Recent NSW statistics are harder to locate, but according to SBS in September 2011 nearly 500 CSG exploration and production wells had been drilled in NSW.[62] In response to immense public pressure the NSW government put a stay on new CSG wells between 2012 and 2014; evidence suggests that since then the government has been cautious about approving new CSG projects, perhaps a reaction to the public backlash it experienced.[63]

---

[57] Nick Evershed, "An unconventional gas boom: the rise of CSG in Australia", *The Guardian*, 18 June 2018.
[58] See Cleary 2012 for an extensive discussion of the environmental impact of CSG wells.
[59] "Factbox: CSG in Australia".
[60] Cleary 2012, pp44-9.
[61] ibid., p41.
[62] "Factbox: CSG in Australia".
[63] Evershed, "An unconventional gas boom: the rise of CSG in Australia".

Shale gas is less well developed but the estimated size of deposits is remarkable: varying estimates suggest that at least 400 and 1000 trillion cubic feet of shale gas sits below the surface of the Australian landscape, much of it located in remote WA and the NT.[64] Mining giants such as Santos are pressing to have access to these deposits.[65]

While noting the domestic consumption of unconventional gas, the market is again driven by export potential. Australia has surged in the global gas trade. In 2017-18 Australian trade in liquefied natural gas (LNG) grew by 38.5 percent.[66] As this decade opened it was announced that Australia had overtaken Qatar to become the world's leading exporter of LNG.[67] By value LNG was the third-ranked export in 2018-19, behind iron ore and metallurgical coal.[68] It is important to note that this is not purely driven by the extraction of unconventional gas; conventional gas projects such as the Gorgon offshore project have also expanded substantially. Nonetheless the booming gas export industry has opened up potential for further profits through CSG and shale gas extraction, and has contributed to a sharp rise in domestic gas prices.

On the whole coal and its subsidiary products are a resource of vast importance to the Australian export economy. As noted earlier, in 2017 metallurgical coal was the second-largest product exported by volume; gas (including shale gas and CSG) was third, while thermal coal was in fourth place. Coal exports alone fetched $67 billion in 2018-19, without taking into account unconventional gas exports. This reflects Australia's position as the world's largest exporter of coal and LNG.

---

[64] Australian Council of Learned Academies 2013.
[65] Santos, "Shale Gas", *What We Do,* https://www.santos.com/what-we-do/production/natural-gas/shale-gas/.
[66] Department of Foreign Affairs and Trade 2019.
[67] Nick Toscano, "Australia tops Qatar as biggest LNG exporter", *The Age*, 6 January, 2020.
[68] ibid.; Sam Jacobs, "Australia is set to become the world's biggest exporter of natural gas by 2019", *Business Insider*, 8 January 2018.

For the greater common good?

In February 2017 Scott Morrison brought a lump of coal into parliament to praise the fossil fuel industry. While it was treated as a bizarre stunt by many, it nonetheless reflected a political reality in Australia. Both mining generally and coal specifically have substantial influence over the operation of the parties of government, both ALP and Liberal. Understanding the economic significance of coal is important to understanding its political weight.

Formally, the mining and energy industries in Australia are among the most tightly regulated in the world. Governments don't merely rubber stamp projects but instead approval comes with extensive conditions attached, related to an array of environmental factors including toxic emissions, water discharge, dust and so on. Larger and riskier projects have considerably more conditions attached.[69]

Yet the seriousness of these conditions could perhaps be gauged by the fact that mining companies seldom if ever object to them. In fact the US mining giant Peabody Coal describes Australia as "a premier location for coal mine development and investment".[70] Similarly in 2012 mining services firm Behre Dolbear gave Australia top ranking as best place to invest in a study of 25 mining nations. As Cleary notes, this is because Australia's supposed best practice in mining regulation is underpinned by a lack of willingness and capacity to enforce its environmental conditions, at both state and federal levels, rendering them effectively meaningless.[71]

There are two useful examples of this from Queensland. In 2013 the state government responded to mass community and farmer opposition to CSG, and established the GasFields Commission to manage the "coexistence" of CSG expansion with farmers, local communities and other stakeholders. In 2012-13 the government pledged $2.5 million for the agency but after taking into account running costs and staffing of one chairperson and six commissioners, this left precious little for on the ground monitoring. Moreover the

---

[69]   Cleary 2012.
[70]   Cited in ibid., p50.
[71]   ibid.

first chairperson came to the role with a reputation for pro-CSG bias: John Cotter had been chair of the farm lobby, AgForce, and had been heavily criticised for failing to defend farmers against mining and CSG development. Early on, as chairperson Cotter signalled, he considered less rather than more regulation of CSG was needed: "If regulation there is impeding their [mining companies'] progress…then it needs to be looked at".[72] This is hardly indicative of a government wanting to be seen to take the regulation of CSG seriously.

The other example is the tragic re-emergence of black lung (pneumoconiosis) and silicosis in Queensland mines, diseases which had previously been eradicated. In February 2019 it was confirmed that over a hundred Queensland miners had been diagnosed with mine dust lung diseases.[73] The official enquiry in 2017 detailed how government regulators had failed to adequately monitor coal dust levels; the health department had failed to consider black lung a serious concern, and mine operators either ignored the risks or tried to shift blame, as well as routinely exceeding maximum dust levels. Many workers were never screened for black lung, while thousands of others were never advised that their lung x-rays were of poor quality and could not be examined for the disease. Others had their x-rays examined by staff with inadequate training to identify early signs of the disease. The health surveillance unit responsible for monitoring miners for dust lung diseases employed only one part-time occupational physician who lacked the capacity to examine the overwhelming stockpile of records. The enquiry revealed that the bulk of these records were simply never examined and were left to degrade.[74] This human tragedy inflicted on miners and their families is a glaring example of the meaninglessness of government regulations where there is no will to even assess compliance, let alone enforce them.

---

[72] ibid., pp31-32.
[73] Megan Hendry, "Black lung advocates say 20 Queenslanders diagnosed with coal dust diseases in a fortnight", ABC News, 27 February 2019.
[74] Coal Workers' Pneumoconiosis Select Committee 2017.

Nor is the lack of meaningful regulation confined to Queensland. Cleary's *Mine-Field* details a regulatory "race to the bottom" where state governments competing with each other for lucrative mining contracts steadily eroded meaningful regulation. In NSW mines approved under the *Environmental Planning and Assessment Act 1979* are expressly exempted from complying with seventeen state laws including the *Native Vegetation Act*, the *Water Management Act* and the *Heritage Act.* State governments frequently offer big mining developments exemption from the usual regulations by giving them "state significance" status or by fast-tracking approval. Cleary also documents a vast array of ways that these regulations allow companies to circumvent or avoid regulation, such as by allowing them to self-report their environmental impact.[75]

Even when regulations are enforced the penalties are weak at best. In March 2012 Whitehaven Coal was found to have seriously breached environmental protection licenses around water pollution at its Narrabri and Tarrawonga mines. It was fined $6,000. A few weeks later it was again found to have breached licenses for releasing waste water into the Goulburn River. For this breach Whitehaven was fined $105,000. This fine sounds more significant but as Cleary points out, it is about the cost of replacing a single tyre on the giant yellow mining trucks that are standard issue at coal mines.[76] In this context regulation looks less like best practice and more like a toothless tiger.

Some have explained this toothless regulatory tiger as a product of the interference of coal companies in parliamentary politics. Cleary and others have done some remarkable research on the direct influence of mining and coal on the political process, particularly with regard to lobbying and the movement of personnel in the halls of power. It is undeniable that the mining industry has a well-oiled political machine that attempts to gain influence through a combination of political donations, lobbying and cultivating extensive political networks in the halls of power.

---

[75] Cleary 2012.
[76] ibid.

The building up of networks between mining and political parties is part of the daily reality of the operation of the Australian state. In NSW the undisclosed donations of former mining entrepreneur Nathan Tinkler is but one example: a highly ambitious businessperson who sought to buy political influence through large donations to the Liberal and National parties. In the wake of the ALP's proposed mining super profits tax (commonly known as the mining tax) there was a substantial increase in mining money directed towards the Liberals and Nationals. Common as well is the cultivation of lobbying networks that means that the Minerals Council has been known to provide public advice on the personnel it thinks should make up cabinet, as was the case when it counselled Julia Gillard not to drop Martin Ferguson from the front bench. Mining bodies have direct access to political power brokers and will willingly apply pressure to meet the needs of the extractive industry.

There is also a revolving door between the mining industry and politics. Again, Cleary paints a damning picture that shows the movement of politicians at the end of their parliamentary careers on to the payroll of mining companies. Former Nationals leader and deputy prime minister John Anderson earned a reputation for being sympathetic to the interests of coal and CSG. After his sudden resignation from politics he took up a non-executive board member position with CSG company Eastern Star Gas. Another former Nationals leader, Mark Vaile, went over to Tinkler's Aston Resources at the end of his career. Nor is the revolving door just reserved for the conservative side of politics: Julia Gillard's one-time chief of staff Amanda Lampe had jumped into politics after working at Origin Energy. Former Queensland ALP deputy premier Keith de Lacey went over to MacArthur Coal after finishing his time in parliament, and former ALP National Secretary Gary Gray took on a position with Woodside as a lobbyist.[77] Martin Ferguson famously went from the ALP front bench to the Minerals Council. [78] The

[77]   ibid., pp84-88.
[78]   Charlie Lewis, "That was then, this is now: Martin Ferguson's head-spinning 180 on union power", Crikey, 9 August 2017.

interconnectedness of personnel between mining and both sides of the parliamentary divide is indicative of how embedded mining is in the operation of government.

Cleary and others are right to criticise the influence of mining on the halls of power.[79] Yet contrary to their arguments, it's important to see that the mining industry does not merely exert influence because of its lobbying efforts or the development of political networks. Rather, the lobbying, networking and movement of personnel is *reflective* of the broader importance of coal and mining to the economic system. The industry is not important because of the lobbying but rather the lobbying has weight because of the importance of the industry. The fact that Australia has a highly profitable coal export industry means that conservative *and* Labor politicians are always keen to meet the needs of miners and go to lengths to ensure the Australian market is accessible and conducive to investment in coal and related industries.

It is impossible to imagine this situation any other way. The centrality of coal to Australian capitalism means that the capitalist state will always serve the needs of coal. The Australian state is not going to be persuaded to abandon a multi-billion dollar export industry, even under the weight of an increasing climate crisis. This is particularly the case because of the fact it is an industry linked to imperialism and therefore of central importance to global capitalism.

This in part explains why the state has been so repressive in its response to climate justice protests. In Queensland the ALP premier Annastacia Palaszczuk has rushed through laws that clamp down on protests and impose significant fines on non-violent protesters, with Liberal-National Party support. The supposedly progressive Labor premier of Victoria Daniel Andrews gave his seal of approval to the violent attacks on the Blockade IMARC protests.[80] An Extinction Rebellion protest in Sydney made international news after police arrested over 30 protesters, imposed draconian bail conditions on

[79]   ibid; see also Krien 2017.
[80]   Simone Fox Koob and Benjamin Preiss, "Premier thanks police, slams 'appalling' anti-mining protesters", *The Age*, 30 October 2019.

them, and held two protesters in remand for more than 24 hours after they refused to sign the bail conditions.[81] This is all happening as a direct response to an impressive wave of environmental activism across the country. While the context of a general increase in police repressiveness during the neoliberal era is partly to blame for this onslaught on the democratic right to protest, the response is an indication that challenges to extractive industries will not be tolerated.

This is further supported by a recent joint police and army counter-terrorism training exercise at the Loy Yang power station in the La Trobe Valley, which certainly indicates the Australian state is prepared and willing to defend coal interests in Australia.[82]

Labor and the unions

Before moving on to discuss the politics of climate justice campaigning in Australia, I want to discuss the politics of coal and the ALP. In the aftermath of the ALP's shock defeat in the 2019 election, much was made of their significant losses in Queensland mining seats. In particular it has been argued that the ALP's position on the Adani mine was a key factor in their defeat, and that the working class is supportive of the coal industry. Since the election Labor has swung to the right on a variety of policies including climate change.

This approach needs to be thoroughly rejected. There is ample evidence that the vast majority of people are not just opposed to the Adani coal mine, but in fact are deeply concerned about the impact of climate change. This is supported by numerous opinion polls.[83] Furthermore it is fair to say that the poor and working class will be

---

[81]   "Dozens arrested at Extinction Rebellion climate protests", Al Jazeera, 7 October 2019.
[82]   "ADF and Vic Police wrap up counter-terrorism training", *Australian Defence*, 21 October 2019. https://www.australiandefence.com.au/defence/joint/adf-and-vic-police-wrap-up-counter-terrorism-training#pUZqRgeiCHUJoQmP.99.
[83]   For example, Matt McDonald, "Are Australians more worried about climate change or climate policy?", The Interpreter, Lowy Institute, 26 June 2019, https://www.lowyinstitute.org/the-interpreter/are-australians-more-worried-about-climate-change-or-climate-policy; Matt Wade, "A record share of Australians say humans cause climate change: poll", *Sydney Morning Herald*, 1 April 2019; Katharine Murphy, "More voters think Australia not doing enough on climate, Guardian Essential poll shows", *The Guardian*, 26 November 2019.

disproportionately impacted by climate change. For a start, they are not in a financial position to afford luxury bunkers to save them from the worst realities of climate change. As a whole, the poor and the working class have an interest in stopping the advance of climate change and the fossil fuel industries as a matter of priority, and the sectional interests of one group – those directly employed in coal and mining related industries – should not trump the interests of the working class as a whole.

It is worth also looking at the position of workers employed in coal and mining related industries. Less than 2 percent of the Australian working class are employed in mining, and less than half a percent are employed in coal.[84] This is not going to sway the electoral fortunes of the ALP across Australia. In any case, the left must be clear that the interests of these workers (as separate from their political opinions) also lie with the dismantling of the coal industry. This of course relates to the question of climate change more broadly, but it is also a question of the living conditions of those who work in or live under the effects of the coal industry.

There is plenty of evidence to suggest that the coal industry cares precious little about the health and wellbeing of those who are impacted by the industry: the cases of black lung in Queensland; the response to the 2014 coal pit fires in Morwell in the La Trobe Valley that left local residents seven times more likely to have a heart attack;[85] the disastrous "clean up" of fly ash after the decommissioning of the Playford B and Northern Power Stations in Port Augusta that left the town covered in potentially toxic ash for weeks and weeks.[86] In reality mining companies give scant consideration for the wellbeing of workers and mining communities.

In the 2019 federal election the miners' union in Queensland, the CFMMEU, declared it wouldn't support candidates that didn't "back" the coal mining industry. We must be clear that this reflects a

---

[84]   Australian Bureau of Statistics 2019.
[85]   Robert French, "Morwell residents seven times more likely to have a heart attack since Hazelwood mine fire", ABC News, 4 September 2017.
[86]   Angelique Donnellan, "Port Augusta Power Station clean-up leaves residents dust-covered and disappointed", ABC News, 16 April 2018.

political problem with the leadership of that union, which shamefully conflates the interests of the mining companies with those of the workers. In fact it is reflective of the political decline of what was once one of the most militant unions in Australia, after decades of class collaboration since the implementation of the Accord.

In any case, we must reject the idea that the ALP in any way opposes coal in Australia, or that electing them is a strategy. At the time of writing Anthony Albanese has repeatedly stated that he refuses to get party political over the bushfires. Perhaps the smoke cloud that descended on Sydney has clouded my judgement, but I can't help but raise the question – if not now then when, Albanese? How many regional centres need to face the prospect of running out of water before the time comes? How many people need to die in out of control bushfires? How many thousands of people need to be huddled on a beach, with no supplies and in desperate need of evacuation, before that blessed time arrives?

The reality is the time will not arrive because there is no "party political" when it comes to coal. Just because Labor has the good sense not to bring a lump of shellacked coal into parliament does not mean it is any different to the Liberal party on this question. In late October, Albanese said that Labor must "embrace" "wealth creation" and "mining" on its way to a "clean energy future". He specifically laboured the point that the coal industry would be key to this.[87] This is nothing more than the ALP pretending to care about climate change while at the same time making it clear to the mining industry that it continues to support coal's dominance in Australia – just as the ALP has always done, at state and federal levels.

Campaigning dead ends

This points to the bankruptcy of strategies put forward by campaign groups that put their faith in trying to persuade the ALP to support them. For example in late 2017 Stop Adani Sydney ran a "Shakeup at Albo's" event, where it declared that Albanese "supports

[87] Rob Harris, "Albanese says Labor must embrace wealth creation, mining sector on way to low-carbon future", *Sydney Morning Herald,* 29 October 2019.

action on climate change, and is a great advocate for renewables". The purpose of the event was to "ask for his [Albanese's] help in stopping the biggest coal mine in history".[88] This was not an isolated event for Stop Adani Sydney. Similarly, the Australian Youth Climate Coalition (AYCC), one of the key organisations behind the student climate strikes, threw its efforts into campaigning for a "#ClimateElection" rather than mobilising for the popular international student strikes in the lead up to the election. While the AYCC did not campaign explicitly for the ALP, it nonetheless organised numerous events, including candidate forums that were clearly aimed at mobilising support for the ALP. During the campaign period the AYCC organised very few events that were *not* oriented towards the federal election.[89]

In the context of the ALP's consistent support for coal these actions ignore political reality and attempt to sow seeds of hope where there is nothing but a long history of betrayal. Albanese cannot be morally persuaded to support the Stop Adani campaign because the ALP is thoroughly committed to capitalism, and all that it entails. The ALP will support coal because it is good for the interests of Australian capitalism.

In a similar vein, this demonstrates the problems with the strategies associated with forms of lobbying or trying to pressure the ALP or other parties to change their policies. Many NGOs and small-l liberals do this. Take Paul Cleary as an example. Cleary has written two books on mining in Australia, the most recent of which, *Mine-field*, is a detailed and interesting exposé of recent developments in CSG and coal mining.[90] Yet his other major contribution to the discussion around mining was a whole book, *Too Much Luck*, dedicated to campaigning for a sovereign wealth fund. Cleary's argument is basically that mining companies should be taxed more and the wealth generated used to fund social services, infrastructure

[88] See "Stop Adani Shakeup at Albo's!", #Stop Adani,
https://www.stopadani.com/stop_adani_shakeup_at_albo_s.
[89] For example see AYCC's list of previous events on Facebook,
https://www.facebook.com/pg/AYCC.org.au/events/?ref=page_internal.
[90] Cleary 2012.

and so on. He provides a wealth of detailed information and data to support his argument.[91]

While this demand is perfectly supportable, Cleary doesn't seem to be aware that the reason governments don't implement his suggestions is not because they don't *understand* the impact of their taxation policies or environmental implications of mining. It is because a sovereign wealth fund does not align with their priorities. The priorities of government in Australia – conservative, Labor, state and federal – are to support what is the most conducive to ensuring mining investments. And what is most conducive to mining investment is ineffectual regulation, low taxation and generous subsidies and other economic support. No major party in Australia will be swayed by a compelling argument for an alternative, no matter how many pages are dedicated to explaining that strategy.

The Greens

While the ALP is clearly wedded to the coal industry, a more leftish seeming strategy can be to look to the Greens as a parliamentary alternative. After all the Greens are a party that campaigned about environmental issues from their foundation and put a strong emphasis on policies around environmental issues and renewable technology. Recently the parliamentary Greens leadership has started discussing the prospect of having an environmental policy framed in the popular language of the "Green New Deal". However the left should be aware of the political limitations of the Greens and both their capacity and willingness to implement the policies that are formally on their platform.

Others have noted elsewhere that the Greens have been on a long term rightward trajectory. There has been a move away from the protest politics that fed into their popularity in the late 1990s and early 2000s, and towards an increased professionalisation of the party.[92] The party today is overwhelmingly committed to

---

[91]   Cleary 2011.
[92]   Ben Hillier, "Into the mainstream: the Australian Greens", *Red Flag*, 2 May 2019.

neoliberalism and market mechanisms to deal with climate change, notwithstanding its socially progressive policies around increasing public transport and a government-owned renewable energy retailer. As a party it labours under the liberal illusion that the fossil fuel industry can be eradicated by tweaks to energy policy and by restrictions on political donations and lobbying efforts, as though the state in Australia was not fundamentally wedded to the coal industry.[93]

Even so one must view with scepticism the Greens' commitment to its policies in practice. The experience of the Greens in government has been one of compromise and negotiation rather than meaningful action. Following the 2010 federal election the Greens were effectively in a coalition government with the ALP under prime minister Julia Gillard. During its time in office the Greens achieved very little by way of winding back the fossil fuel industry. The one act it can point to, and that it actively defends on its website, was that it negotiated to support the passage of the carbon tax through parliament.[94] This was a regressive tax that pushed the cost of carbon emissions on to the consumer, with an increased cost of electricity for the average family of around 10 percent. The energy industry and large business typically passed on all or part of the cost of the tax to their customers, and the Treasury estimated that the carbon tax contributed to an increased cost of living and rise in the Consumer Price Index.[95] Moreover the carbon tax contributed to the ideological normalisation of neoliberalism by green-washing the introduction of another consumer tax, rather than placing the burden of reducing carbon emissions squarely on the shoulders of the mining and energy industry. This is hardly a history that offers any inspiration to those who genuinely want to see the abolition of the coal industry.

---

[93] For example, see their renewable energies policy, Australian Greens, "Renewable economy & climate change", https://greens.org.au/platform/renewables.
[94] "The Greens and CPRS", https://greens.org.au/cprs.
[95] Irigoyen 2017.

An Australian Green New Deal?

In the wake of developments in US politics there has been discussion recently of an "Australian Green New Deal". The idea has entered the vernacular of the Greens and even sections of the Labor right such as Chris Bowen. Popularised by liberal Democrats in the US such as Alexandria Ocasio-Cortez, the Green New Deal calls for significant state intervention to reduce carbon emissions, with government investment in technology, infrastructure and public services to address the climate crisis. As well the Green New Deal addresses in part questions of social justice with an emphasis on green job creation and social policies to improve living standards for the poor, such as public housing programs.

While noting the Greens and ALP have both adopted the language of a Green New Deal, I am more concerned with the more left wing versions of the proposal. To this end I want to address Dino Varrasso's recent *Jacobin* article about an Australian Green New Deal. [96] Varrasso has outlined in detail what he considers an antipodean Green New Deal might look like, including:

- workers from mining and coal power stations being reskilled and retrained into green industries;
- nationalising the electrical grid and de-marketisation of coal-fired power supply;
- investment in renewables technology, expansion of public transport and the building of a high speed rail network;
- building energy efficient medium to high density public housing in cities, and
- investing in new forests.

He also addresses how governments could pay for this, such as by increasing taxation, cutting funding to private schools, abolishing subsidies for mining companies, and so on.

Varrasso describes his argument as "practical but utopian", but in fact it is just utopian. This is most immediately obvious in the fact that he makes no meaningful strategic argument about how such a

---

[96] Varrasso 2019.

proposal would be achieved. He spends considerable time detailing potential government policies and how they could be paid for, but makes only a few brief comments at the end of the article about mass movements and an ambiguous statement about the need for a *socialist* Green New Deal. One can also reasonably infer that Varrasso supports a project of government reform, backed by mass movements and trade unions, as per his closing remarks. However he is studiously vague about the political forces that would lead this reform agenda, notwithstanding some critical remarks about the Greens and ALP and their commitment to neoliberalism. In that context, making brief and vague references to mass movements, trade unions and socialism at the end of a reasonably long article is not a strategy – it ends up providing a left cover for a governmental approach within the framework of capitalism.

Yet based on the analysis provided in this essay, we should be clear that this is a fundamentally mistaken approach. It is the equivalent of Saudi Arabia abandoning oil. There is a looming and unanswered question in Varrasso's argument about how such a substantial project of political reform could be achieved, given that even the reasonably popular Rudd government could not implement even a relatively minor mining tax.

What the mining tax debacle demonstrated is that as long as society continues to be organised around the interests of capital, there will be a strong drive to utilise the vast coal wealth that lies beneath the Australian soil. While popular movements may be able to stop a single coal mine or a set of gas fields, to stop the fossil fuel industry as a whole would require a fundamental transformation of the entire political and economic system. Underlying Varrasso's flippancy about this is the implication that such a transformation is *unnecessary*, and all it will take to "facilitate a rapid transition" to a fossil fuel free society is a government with the political will to nationalise the electricity grid and disincentivise coal-powered generators.[97]

Indeed this is the most important and dangerous argument of all, one that is at the heart of all Green New Deal proposals. The case is

---

[97]   ibid.

that a new round of wealth-producing, poverty-alleviating and environmentally sustainable capitalist economic growth is possible, if only governments invested in and subsidised green technology. While this may be true in the abstract and provides good fodder for left-sounding reformist articles in *Jacobin,* it is not likely to be tested in the real capitalisms of Australia or the USA. Any abandonment of the fossil fuel industry in economies "blessed" with access to these natural resources will not come within the framework of capitalist social relations. In a world structured around profit and the accumulation of value, Saudi Arabia and the USA won't give up oil, and Australia won't give up coal. Achieving that will require more than merely electing left wing figures to positions of power, and more even than mass movements to put pressure on a capitalist government. It will require the total dismantling of capitalism.

Conclusion

The purpose of this article has been to outline how coal is embedded in the economic and political structures of Australia. The fact that Australia has vast coal resources has shaped its history and present, both as a highly valuable export industry as well as the development and delivery of energy supply. This vital economic role has given coal vast influence over Australian politics, and the state in Australia has a long record of supporting the coal and mining industries in a variety of ways. In line with this both conservative and Labor governments, at state and federal level, do everything in their power to ensure that conditions are conducive and attractive to coal investment.

It follows that to challenge the coal industry in Australia will require fighting for a society that values people and the planet more than profit – a socialist society. The alternative to such a society is simply a world that continues to burn. This means that while socialists should support every movement that wishes to challenge the coal and broader fossil fuel industries, we need to build the forces of explicitly anti-capitalist and revolutionary organisations. This is the key task of those today who truly wish to end the coal industry, and all of the fossil fuel industries that are sending us hurtling towards environmental disaster.

References

Australian Bureau of Statistics 2019, "Labour Force, Australia, October 2019", cat. no. 6202.0.

Australian Council of Learned Academies 2013, "Engineering Energy: Unconventional Gas Production", *Securing Australia's Future*, 6, https://www.shale-gas.com.au/wp-content/uploads/2014/05/ACOLA-Final-Report-Engineering-Energy-June-2013.pdf.

Cleary, Paul 2011, *Too much luck: The mining boom and Australia's future*, Black Inc.

Cleary, Paul 2012, *Mine-field: The dark side of Australia's resources rush*, Black Inc.

Coal Workers' Pneumoconiosis Select Committee 2017, *Black lung white lies: Inquiry into the reidentification of Coal Workers' Pneumoconiosis in Queensland*, Report No.2, 55th Parliament of Queensland, https://www.parliament.qld.gov.au/Documents/TableOffice/TabledPapers/2017/5517T815.pdf.

Cunningham, Michelle, Luke Van Uffelen and Mark Chambers 2019, "The Changing Global Market for Australian Coal", *Reserve Bank of Australia Bulletin*, September, https://www.rba.gov.au/publications/bulletin/2019/sep/pdf/the-changing-global-market-for-australian-coal.pdf.

Deery, Phillip 1995, "Chifley, the Army and the 1949 Coal Strike", *Labour History*, 68.

Department of Foreign Affairs and Trade 2019, "Composition of Trade Australia 2017-18", January, https://dfat.gov.au/about-us/publications/Documents/cot-2017-18.pdf.

Department of Resources, Energy and Tourism and Geoscience Australia 2010, *Australian Energy Resource Assessment*, Commonwealth of Australia, https://d28rz98at9flks.cloudfront.net/70142/70142_complete.pdf.

Geoscience Australia 2013, "Black Coal", *Australian atlas of minerals resources, mines and processing centres*, http://www.australianminesatlas.gov.au/aimr/commodity/black_coal.html.

Goodman, James, and David Worth 2008, "The minerals boom and Australia's 'resource curse'", *Journal of Australian Political Economy*, 61.

Hughes, A. 2018, "Australian Resource Reviews: Brown Coal 2017", Geoscience Australia, http://dx.doi.org/10.11636/9781925297997.

International Energy Agency 2018, *Coal 2018: Analysis and Forecasts to 2023*, IEA Market Report Series, https://doi.org/10.1787/25202723.

Irigoyen, Claudia 2017, "The Carbon Tax in Australia", *Centre for Public Impact*, 5 May, https://www.centreforpublicimpact.org/case-study/carbon-tax-australia/.

Krien, Anna 2017, "The Long Goodbye: Coal, Coral and Australia's Climate Deadlock", *Quarterly Essay*, 13 August.

Malm, Andreas 2016, *Fossil Capital: the Rise of Steam Power and the Roots of Global Warming*, Verso.

Martin, C.H. and Alan J. Hargraves 1993, *History of coal mining in Australia: the Con Martin memorial volume*, Australian Institute of Mining and Metallurgy.

Needham, Stewart 2008, "The potential for renewable energy to provide baseload power in Australia", Research Paper no. 9 2008–09, Australian Parliament, https://www.aph.gov.au/About_Parliament/Parliamentary_Departments/Parliamentary_Library/pubs/rp/rp0809/09rp09.

Pearse, Guy 2009, "Quarry vision: coal, climate change and the end of the resources boom", *Quarterly Essay*, 33.

Queensland Department of State Development, Infrastructure and Planning 2014, "Carmichael Coal Mine and Rail Project: Project Overview", Completed EIS projects, 9 July, http://www.statedevelopment.qld.gov.au/coordinator-general/assessments-and-approvals/coordinated-projects/completed-projects/carmichael-coal-mine-and-rail-project.html.

Varrasso, Dino 2019, "Australia needs a Green New Deal", *Jacobin*, https://www.jacobinmag.com/author/dino-varrasso, 11 March.

GILBERT ACHCAR ON THE UNDYING REVOLUTIONS IN THE MIDDLE EAST AND NORTH AFRICA

Gilbert Achcar is a Professor of Development Studies and International Relations at SOAS University of London. He is the author of numerous books on the Middle East, including *The People Want: A Radical Exploration of the Arab Uprising* and *Morbid Symptoms: Relapse in the Arab Uprising*. He was interviewed for the *Marxist Left Review* by Darren Roso.

Let's return to what now seems to be a distant memory: the revolutionary shockwave that swept the Arab world in 2011. You argued in your book, *The People Want: A Radical Exploration of the Arab Uprising*, **that these events were only the beginning of a protracted revolutionary process owing to the specific nature of capitalism in the Middle East. Could you explain these dynamics of political economy in the Arab world and their relationship to forms of authoritarian rule?**

To begin with a general consideration, it is obvious now that we are witnessing a severe global crisis of the neoliberal stage of capitalism. Neoliberalism developed as a full-fledged capitalist stage since the enforcement of its economic paradigm in the 1980s. This

---

Darren Roso's book *Daniel Bensaïd: From the Actuality of Revolution to the Melancholic Wager* is forthcoming with Brill Historical Materialism. He is currently editing translations of Bensaïd's political writings.

stage has gone into crisis since the Great Recession a decade ago. The crisis is unfolding under our eyes, resulting in ever increasing social upheavals. If you look today at what is occurring in Chile, Ecuador, Lebanon, Iraq, Iran, Hong Kong and several other countries, it looks like the boiling point is reached by more and more countries.

The events in the Arab region fit into that general global crisis, to be sure. But there is something specific about that regional upheaval. There, the neoliberal reforms were carried out in a context dominated by a specific type of capitalism – a type determined by the specific nature of the regional state system that is characterised by a combination in various proportions of rentierism and patrimonialism, or neopatrimonialism. What is mostly specific to the region is the high concentration of fully patrimonial states, a concentration unequalled in any other part of the world. Patrimonialism means that ruling families own the state, whether they own it by law under absolutist conditions or just in fact. These families regard the state as their private property, and the armed forces – especially the elite armed apparatuses – as their private guard. These features explain why the neoliberal reforms got their worst economic results in the Arab region of all parts of the world. Neoliberal-inspired changes achieved in the region resulted in the slowest rates of economic growth of any part of the developing world and, consequently, the highest rates of unemployment in the world – specifically youth unemployment.

The reason for this is not difficult to understand: the neoliberal dogma is based on the primacy of the private sector, the idea that the private sector should be the driving force of development, while the state's social and economic functions must be curtailed. The dogma says in a nutshell: introduce austerity measures, trim the state down, cut social expenditure, privatise state enterprises and leave the door wide open to private enterprise and free trade, and miracles will happen.

Now, in a context lacking the prerequisites of ideal-typical capitalism, starting with the rule of law and predictability (without which long-term developmental private investment cannot happen), what you end up getting is most of private investment going into quick profit and speculation, especially in real estate along with construction, but not in manufacturing or agriculture, not in the key productive sectors.

This created a structural blockage of development. Thus, the general crisis of the global neoliberal order goes in the Arab region beyond a crisis of neoliberalism into a structural crisis of the type of capitalism prevailing there. There is therefore no way out of the crisis in the region by a mere change of economic policies within the continued framework of the existing kind of states. A radical mutation of the whole social and political structure is indispensable, short of which there will be no end in sight to the acute social-economic crisis and destabilisation that affects the whole region.

That's why such an impressive revolutionary shockwave rocked the whole region in 2011, rather than just mass protests. The prospect was truly insurrectionary, with people chanting "The people want to overthrow the regime!" – the slogan that has become ubiquitous in the region since 2011. The first revolutionary shockwave of that year forcefully shook the regional system of states, revealing that it had entered a terminal crisis. The old system is irreversibly dying but the new cannot be born yet – I'm referring here, of course, to Gramsci's famous sentence – and that's when "morbid symptoms" start appearing. I used that phrase in the title of the 2016 sequel to my 2013 *The People Want.*

Is it true to say that neoliberal measures in the Arab world have accelerated despite the revolutionary surge? Egypt's food prices are rising along with electricity and fuel prices, and the conservative estimates of the World Bank say about 60 percent of Egyptians were "either poor or vulnerable", all this while the regime has renewed its crackdown on street protesters. Can you talk about the relationship between counter-revolution and accelerated neoliberalism?

Egypt provides a very good example of this, indeed. When the Great Recession hit in 2008, many believed that it heralded the end of neoliberalism and that the pendulum would swing back towards the Keynesian paradigm. That was a huge illusion, however, for the simple reason that economic policies are not determined by intellectual and empirical considerations; they are determined instead and above all by the balance of class forces.

The neoliberal turn has been steered since the 1980s by fractions of the capitalist class, those with a vested interest in financialisation. In order to bring a new shift away from that, there needs to be a change in the social balance of forces, impacting the balance between fractions of the capitalist class itself, a change equivalent at least to that which took place in the 1970s and 1980s.

This did not happen yet, and the progressive forces opposed to neoliberalism have not yet proved strong enough to impose change. The neoliberals are still running the show: they claim that the reason of the global crisis is not neoliberalism but the lack of a thorough implementation of its recipes. Although they resorted massively in 2008-9 to measures contradicting their own dogma, such as the huge bailout of the financial sector by means of state funds, they quickly reverted to more and more of the same neoliberal policies pushed further and further.

That's exactly what we've got in the Arab region, despite the gigantic revolutionary shockwave that shook the whole region in 2011. Almost every single Arabic-speaking country saw a massive rise of social protest in 2011. Six of the region's countries – that is more than a quarter of them – witnessed massive uprisings. And yet, the "lesson" according to the IMF, the World Bank, those guardians of the neoliberal order, is that all this happened because their neoliberal recipes hadn't been implemented thoroughly enough! The crisis, they claimed, was due to insufficient dismantling of remnants of yesterday's state-capitalist economies. They asserted that the solution is to end all forms of social subsidies, even more radically than what had already occurred.

However, the reason that governments of the region did not do *more* of that indeed was because they were afraid to do so. This isn't Eastern Europe after the fall of the Berlin Wall, when people swallowed the very bitter pill of massive neoliberal changes in the hope that it would bring them capitalist prosperity. In the Arab world, people are not willing to pay the price for that because they have no illusions that their countries will turn out like Western Europe as the Eastern Europeans were brought to believe. Therefore, in order to impose further neoliberal measures on the people, brutal force is required. Egypt is hence a very clear illustration of the fact that the implementation of neoliberalism does not go hand in hand with democracy as Fukuyama's "end of history" fantasy claimed thirty years ago.

Egypt clearly shows that in order to implement thoroughly the neoliberal program in the Global South, dictatorships are needed. The first such implementation was in Pinochet's Chile, of course. In Egypt, it is now the post-2013 dictatorship led by Field Marshal Sisi – the most brutally repressive regime that the Egyptians have endured in many decades. It has gone the furthest in implementing the full neoliberal program advocated by the IMF, at a huge cost to the population, with a steep rise in the cost of living, food prices, transport prices, everything. People have been completely devastated. The reason why their anger did not explode in the streets on a massive scale is that they are deterred by state terror. But the full implementation of the IMF's neoliberal recipes has not and will not produce an economic miracle. Tensions are thus building up and sooner or later the country will erupt again. There was already some limited explosion of popular anger last September; sooner or later, there will be a much bigger one.

Though contexts differ, and specificity is always important, why did barbarism maintain its head start over the workers' and democratic movements throughout the Arab world? What, and why, were the turning points of defeat in the region since 2011? What is the state of the Egyptian left and the workers' movement in the face of Sisi's ultra-neoliberalism and his authoritarian brutality?

Unfortunately, both the left and the workers' movement in Egypt are in bad shape. They have suffered a painful defeat – not only due to the brutal comeback of the repressive state, but also because of their own contradictions and illusions. The major part of the Egyptian left has pursued a politically erratic trajectory, switching from one misconceived alliance to another: from the Muslim Brotherhood to the military. In 2013, most of the left and the independent workers' movement supported Sisi's coup very short-sightedly, subscribing to the illusion that the army would put the democratic process back on track. They thought that getting rid of Morsi and the Muslim Brotherhood, after their year in power, would reopen the way to furthering the revolutionary process even though it was brought about by the military.

It sounds rather silly, but they did genuinely hold this illusion, which the military fostered in the initial post-coup phase. The military even co-opted the head of the independent workers' movement into their first post-coup government. This terrible blunder discredited the left as well as the independent workers' movement. As a result, the left wing opposition is much weakened and marginalised in today's Egypt.

I'm not speaking here of the Marxist radical left, which has always been marginal, although it played a disproportionate role at times during the revolutionary upheaval of 2011-13. I'm speaking of the broader left, the one that used to appeal to large masses. This broader left has lost much of its credibility after 2013. This is actually one crucial reason why people have not mobilised massively against the new neoliberal onslaught. When there is no credible alternative, people tend to assimilate the regime's discourse that says: "It's us or chaos, us or a Syria-like tragedy. You must accept our iron heel. It will be tough, but at the end of the day you will find prosperity". The Egyptians do not really buy the last promise – prosperity – but they are still paralysed by the fear of falling into a situation much worse still than what they are enduring.

Linked to all that is another specificity of the regional revolutionary process, of which Syria is the most tragic illustration. We already discussed a first specificity – the structural crisis that is peculiar to the Arab world in the context of the general crisis of neoliberalism. The other specificity is that this region has experienced the development over several decades of a reactionary oppositional current, which was promoted for many years by the United States alongside its oldest ally in the region, the Saudi kingdom. I mean Islamic fundamentalism, of course – the whole spectrum of this current, whose most prominent component is the Muslim Brotherhood and whose most radical fringe includes al-Qaeda and the so-called Islamic State (aka ISIS).

Islamic fundamentalism was sponsored by Washington as a main antidote to communism and left wing nationalism in the Muslim world during the Cold War. During the 1970s, Islamic fundamentalists were green-lighted by almost all Arab governments as a counterweight to left wing youth radicalisation. With the subsequent ebb of the left wing wave, they became the most prominent opposition forces tolerated in some countries, such as Egypt or Jordan, and crushed in others such as Syria or Tunisia. They were, however, present everywhere.

When the 2011 uprisings started, Muslim Brotherhood's branches jumped on the revolutionary bandwagon and tried to hijack it to serve their own political purposes. They were much stronger than whatever left wing forces remained in the region, very much weakened by the collapse of the USSR, while the fundamentalists enjoyed financial and media backing from Gulf oil monarchies.

As a result, what evolved in the region was not the classical binary opposition of revolution and counter-revolution. It was a triangular situation in which you had, on the one hand, a progressive pole – those groups, parties and networks who initiated the uprisings and represented their dominant aspirations. This pole was organisationally weak, except for Tunisia where a powerful workers' movement compensated for the weakness of the political left and allowed the uprising in this country to score the first victory in bringing down a president, thus setting off the regional shockwave. On the other hand, there were two counter-revolutionary, deeply reactionary poles: the old regimes, classically representing the main counter-revolutionary force, but also Islamic fundamentalist forces competing with the old regimes and striving to seize power. In this triangular contest, the progressive pole, the revolutionary current, was soon marginalised –

not or not only due to organisational and material weakness, but also and primarily because of political weakness, of the lack of strategic vision.

The situation became dominated therefore by the clash between the two counter-revolutionary poles, which escalated into a "clash of barbarisms", as I call it, of which Syria is the most tragic illustration, with a most barbaric Syrian regime confronting barbaric Islamic fundamentalist forces. The huge progressive potential that was represented by the young people who initiated the uprising in Syria in March 2011 got completely crushed.

Many of these young people left the country, because they couldn't survive either in regime-held territories or in territories held by Islamic fundamentalist forces. Much of the Syrian progressive potential was thus scattered in Europe, Turkey, Lebanon and Jordan. Some of it survives inside the country but, as long as the war situation lingers on, it will be difficult for it to re-emerge.

The Kurdish situation in Syria is a different story. The Kurdish PYD/YPG in North-East Syria is undoubtedly the most progressive of all the armed forces active on the ground in Syria, if not the only progressive force. They managed to develop and extend the territory under their control with US backing, because Washington under Obama saw them as efficient foot soldiers in the fight against ISIS. They had their own stake in fighting ISIS, of course, since it is a deadly enemy for them. Their first direct cooperation with the US was indeed in the battle of Kobane in 2014, when US air support including airdrops of weapons was decisive in allowing the Kurdish fighters to roll back ISIS's offensive. There was thus a convergence of interests between the US, providing air support as well as other means and resources, and the YPG, providing troops on the ground.

That is what Donald Trump has let down, stabbing the Kurds in the back and opening the way to Turkey's colonial-nationalist and racist onslaught against them. Their situation has become extremely precarious as they are now caught between Turkey's hammer and the Syrian regime's anvil, between Turkish chauvinism and Arab chauvinism – two projects of ethnic cleansing, converging on the project to replace Kurds with Arabs in Syria's border areas with Turkey. Moscow is helping both in this endeavour.

But the PYD/YPG failed to join up consistently with the rest of the struggle against Assad's murderous regime...

I wouldn't put the main blame on them: none of the Syrian armed opposition forces was open to a true recognition of the Kurds' democratic and national rights. To be sure, the PYD/YPG are not some reiteration of the Paris Commune as some tend to portray them quite naively. And yet, with all their limitations and without fostering illusions about them, they represent the most progressive significant organised force on the ground in Syria. If we take the status of women as our main criterion – and it should always be a crucial criterion for progressives – there is no match for the PYD/YPG. Add to this that their co-thinkers in Turkey lead the Peoples' Democratic Party (HPD), the only progressive and feminist major political force in that country.

What were the most significant theoretical and political lessons to draw out of the previous cycle of revolutionary struggle for Marxists? We often hear the argument that Marxism is "Orientalist" and is thus unsuited to non-Western societies. Michel Foucault's attitude towards the Iranian revolution (1979) was an example of the attempt to find salvation in a non-Western religious Otherness, declaring an end to universal visions of human emancipation, class politics and Marxian theoretical instruments to understand the world.

So why do you believe that Marxist theory is better equipped to make sense of the revolutions and counter-revolutions throughout the Middle East and North Africa? What are the prospects for a new generation of Arabic-speaking Marxists activists to develop since 2011, and to what extent has this started taking place?

The Orientalist vision of the region is that it is doomed to be eternally stuck in religion as part of its cultural essence, and that religion explains everything and has always been the key motivation of the region's populations. That is a completely flawed vision, of course, which is also very impressionistic in that it ignores the past and believes that the present is going to last forever.

Looking at the Middle East and North Africa in recent years, one may get indeed the impression that Islamic fundamentalist forces are prominent everywhere. However, that wasn't the case a few decades ago, especially in the 1950s and 1960s, when these forces were marginalised by much stronger left wing forces. I was asked to write a preface to the re-edition of Maxime Rodinson's *Marxism and the Muslim World* a few years ago. This collection of articles, most of which were written in the 1960s, discusses a part of the world where left wing currents were dominant. I had therefore to inform or remind the readers of this historical fact, lest they be bewildered in reading the book.

Few realise today that in the 1950s and 1960s, it was widely assumed that the Arab region was under communist ideological hegemony. A Moroccan author published in 1967, in French, a book entitled *Contemporary Arab Ideology*, where he discussed what he called "objective Marxism" as an ideology that was diffuse in the region. By this phrase, he meant that people used Marxist categories and ideas, most of them without even being aware of their origin.

Or take a country like Iraq – a good example. Today, clerics and mullahs dominate the political scene, especially among the Shiites. But if you fast backward to the late 1950s, you'll find that the major struggle in the country opposed Communists to Baathists, the latter subscribing to a nationalist ideology that described itself as socialist. The Communists were particularly influential among the Shiites and were able to mobilise hundreds of thousands of people in demonstrations. So, think of *that* Iraq and of *today's* Iraq: a wide gulf is separating them. But it proves that there is nothing in the genes of the region's populations that dooms them to abide by the political guidance of religious forces.

The most popular political leader in modern Arab history was indisputably Gamal Abdel-Nasser – Egypt's president between 1956 and his untimely death in 1970. He went as far to the left as possible within the boundaries of bourgeois nationalism, implementing a sweeping nationalisation of the economy along with successive agrarian reforms, promoting state-led industrial development, and bringing a substantial improvement in labour conditions, all this on an anti-imperialist and anti-Zionist backdrop.

Although it occurred under harsh dictatorial conditions, this was a very progressive phase in Egypt's history, and it was emulated in several Arab countries. When you contemplate that history, you realise that the role of Islamic fundamentalism in recent decades is not rooted in some cultural essence, as the Orientalist view would have it. It is rather the product of specific historical developments. As we discussed already, it is partly the product of Washington's protracted and intensive use of Islamic fundamentalism in cahoots with the most reactionary state on earth, the Saudi kingdom, in fighting Nasser and the USSR's influence in the Arab region and the Muslim world.

When the Arab Spring (as the uprisings were called in 2011) blossomed, a new generation entered the struggle on a mass scale. The bulk of this new generation aspires to a radical progressive transformation. They aspire to better social conditions, freedom, democracy, social justice, equality, including gender emancipation. They reject neoliberal policies and dream of a society in sharp contrast with the programmatic views of those Islamic fundamentalist forces that hijacked or tried to hijack the uprisings and lead them towards their own goals.

There is a huge progressive potential in the region, and we have seen it coming back to the fore in the second revolutionary shockwave that is presently unfolding. It started in December 2018 with the Sudanese uprising, followed since last February by the Algerian uprising, and since October by massive social and political protests in Iraq and in Lebanon. Sudan, Algeria, Iraq and Lebanon are boiling, and all other countries of the region are on the brink of explosion.

What about the role of Stalinism in the Arab world?

The Soviet Union and the communist parties under its leadership have represented the dominant form of "Marxism" in the region for decades. There have been several important communist parties in the region, all narrowly linked to Moscow. This meant that the self-described Marxist literature was heavily dominated by Stalinism in the region in the 1950s and 1960s. With the global emergence of the New Left in the late 1960s and the 1970s, new translations allowed access to critical Marxist and anti-Stalinist Marxist authors in Arabic.

The rise of a New Left in the Arab region was boosted by the June 1967 defeat of the Arab armies in the so-called Six-Day War, which dealt a major blow to Nasser and his regime. A large section of the youth got radicalised beyond both Nasserism and Stalinism, into what often was radical nationalism in a "Marxist" garb rather than plain Marxism. The Arab New Left grew significantly in the late 1960s and early 1970s, but it failed in building an alternative to the old left, let alone an alternative to the powers that be.

That is the period when the regimes used Islamic fundamentalism to nip the New Left in the bud. Most, if not all, Arab governments unleashed and helped Islamic fundamentalist groups in the 1970s, especially in the universities, as an antidote to the new left wing radicalisation. They thus contributed significantly to the failure of the radical left.

Of course, the latter bears the main responsibility for its own defeat. It lacked political maturity and strategic acumen. The new radicalisation did not go far beyond previously dominant superficial and dogmatic "Marxism", heavily influenced by Stalinism. Marxism was generally reduced to a few clichés. There were exceptions, of course, but overall original Marxist intellectual production in Arabic remained very limited – leaving aside contributions by Marxist thinkers from the region who lived abroad and wrote in European languages, such as the late Samir Amin. The most prominent exception was Hassan Hamdan, know under the pen name of Mahdi Amel. He was the most sophisticated intellectual of the Lebanese Communist Party and was assassinated by Hezbollah in 1987. An anthology of his writings will come out soon in English translation.

Let's return to the present: the Algerian uprising and Sudan's revolution reignited hope, as have the courageous protests in

Egyptian streets and Lebanon's assemblies in Riad al-Solh square calling to topple the current regime. At the risk of asking an impossible question, to what extent have ordinary people in the region learnt political lessons from the earlier wave of struggle? What kind of mass dynamic is involved here? How have the oppressed and exploited learnt through the experience of mass struggle? Have they learnt?

They have definitely learnt. Protracted revolutionary processes are cumulative in terms of experience and know-how. They are learning curves. The peoples learn, the mass movements learn, the revolutionaries learn, and the reactionaries learn as well, of course, everybody learns. A long-term revolutionary process is a succession of waves of upsurges and counter-revolutionary backlashes – but they are not mere repetitions of similar patterns. The process is not circular, it has to move forward or else it degenerates.

People grasp the lessons of previous experiences and do their best not to repeat the same errors or fall into the same traps. This is very clear in the case of Sudan, but also for Algeria and now for Iraq and Lebanon too. Sudan and Algeria, along with Egypt, are the three countries of the region where the armed forces constitute the central institution of political rule. Of course, armed apparatuses are the backbones of states in general, but it is direct military rule that is peculiar to these three countries in the Arab region.

Their regimes are not patrimonial. No family owns the state to the point of making whatever they wish of it. The state is rather dominated collegially by the armed forces' command. These are "neo-patrimonial" regimes: this means that they are characterised by nepotism, cronyism and corruption, but no single family is in full control of the state, which remains institutionally separate from the persons of the rulers. That explains why in the three countries the military ended up getting rid of the president and his entourage in order to safeguard the military regime.

That's what happened in Egypt in 2011 with the dismissal of Mubarak, and this year in Algeria with the termination of Bouteflika's presidency, followed by the overthrow of Bashir in Sudan, all three carried out by the military. However, when it happened in Egypt, there were huge popular illusions in the military, which were renewed in 2013 when the military deposed Muslim Brotherhood president Morsi.

These illusions were not reiterated in Sudan or Algeria in 2019. On the contrary, the popular movement in the two countries has been acutely aware that the military constitute the central pillar of the regime that they wish to get rid of. The movement in both countries understands very well that when they chant "The people want to overthrow the regime", they mean military rule as a whole – not the presidential tip of the iceberg alone. They grasp this very clearly in both Algeria and Sudan, unlike what happened in Egypt previously.

But in Sudan there is more than that difference. There is a leadership that embodies the awareness of the lessons drawn from all previous regional experiences. This is mainly due to the foundation of the Sudanese Professionals Association (SPA), which started in 2016 with teachers, journalists, doctors and other professionals organising an underground network. As the uprising that started in December 2018 unfolded, the association developed into a much larger network involving workers' unions of all key sectors of the working class. It has been playing the central role in the events on the side of the popular movement. The SPA was also instrumental in the constitution of a broad political coalition involving several parties and groups. They are presently engaged in a political tug of war with the military. They agreed temporarily on a compromise that instituted what can be described as a situation of dual power. The country is ruled by a council in which the leadership of the people's movement is represented alongside the military command. This is an uneasy transitional period that can't last very long. Sooner or later, one of the two powers will have to prevail over the other.

But the key point here is that the Sudanese experience represents a massive step forward compared with everything we have seen since 2011, and this is thanks to the existence of a political astute leadership. The SPA didn't foster any illusions about the military. They are as radically opposed to military rule as they are to Islamic fundamentalism, especially that both were represented in the regime under Omar al-Bashir. They uphold a very progressive program, including a remarkable feminist dimension. This is a very important experience which is very closely observed all over the region.

The popular movement in Algeria is amazing for having been staging huge mass demonstrations every week for several months now. But it has no recognised and legitimate leadership. Nobody can claim to speak in its name. This is an obvious weakness, in stark contrast with Sudan. The forms of leadership naturally change over time, but we haven't entered some postmodern age of "leaderless revolutions" as some want us to believe. The lack of leadership is a crucial impediment: a recognised leadership is crucial in order to channel the strength of the mass movement towards a political goal. This they have in Sudan, but not in Algeria, and not yet in Iraq or Lebanon.

In both Iraq and Lebanon, however, people inspired by the Sudanese example are trying to set up something like the SPA. There are beginnings in that direction, involving university teachers along with various professionals. In Lebanon, they created an Association of Professional Women and Men, clearly inspired by the Sudanese model. That clearly shows how learning from experience functions at the regional level.

Could you further elaborate about the most significant aspects of the mass movements in Iraq and Lebanon?

Both movements share a remarkable particularity in that both countries, Iraq and Lebanon, are characterised by a sectarian political system.

In Lebanon, it has been institutionalised by French colonialism after World War I in a form close to the country's present political system. In Iraq, it was established by the US occupation, much more recently. Such sectarian political regimes thrive off sectarian divisions, naturally. In their context, religious sectarian divisions become the defining feature of political life and government. Sectarianism is a very pernicious and effective tool in diverting class struggle into religious strife. It's an old recipe, a version of "divide and rule":

thwart any horizontal solidarity of class versus class by turning it into a vertical clash between sects. Bourgeois-sectarian nepotistic leaderships secure the allegiance of members of the popular classes belonging to their sectarian community by stoking sectarian divisions and rivalries.

In both Iraq and Lebanon, the accumulation of social grievances resulting from a very wild form of capitalism that crushes ordinary people and deteriorates their standard of living has created a huge resentment. The social explosion was triggered by a political measure in Iraq – the dismissal of a popular military figure – and an economic one in Lebanon – a projected tax on VoIP communications. These measures provoked a formidable outburst of popular anger. In Lebanon, to everybody's surprise, the outburst covered the whole country and involved people belonging to all sects. In Iraq, it has been mostly confined to the Arab Shiite majority, but this is equally significant since the ruling clique itself is Shiite. The movement in both countries has thus strongly repudiated sectarianism in favour of a renewed sense of popular-national belonging.

In Lebanon, sectarianism was so entrenched historically that it appeared as a very difficult barrier to break. It was therefore very amazing to see people belonging to all religious communities participate in an uprising whose key slogan has become the Arabic equivalent of the Spanish-language "Que se vayan todos!" (All of them must go!), which was the key slogan of the December 2001 popular revolt in Argentina. The Lebanese version says "All of them means all of them" – a way of insisting on the repudiation of all ruling class members, with no exceptions. "Us vs. them" shifted from sect vs. sect to a revolt of the people from below against all members of the ruling caste at the top, whichever religious-political sect they belong to, whether Shiite, Sunni, Christian or Druze.

Hezbollah was not spared – and that is even more striking since a sort of taboo regarding the party, and particularly its leader, had been enforced until then. It was astounding to see that people went into the streets in the regions under Hezbollah's control despite the party's clear stance against the popular movement. Since then, there have been successive attempts to intimidate the popular movement by thugs belonging to Hezbollah and its close ally Amal, the two Shiite sectarian groups.

In Iraq, parties and militias linked to the Iranian regime engaged in repressing the popular revolt at a much higher scale, with much killing. That is because Tehran's tutelage over Iraq's government is a major target of the popular revolt. The recent explosion of anger within Iran itself was likewise met with brutal repression. Iran's theocratic regime thus confirms that it is one of the main reactionary forces in the region on a par with its regional rival, the Saudi kingdom. This was already clear from its brutal repression of the democratic popular movement within Iran in 2009 as well as from its massive contribution to the Syrian regime's counter-revolutionary drive starting in 2013 and from its heavy-handed repression of the social protests that flared up again in Iran at the end of 2017 and early 2018.

The role of women in the second wave of the revolutionary process in the Arab region is another very important feature, and a further indication of the higher degree of maturity achieved by the popular movements. In Sudan, Algeria and Lebanon, women have participated massively and very visibly in the demonstrations and mass rallies as well as in heading them. In the three countries, feminists have been a crucial component of the groups involved in the uprisings. Even in Iraq, where women were hardly visible in the initial stage of the protests, they are getting increasingly involved, especially since the students joined the mobilisation.

The big question now is: will the popular movements in Algeria, Iraq and Lebanon succeed in finding ways to organise, like their Sudanese brothers and sisters did, in order to amplify their struggles' impact and achieve major steps towards the fulfilment of their goals, or will the ruling classes manage to quell each of these three uprisings and defuse it? Without being optimistic, due to the very vicious nature of the regimes that govern this part of the world, I have a lot of hope. My hope, however, is based on the knowledge that a huge progressive potential exists, while I am perfectly aware that in order to be realised, a lot of struggle, organisation and political acumen are needed.

ISABELLE GARO ON MARX'S STRATEGIC THOUGHT AND THE SPIRIT OF REVOLT

Interview and translation by DARREN ROSO

Isabelle Garo is an esteemed Marxist writer on the French left. She has written substantially on the connections between Marxism, politics and philosophy, and is currently helping to translate the collected works of Marx and Engels into French.

In this interview with *Marxist Left Review*'s Darren Roso, she discusses the political and philosophical challenges faced by the Marxist left today, assesses the theoretical contributions of Alain Badiou and Ernesto Laclau, and makes the case for a dynamic and politically engaged return to the revolutionary spirit of Marx's writings. Garo has published *Marx, une critique de la philosophie* (Seuil, 2000), *L'idéologie ou la pensee embarquée* (La Fabrique, 2009), *Foucault, Deleuze, Althusser & Marx: La politique dans la philosophie* (Demopolis, 2011), *Marx et l'invention historique* (Syllepse, 2012), *L'or des images – art, monnaie, capital* (La Ville Brûle, 2013).

Let's begin with a short balance sheet of our current context. Your opening chapter announces that an emancipatory political project is in tatters – it has broken down. Why have you raised communism and strategy and deliberately sharpened the question of revolutionary politics today? What is it exactly you want this book to achieve and why?

The present context in France and across the world is quite bad for the exploited and oppressed in general, as also for the organised workers' movement. This long term weakening in the conditions of capitalist crises gave the green light to the ruling classes to take out their revenge at the end of the 1970s and wind back the limited but real social gains of the post-war period. The neoliberal policies imposed by the ruling classes haven't ceased today to be reinforced – with their procession of social regression, reinforced exploitation and inequalities, financialisation, the commodification of all human activities, as well as repression and militarisation, all that in a context of persistent crisis that weakens capitalism and sharpens its inter-imperialist tensions. The threat of further economic tremors and the patently manifest effects of the climatic and environmental crisis are added to the list of human–inflicted damage, which hit the poorest, women and migrants the hardest.

Resistance with its many examples is strong in the face of this unprecedented global situation within which all these dimensions interact, but it remains fragmented. With the general capitulation of social democratic organisations to the cult of the market and the collapse of the Stalinist regimes, with the weakening of militant trade unionism, the challenge facing the radical left is enormous. Meanwhile the far right and racism are being propped up and instrumentalised by the neoliberal governments barely able to maintain stable electoral majorities.

But this picture would be incomplete if it left out the vivacity of social struggles all over the world. The *Gilets Jaunes* (Yellow Vests) movement in France, unprecedented and disparate – but powerful and durable – continues to mark the present situation all the while accelerating the decomposition of the existing political landscape. People are rising up in country after country against social injustice and authoritarianism. Capitalism is seen for what it really is – *irreformable* – guided by its most destructive and murderous trends. Despite the many avenues present in the movements (degrowth, universal income, the commons, ecological enclaves and libertarian insurrection, etc.), we don't have a credible and common alternative.

Sometimes the lines of struggle seem divorced from one another, for instance here the defence of the environment and over there is feminism, and there the struggle against racism and over here the defence of public services that still may exist.

This generalised radical crisis is fraught with threats but it also calls for the revival of strategic reflection, after its long "eclipse" as Daniel Bensaïd called it. This reflection bears upon the alternative that must be rebuilt, but it also raises questions of the organisation and reorganisation of our political and social forces that are too often trapped in electoralist logics or naïve ultra-leftist insurrectionalist fantasies.

In these conditions, it is urgent to reflect on the way – even on the theoretical level – these existing emancipatory struggles can be unified without claiming to dictate the exact path they must follow or unifying them bureaucratically from above.

We must also return to questions pertaining to the rebuilding of militant and revolutionary culture – after decades of defeats and assaults, of uninterrupted propaganda from the ruling class media, of demonisation of revolution, disqualification of the vocabulary necessary to thinking about and speaking of any alternative, and therefore of building it.

My project began with this overall ideological situation, and its contradictions, by first moving through the relative return of the communist question on the theoretical terrain at a moment when its political disqualification is complete. I tried to precisely analyse the approaches of certain authors who have taken up the communist question while also situating them in their context and taking the time to re-examine the construction of a strategic alternative to capitalism. Because to actively participate in the revival of such strategy also takes place on the theoretical terrain.

You reverse the order of presentation by beginning with the most up to date philosophers who are read on the left (Alain Badiou, Ernesto Laclau and Antonio Negri) before treating Marx's ideas on emancipation and strategy. Why do you think it is important for a Marxist to take philosophers head-on? Aren't philosophers

ordinarily concerned with the search after Truth and the Good emptied of politics? You have elsewhere written a book about the relation of Michel Foucault, Gilles Deleuze and Louis Althusser to Marx – how do you understand the relations of philosophy, politics and history and why must you relate Marxism and philosophy? I take it that you do your best to show that Marxists take specific positions on philosophical questions.

Your question has many components. With respect to the inverse order of my presentation, it testifies to the fact that my work does not follow a history of ideas, even if I believe that the greatest care is required when one moves through a critical and contextualising reading. My purpose is to begin with the present and to return to it, by passing through that which could help us radically transform it. To commence with an analysis of current philosophical works seems pertinent to me for many reasons. First because it is on this terrain that the communist and socialist questions are re-emerging, in France at least. Second because the authors I have chosen have all upheld an extremely critical relation to Marx and to Marxism. This gives a political dimension to their works that allows a return to reading Marx from a contemporary point of view. Last because their works, the reception of which is important, are all vectors of a complex repoliticisation of left wing intellectual debate that is revitalising the question of social transformation. These authors therefore invite debate and offer points from which strategic reflection can be kicked off again.

But you also raise the question of philosophy, as an eternal form situated beyond historical contingencies without any or hardly any transformative will. If the philosophers of whom I spoke in this book and my earlier one are in fact inheritors of this model of *philosophia perennis* [perennial philosophy], they belong to a tradition whose relation to the political is constitutive and singular. To capture it briefly: the French philosophy that emerged in the 1970s tried to redefine the notion of intellectual engagement. Sartre's great stature served as a foil, because he was a fellow traveller of the Communist Party and a spokesperson for international causes.

There was a profound ideological turn in France at this time, an intellectual and media offensive against Marxism and the communist project under the slogan of anti-totalitarianism, and this discredited the universal Sartrean form of the intellectual. Michel Foucault and Gilles Deleuze (among others), who were at once removed from but tied to this general climate, participated in this transformation of the intellectual and political landscape in their own way; they both did so by originally reworking the philosophical terrain of it and by proposing micro-political orientations which were ambiguous but in opposition to the organisations of the workers' movement, a rupture with the very notion of class struggle and with any perspective of the abolition of capitalism.

These brilliant and innovative non-Marxist theoreticians durably impacted their time and the history of philosophy while participating in the post-modern rejection of "grand narratives" that often targeted a caricatured Marxism. Importantly, they were able to reconcile opposites: academism and its radical critique; the rejection of institutions and their expert use; the will towards political renovation and a growing tendency towards mass depoliticisation interrupted by May '68.

The authors I studied in this book inherit many of these characteristics. But because they are intervening in a very different context, they are also distant from them on many points: capitalism has not stabilised, quite the contrary, and resistance was scattered by the crisis of the Fordist-Keynesian compromise and the ruling classes' thirst to win back their gains indeed weakened forms of class struggle on our side. Though all those I have chosen to discuss uphold an offensive conception of critical intervention, and though they put the discussion with Marx and Marxism at the heart of their own elaboration, they advocate a turn to a very different path that they suggest is capable of sustaining a possible social and political transformation at a time when the ruling classes are everywhere leading an intensifying social war.

One of the most striking features of this present conjuncture is therefore the return of the theme of communism on the theoretical terrain, more exactly the philosophical terrain. This positive use of the term "communism" remains a marginal one, but up to a certain point it reactivates the hope that was once invested in it, all the while remaining divorced from concrete political perspectives. And it is here that we find certain constant themes of a certain type of contemporary philosophical intervention: *usefully radicalising the critique of the existing world, it also tends to avoid the question of transitions and mediations, that is to say, the question of the means and organisations (concentrating instead on the ends), cut off from the building of social and political mobilisations.*

From this angle, Alain Badiou, Ernesto Laclau and Toni Negri, among others, all share two distinctive traits: on the one hand, they illustrate the durable fragmentation of alternatives and the cordoning off of previously related themes, in privileging certain lines to the detriment of others. So Badiou focuses on the state and the party, Laclau on hegemony, and property for Negri and the theorists of the commons; on the other hand, they try to repoliticise theory but it remains within the fold of theory itself. In other words, this repoliticisation of theory remains dependent on the displacement of politics by philosophy (a shift from politics to philosophy), and that is congruous with, and reactualises, the very same critique of Marxism developed between the 1960s and 1980s.

This is why I think it's important to delicately evaluate this displacement which is neither a flight away from politics nor a direct taking up of politics, but rather the symptom of its crisis and an aspiration towards its renewal. And it's also necessary to seize the moment, in the purview of the revitalisation of collective reflection as to the alternative to capitalism by starting from the paradox of this politics that refers to "communism" – the sign of the problematic links between an emancipatory project and its concretisation.

I'd like you to outline your critique of Alain Badiou. In Australia you can make a career in philosophy out of an obsession with Alain Badiou. Of course, this is divorced from any commitment to radical politics beyond a banal verbalism, and it's an example of the way Anglophone academics spend their lives propagating the

ideas of whoever is *à la mode* on the continent. They naively treat Badiou's relation to Maoist politics as a historical curiosity – tell a few jokes about Badiou's Maoism, show your leftist credentials and then move on to the serious business of abstract philosophy. But you argue that in fact Badiou's philosophical production is intimately part of his Maoist political project and, while creative, both of these projects have their limitations. Why?

Well the first thing to underline is that Alain Badiou is one of the most stimulating philosophers alive today, one of those rare thinkers who is known and renowned for intransigently brandishing the banner of communism. One can reproach him for making a banner out of it (which tends towards schematism) and neither must one adhere to the philosophical construction that is indissociable from it in his work. But at a time when celebrity pseudo-intellectuals reign supreme, who are downright mediocre and wilfully collaborate in the rise of reactionary and racist ideas in France, Badiou is a laudable exception. His reception is a complex question from this point of view: if one remains focused on the epigones, one could correctly denounce an empty rhetoric that is merely gestural. But the greatest part of his audience is far away from all academic ambition and is actually searching for a renovated theoretical-political orientation. I'm addressing this kind of readership.

In order to do this, it seemed more interesting to situate the authors I discuss in their time and their trajectory – simultaneously intellectual and political – than to just contradict them. Badiou's example is fascinating. He was born into a well-cultured left wing family (in 1937 – his father was in the resistance, mayor of Toulouse and a founder of the Unified Socialist Party). He undertook his philosophy studies at the prestigious *École Normale Supérieure* in Paris at a time when Louis Althusser taught there and regrouped around him a plethora of brilliant young philosophers. Althusser was also a critical militant of the French Communist Party, and he would never leave it. When the internal political debates hit and were crossed through with international questions as well as the opposition between the USSR and China, some of Althusser's students came closer to the Chinese road and founded the Union of Marxist-Leninist Communists in France (1969): Badiou was part of this. He subsequently founded the Political Organisation (1985) which continued this same strategic orientation and was marked by a virulent rejection of the state and institutional forms in general, parties and trade unions included.

Badiou never reneged on his strategic choices but his initial orientations underwent considerable transformations, profoundly structuring his philosophical reflection even to the ontological and mathematical dimension which purifies his theses. We can say that with him a certain form of French philosophy of the 1970s, which was elaborated over a period of political retreat, conserved the spirit of protest and aspirations that are reawakening and renewing themselves today.

Hence if communism is for him an Idea, his purpose is absolutely not to affirm the primacy of theory *over* reality: the Idea according to Badiou is not a norm that is outside the historical process but an immanent norm, whose resurgence punctuates history to the tune of its repeated failures. An Idea is thus not destined to be realised (in the victory of communism) but to manifest itself in history, its defeats not impeding but actually guaranteeing its eternal return. And so also its eternal defeat! But this thesis should be discussed. It goes hand in hand with a re-exploration of the dialectic and a critique of representation (in the philosophical and political meaning of the term) which implies a rejection of institutions and a critique of democratic forms as if they are destined to bureaucratic relapse.

Communism is conceived of as a permanent popular mobilisation. It exists only as a historical convulsion, not as an instituted alternative: this exalting or exalted conception leans towards historical pessimism. Above all this ontology of history prevents thinking through the non-delegated forms of representation, associated with the control and the revocability of those elected. It abandons the exploration of radically democratised forms of communism of a new generation, concerned to renew collective planning over social life while also being against barracks socialism and the free market.

It is exactly this type of question that we are today confronted with. It invites us to critically debate Badiou's proposed reading of Marx, when the latter analysed the Paris Commune, its institutional inventions and its forms of mobilisation. More generally, Badiou's hostility to "socialism" goes back to his refusal to pose the question of dialectical articulation and mediations that are so urgent to revisit today, if we want to finally succeed in exiting from capitalism and constructing a viable and democratic social organisation.

Your chapter on the late Ernesto Laclau is very valuable. With the renewed prospects of socialist electoralism, left reformist currents have looked to Laclau's defence of left populism as a way of politically organising. Omar Hassan has written about this in an article titled "Podemos and left populism" in this journal.[1] When Laclau and Mouffe's book *Hegemony and Socialist Strategy: Towards a Radical Democratic Politics* was first published, the *New Left Review* ran Norman Geras' incisive criticisms of their philosophical presuppositions, political arguments and cheap digs at Marx.[2] Geras argued that the reach and hold of ideas is not always a direct function of their truth or quality, and that Laclau and Mouffe had blurted out an ex-Marxism without substance that in fact led to an impasse. Geras argued that socialist thought faced a two-fold difficulty. On the one hand socialist thought must understand the world, and to discover truths about the world is a many-headed collective effort involving open debate. On the other hand, socialist thought confronts different forms of hostility, "pressed in from all directions by those ready to write it off, deride it, belittle both its hopes and achievements as illusion or dross".[3] Laclau and Mouffe had met this two-fold difficulty

---

[1] Omar Hassan, "Podemos and left populism", *Marxist Left Review*, 11, 2016, Summer.

[2] https://newleftreview.org/issues/I163/articles/norman-geras-post-marxism.pdf and https://newleftreview.org/issues/I169/articles/norman-geras-ex-marxism-without-substance-being-a-real-reply-to-laclau-and-mouffe.pdf.

[3] https://newleftreview.org/issues/I169/articles/norman-geras-ex-marxism-without-substance-being-a-real-reply-to-laclau-and-mouffe.pdf.

improperly by taking intellectual short cuts that led back to liberal democratic criticisms of Marxism which have already been answered many times over. Thus, Laclau and Mouffe reinforced the anti-Marxist backlash going on at the time in several European countries to the benefit of bourgeois parliamentary democracy. Can you take us through the key steps of your critique of Laclau?

That's right – the works of Laclau and Mouffe have been widely criticised, particularly in the Anglophone world, and fuelled the debate on the question of socialism and also on strategy and hegemony, and this it to their merit. In the end, we can judge their contributions to be paltry and that their proposed political orientation had nothing whatsoever new to it: I share this criticism. But on this point again it is necessary to read Laclau's texts closely, on account of the impact they have had today on a part of the radical left, and again considering the intellectual and political trajectory that sheds light on the theses he argued for.

Before elaborating on these remarks, we must begin by noting that Laclau's profile is quite different from Badiou's. Laclau was born in Argentina and was trained in a singular Argentinean political culture. He was a member of a far left party that decided to support Peron, who was deemed anti-imperialist. He constantly reaffirmed his faithfulness to his initial commitment, even if he evolved towards liberal institutional choices later on. And actually, we can take Peronism to have remained the matrix of Laclau's later conception of populism as the construction of an alliance beyond the boundaries of class, which involves the articulation and aggregation of diverse demands (that can even be incommensurable) that can be embodied in the figure of a leader.

From this vantage point, one can say that Laclau is one of the rare authors to stand on the ground of strategic reflection, even if he reduces the field solely to the question of winning hegemony within the framework of existing institutions and capitalism. We can say that his work consorts with the contemporary ideological turn, without analysing it but also without giving up political intervention. And his methods are subtle.

Hence for instance, Laclau argues that social classes only exist through their struggles. This thesis is also Marx's. But Laclau radicalises it to the point of cutting off the definition of this struggle from all conflicts of social and economic interest, anchored in the very structure of the capitalist mode of production. Because no class is an alternative, it must be given to it from the outside: the leader is a demiurge, working for the political unification of a social world that is fragmented by definition. The success of this intervention depends only on the judicious selection of a demand or of one "interpellation" among others, able to catalyse them. Hegemony finds itself redefined as a tool to access social and political power such as it stands, very far indeed from the notion that is borrowed from Gramsci.

More generally, Marxism in Laclau's eyes is simultaneously an obsolete theory and a reservoir of notions to redefine, a vocabulary to renew. The way he debates Marx's theses is often devoid of any rigor. Laclau knows he can count on a general lack of knowledge when it comes to Marx, Marxism and the failures of statised socialism, by attributing to Marx the project of a communism that is summed up in the "dictatorship of the proletariat" and in playing with the sinister resonances of the term "dictatorship" throughout the twentieth century.

Because of this pruning operation, emancipatory strategy is redefined as the fabrication of an effective subterfuge, of a unifying myth, close to the ideas developed by Georges Sorel at the turn of the twentieth century (his nationalist and anti-Semitic side would distance him from all emancipatory perspectives). The essential point for Laclau is to begin the linguistic and rhetorical turn of socialism, with only "discursive constructions" being able to confer a provisional coherence to a social world that is fundamentally fragmented and malleable, blind to its own future. This is what the word "populism" means in strategic terms: not the popular will, but in reality, its opposite, the construction of a people by the strategist who presents himself as its expression, its incarnation, and not as its representative or its delegate subject to collective control.

Laclau elaborates a very particular style that is in profound agreement with this compass-less strategy. It is deeply eclectic, heteroclite even, mixing the most diverse references, from Kautsky to Barthes, from Gramsci to Wittgenstein, from Marx to Schmitt – conforming to the image of a fragmented social world he describes; this is carried out while trying to rhetorically illustrate and legitimise a pragmatist politics that disguises itself as a radical innovation. From this point of view, when Laclau defines political intervention as the discursive elaboration of a demand that pre-exists it, he actually correctly describes what is in fact the manner in which his own theory is built!

This alternative to the alternative ultimately takes liberal democracy's word for good coin. Laclau began by decoupling socialism and communism: his double rejection of political mediations and anti-capitalist goals eventually led him to propose what one could call a "post-socialism" – a political pendant of post-Marxism – that is nothing more than bourgeois parliamentary democracy led back to its own abstract and empty ideal: the pluralism of opinions. At a time when democracy is decomposing, to recall the slogans of classical liberalism can seem quasi-subversive! But fundamentally, Laclau's goal is merely to rehabilitate intervention in the institutional political field as it currently stands, by acknowledging the growing popular rejection of it while also reaffirming its unsurpassable horizon. This conception calls for debate, given the resonance it today has in France and Spain.

I'd like to move now to your chapters on Marx, on emancipation and strategy respectively. You are against reading Marx in a purely Marxological way and insist on the political dimensions of Marx's work. You call for a renewed political reading of Marx and communism, anchored in the critique of political economy. What did you want your readers to draw from your chapter on Marx, communism and emancipation?

This question forms the heart of the book. I am one of those who considers Marx's thought to have an unparalleled ability to encourage a critical analysis of capitalist relations of exploitation and domination, which are constantly changing. Far from being descriptive, this analysis is part and parcel of the perspective of a radical transformation of social reality, which is its condition even more than its consequence. It is precisely this critical potential – at once theoretical and militant – always in need of readjustment and being brought up to date, which manifests itself particularly in the strategic field, in a way that has hardly been touched on enough until now.

Far from presenting Marx as the bearer of an eternal truth, with a view of giving a lesson to all those who deviate away from such eternal truth, the purpose of my book is actually the opposite: since authors today are renewing themes of communism (and socialism), since the question of the alternative always searches for, and forges itself, within the social relations and existing ideas, let us start from these contemporary questions to reread Marx in their light and ask the great question that concerns us all anew: that of the abolition of capitalism.

The chapters dedicated to Marx are focused on the constant development of his conception of communism which is never a project he has readymade answers for, but neither is it an evanescent and indefinable notion. The term names the complex process of building a political path of the radical contestation of capitalism, the permanent invention of the theoretical and practical means to achieve it, all the while sketching the outlines of the society to invent.

This is why we can say Marx's communism is *strategic* and is far from many historical interpretations that ossify and simplify his arguments.

Marx's questions are still our own: what are the contradictions of capitalism and how to intervene into it? How to build organisations that lead social struggles to their revolutionary terminus? How to confront the question of the state and democracy? How to conjoin and mobilise different social forces bearing emancipatory projects that are not necessarily the same? The revolutions of the nineteenth and twentieth centuries have faced all of these obstacles. To return to Marx from this vantage point is not at all to look for readymade answers, but to raise questions that still concern us and to find analyses that retain – in many ways – an unparalleled power if we reactivate the political scope of them.

When Marxism was under attack in France and Italy in the 1980s, one of the key arguments mobilised against its adherents was that it lacked a specific "politics". They basically said that Marxism dissolves politics into economics. You have coedited *Political Marx* and tried to show the political content of Marxism and I find your chapter on Marx's communism as strategy a further contribution to this debate. You insist on the revolutionary potential of labour power, and you claim that this potential has political and epistemological consequences (that reformists and liberals fail to comprehend) which tie critical knowledge and political rebellion together. Why should Marx be read with an eye to communism as strategy? What were the key moments in the development of Marx's strategic thought, and why do they matter for our present?

This reading of Marx as an anti-political author remains the dominant interpretation today. It is correct in one way if we consider that Marx fundamentally redefines the notion of politics, by refusing to cut it off from economic and social dimensions, inaugurating a "critique of political economy" that articulates them. But above all, Marx's analysis bears on the contradictions and on the manners of intervening into them: far from proposing a model of the ideal society, prior to its historical construction and taken to polish off the meaning of history in a definitive sense, Marx calls "communism" a political construction based on the class struggle. And in days gone by, as today, the struggles of ideas take part in these class struggles.

One of the central tenets of this Marxian communism concerns the transformations of the relations of property, which form the legal structure of capitalism. Today, it is common to encounter a critique of capitalism that denounces consumerism and consumers, who are judged incurably intoxicated by the dependence on commodities. This critique disarms action and fails to understand the complexity of the wage relation, where the conditions of life and the spirit of revolt, the aspiration to social justice and the adhesion to the competitive vision of the world, and the whole gamut of their interrelations, are tied together. It also misses the dimension of individuality as a contradictory place where aspirations, constraints and consent collide.

It is at this precise point that communist intervention takes on its full meaning, as a politicisation and collective organisation of this social rage that is everywhere today being felt again, and which takes contradictory – regressive as well as emancipatory – forms. Marx thinks it through in a powerful way: as the abolition of large scale capitalist property and of the regime of wage slavery, and as the appropriation of the self (individual and collective) aiming towards the development of autonomy, human faculties, collective social control, of the reorganisation of time. For Marx, capitalist social relations organise the theft of human activity and its products, this fundamental dispossession affecting the human subject with full force.

The central motor power of the class struggle is the propertyless taking back the proceeds of their exploited labour. This is a central place where a possible forming of class consciousness can take shape. The associated producers must take back that which they never actually had, but which they are clearly lacking: the collective control of their working conditions, the production and distribution of wealth that is produced by them.

Once the extent of this re-appropriation is redefined, which involves the development of unprecedented potentialities, the difficulty lies in making it a credible and mobilising political objective, placed at the heart of revolutionary strategy: it is precisely this question that Marx tackles both in *Capital* and in the political writings, whether they be interventions or analyses, weaving the question of ends and mediations (means) into a coherent whole.

The question of communism must therefore be posed at the heart of the "laboratory of production": against bourgeois political economy, Marx argues loud and clear that "labour is the substance, and the immanent measure of value, but has itself no value".[4]

---

[4]   Marx, *Capital*, 1, chapter 19: "The Transformation of the Value (and Respective Price) of Labour-Power into Wages", https://www.marxists.org/archive/marx/works/1867-c1/ch19.htm.

It's precisely here that exploitation and domination are knotted together and clash with the social rage they evoke, forming a contradiction that is as economic as it is social and individual: "That which comes directly face to face with the possessor of money on the market, is in fact not labour, but the labourer", Marx writes.[5] It is the workers' faculties that are simultaneously forged and denied, their emancipation that is met and denied, that drives the producers to struggle for the shortening of the working day and, in the end, against capitalism as such. The question of property widens here to the question of emancipation. We are far from having a communist program that remains exterior and anterior to the class struggles and its actors.

The book ends with an argument for what you call a "strategy of mediations". What is this, and why is it necessary?

Strategy, for all those who want to abolish capitalism and who think a revolutionary perspective fitting for our time is relevant, commences by understanding the difficulty and the complexity of such a historical process. Humanity has never yet succeeded in organising collective mastery over its becoming and future. Now under the penalty of extinction, we must accomplish this colossal effort without any further delay. This is why the construction of an alternative resides not only in the theoretical elaboration of another world, but, on the one hand, in the ability to connect it to a project of radical transformation and, on the other hand, to connect it to the collective mobilisations and individual aspirations as they exist today.

To bring these two sides – project and resistance – into a coherent project is the political task *par excellence*. It moves through the invention of mediations. Mediations aren't merely means, still less stages, but living forms. They are democratic forms of organisation, of mobilisation and struggles, programs and collectively elaborated projects. But they also constitute an activist culture that participates in the reconstruction of forms of life – social and political – that are inviting and able to grow. In short, these are the multiple forms of

---

[5] ibid.

class struggle conscious of its conditions and finalities, and of their inseparable character.

The task is possible, as difficult as it seems: it is enough to have participated in a long strike or a mobilisation that has lasted some time to know just how quickly and with what intensity the shared joy of a true social life that is intense and rich, of labour reconsidered, of time liberated, can flower in these moments of struggle. How can these possibilities spread, consolidate themselves and discuss matters further? Reflections in action and theorising interventions, they are situated at the meeting point of existing structures, parties, trade unions, associations, all the while having to go beyond their institutional contours in a constructive way.

How is it possible to rally this dynamic without choking it, in fighting against the alienating logic of politics as well as the purely spontaneous outbursts that have no future? How to escape the double pitfall of utopianism without struggle and struggles without hope? It is the perspective of such a strategic revival that we must explore, in taking up the best of what the socialist and communist traditions have left for us to use and explore. One book is unable to give the answers, but the current absence of strategic debate in the strong sense of the term for the moment fuels the dispersion of protest. But the lack also fuels the proliferation of theoretical solutions that are intended to be final, panaceas destined to benefit from the crisis of concrete alternatives.

My book is intended to contribute to this revived confrontation, all the while demanding the project of a collectively decided abolition of capitalism.

That which is called, yesterday as today, a *revolution.*

REVIEW: WORKERS' ANTI-WAR RESISTANCE IN JAPAN

SHOMI YOON

Masao Sugiura, *Against the Storm: How Japanese Printworkers Fought the Military Regime, 1935-1945* (trans. Kaye Broadbent and Mana Sato). Interventions, Melbourne, 2019.

Against the Storm is a compelling memoir of the struggles of printworkers' leader Masao Sugiura, active at the height of Japanese militarism during the Pacific War. Sugiura recounts his experiences in the *Shuppankō Kurabu* (The Print and Publishing Workers Club), demonstrating how Japanese workers struggled against the imperial state, and pushed to defend the rights of workers and the unemployed.

Few readers – Japanese or non-Japanese – will be familiar with this history of Japanese anti-war resistance. The dominant narrative asserts that every Japanese worker was sycophantically loyal to the emperor and the war effort. This myth was one of the main motivations for Sugiura to write his memoir of resistance. He wanted to preserve a record of workers' war-time resistance to show that "the print and publishing industry union movement continued, preventing the organisation of workers from completely disappearing". Translators Kaye Broadbent and Mana Sato bring this history to English readers for the first time.

Shomi Yoon is a member of the International Socialist Organisation Aotearoa/New Zealand, an editor of *Socialist Review*, and active in the teachers' union Te Wehengarua Post Primary Teachers' Association.

Against the Storm gives a rich and detailed history of how workers organised against the war and for their own interests in one of modern Japan's darkest times. Sugiura incorporates diverse sources ranging from personal memoir, quotes from activists and even Special Police archives.

For activists and socialists today this memoir contributes a number of invaluable lessons.

Firstly, a political group's organisational structures must be flexible and adaptable to changing political circumstances. The Club started out as a Society, which operated as a trade union. Sugiura's own politicisation came while being on the strike committee at Tokyo Printing in 1935. Club leader and covert Japanese Communist Party (JCP) member Shibata Ryūichirō led the committee. The strike ended in defeat but drew in new layers of activists to organised industrial politics. Shortly after this, the anti-war JCP was effectively smashed by the state. One CP member describes it as the "period when our lives were advancing into darkness". Leaders Iwata Yoshimichi and Kobayashi Takiji were tortured to death by the police, and state violence broke the party.

Increased state repression prompted Shibata to argue for a different approach for the Society, focusing on social activities for workers instead of open politics. He was adamant that they would be "destroyed if it took a more militant approach". Shibata insisted that they should become a social club to avoid detection by the Special Police and be able to reach a mass audience: "whatever small and routine thing we do, we are assisting workers, gathering members, and developing them and raising their class consciousness".

The Club began to organise cultural and sporting activities and events; raise train fares and funds for unemployed members; it put on theatre performances and established book clubs, tramping clubs, even haiku clubs.

The Club never reached that mass base Sugiura hoped for, peaking at around 1,500 members. Nevertheless growing from 200 during the period of the most intense state repression was an admirable achievement, and required courage and tenacity from activists. The 1930s were a bleak time for youth. Sugiura describes a cartoon where a young person faces three roads: "one was the road to suicide, another was the road to decadence and the third was the road to Marxism". The Club nurtured and developed new layers of activists who had no other outlet towards a political direction.

The second lesson Sugiura impresses on readers is the old leftist adage that workers will always resist. "Even during the darkness of wartime", Sugiura recalls, "no matter how much the government increased the repression, the dissatisfaction with the war spread among those living at the bottom of society. There were endless instances of people making anti-war remarks at meetings or distributing dangerous literature…". Sugiura quotes anti-war comments scribbled on the 1942 election ballot papers, such as "You cannot fight on an empty stomach", or "The government is our enemy, what are small business owners to do?" Resistance was not always open. Some expressed discontent by turning up to work late or leaving early, moving from factory to factory illegally, working only when the supervisor was present, or even behaving violently towards supervisors and managers.

The Club attempted to connect these frustrations and demands covertly through social activities. Activists were schooled on how to evade the police by avoiding police boxes (small booths acting as mini-police stations on the side of major streets), learning to memorise addresses, keeping safe in political settings, and how to talk to potential recruits. Sugiura details methods for meeting new recruits in the factories, such as by conducting surveys on the cultural interests of the workplace – this could be used to invite potential recruits to a film appreciation group or hiking club.

When state repression intensified, it was only a matter of time before the Club leaders were arrested: Sugiura, Shibata and Shiraishi were all arrested in 1942, and remained imprisoned until the end of the war. Shibata tragically died in prison six months before the war finished, just 38 years old. Sugiura recounts the anguish and grief of losing his comrade and mentor. Sugiura's wife was also killed during the US mass bombing of Tokyo.

The third and final lesson Sugiura offers is the necessity of continuing to build an organisation even though the political situation seems futile. As soon as the war concluded, there was a flourishing of democratic movements from below. Comrades active in the Club threw themselves into the democracy movement. Union membership in late 1945 was 600,000, rising to 6.7 million by June 1948. A May Day demonstration attracted 2 million workers nationwide in 1946. As the translators note, the Club could remain relevant precisely because "the overwhelming determination of Sugiura and many other activists to keep union traditions alive in Japan during the period of militarism bore fruit very early in the post-war period and many Club members were at the centre of this activity". After the war, club members helped print the JCP newspaper *Akahata* (Red Flag), and build the "foundation for democratic print works throughout the country". As a Club commemorative event noted, "because Club members …kept the flame of the print and publishing workers' struggle, despite all the repression they had to endure [they] passed on their revolutionary tradition and noble spirit of self-sacrifice."

Against the Storm is a valuable memoir told from the experiences of a rank and file print worker. It helps us to understand the mindset of an activist in the most difficult of times, reflect on organisational structures, and explore the different debates among print workers during military rule in Japan. Masao Sugiura's memoir is an essential record and historical monument.

REVIEW:
THE POLITICS OF THE
INDONESIAN UNION MOVEMENT

BEN REID

Max Lane, *An Introduction to the Politics of the Indonesian Union Movement.* ISEAS, Singapore, 2019.

Between 2009 and 2015, sections of Indonesia's nascent trade union movement attempted to enter the political fray. Many political and trade union activists hoped that an independent workers' party could emerge. These hopes floundered, and key trade union leaders instead ran for political office with existing parties, even endorsing authoritarian and anti-human rights policies. Max Lane presents a sobering assessment of these trends, largely focusing on comparatively strong areas of trade union organisation among the industrial belt on the outskirts of Jakarta.

Trade union coverage in Indonesia is a mere 3 percent of the labour force, or 5 million members. This low union density is a product of both political and historical factors. The independence struggle against Dutch colonisers had resulted in a strong influence of radical nationalism and the left in Indonesia before 1965. Then President Sukarno's attempts to allow the Indonesian Communist Party into government resulted in a pre-emptive wave of repression and mass killings by the army and Islamist organisations. These

Ben Reid, a long-term socialist activist, has researched and written extensively on Southeast Asian politics. He is the author of *Philippine Left: Political crisis and social change* (2000, Manila and Sydney: Journal of Contemporary Asia).

effectively destroyed the left and ended Sukarno's rule. The subsequent "New Order" dictatorship of President Haji Mohamed Suharto and his GOLKAR party (*Partai Golongan Karya* [Party of Functional Groups]) lasted until 1998.

While Suharto presided over what appeared to be a steadily growing capitalist economy with substantial petroleum export revenue, only a small section of the population benefited. Industrialisation remained limited, poverty levels high, and the Suharto family and other members of his clique of supporters siphoned off much of the proceeds of economic growth.

However, at least three currents of trade unionism emerged. First and notionally largest was the regime-sponsored SPSI (*Serikat Pekerja Seluruh Indonesia* [All Indonesian Workers' Union]). It largely functioned to dampen down any militancy amongst the country's growing labour force.

Second, a dissident current emerged as the SBSI (Serikat Buruh Sejahtera Indonesia [Indonesian Workers' Welfare Union]), in 1992. It brought together dissidents from the SPSI and non-government organisations.

Third, there were more radical and dissident currents. The most notable was probably the PPBI (*Pusat Perjuangan Buruh Indonesia* [Centre for Indonesian Working Class Struggle]). It was aligned with the radical PRD party (*Partai Rakyat Demokratik* [People's Democratic Party]) that originated among student activists.

Amid growing political opposition and the impacts of the 1997-8 Asian economic crisis, Suharto was toppled in 1998, and a period of "*reformasi*" (reform) followed. Notionally free elections were held in 1999.

Trade unions adjusted slowly to the *reformasi* period, and remained quite weak after 1999. None had played a direct role in bringing down the regime. Repression and harassment against unionists continued. The pace of political struggle declined, while elite-based political parties consolidated, and the small radical left fragmented.

Nevertheless, some strong points of organisation emerged. Some of the old political demarcations in the unions broke down. A plethora of organisations emerged in the factory belt outside Jakarta. The most significant were the KSPI (*Konfederasi Serikat Perkerja Indonesia* ([Confederation of Indonesian Trade Unions]) and its main affiliate the FSPMI (*Federasi Serikat Pekerja Metal Indonesia* [Indonesian Metal Workers' Union Federation]).

The FSPMI increasingly consolidated a base of members in the manufacturing sector after 2000, especially in motorcycle and car assembly plants. Officials from the SPSI tradition even allowed radical activists from the dissident trade union currents to play an organising and educational role. A well organised "Garda Metal brigade" was formed that was crucial to the success of demonstrations and pickets.

These newly consolidated unions took up political issues, mobilising a national campaign of mobilisations and demonstrations between 2008 and 2011, after Indonesia's Congress failed to implement its 2004 Bill on Social Security Providers. In 2012 unions campaigned for wage rises, including an increase in the minimum wage. There was a considerable upswing in strikes and protests, culminating in a 2 million strong "national strike" in October. Workers successfully forced large wage increases.

After this, the momentum suddenly halted. Trade union, business and government figures signed a declaration of industrial harmony. The presence of leftists and other activists from the dissident trade union tradition in the FSPMI was quickly curtailed.

FSPMI leaders made a highly opportunist turn to electoral tactics. Rather than form an independent workers' or labour-based party, its leaders ran as candidates for numerous elite-based parties. From 2013 the "*Go Politik!*" campaign substituted for workplace organising and participation in mobilisations and alliances. Disgracefully, Said Iqbal, a central leader of the FSPMI, became a supporter of Prabowo Subianto's presidential campaign. A Suharto-era general, Prabowo was associated with many accusations of human rights abuses. He and his *Gerindra* party (*Partai Gerakan Indonesia Raya* [Great Indonesia Movement Party]) had only split from GOLKAR in 2008.

By late 2013, any rallies and demonstrations that were called were turned into pro-Prabowo gatherings. Other federations and groupings – confusingly – supported rival Joko Widodo's candidacy.

Indonesian electoral politics was now a contest between two rival camps committed to a neoliberal model of economic development, and with only marginally different policies. Widodo tempered these policies with some moderate social reforms, such as expanding subsidised public health. Prabowo largely shared the same outlook but wanted a more disciplined approach to development and increasingly cultivated ties to conservative political Islamist currents.

Lane concludes rather ominously:

> [T]he "ideological" basis for organizing, mobilizing and agitating… [centres on] the phenomenon called "populism" – an agitational appeal to a broad coalition of the various segments of the poor and popular classes against the elite or against groups identified as the cause of popular poverty and economic backwardness… This has become an increasingly evident feature of contemporary Indonesian politics, and of political contestation within organised labour… reflected in the KSPI/FSPMI's and other unions' alliance with the Islamic populism initially targeted against…President Widodo. That populism alleges that Chinese, infidel communists and false Muslims are the cause of the suffering of the popular classes…

The dissident trade union tradition of support for social mobilisation for social and political mobilisations, therefore, faces serious challenges.

Lane presents this sobering analysis well. However, when absorbed in a case study it is important to remember that not all readers share the same level of interest or background knowledge. Some of the "blow by blow" narrative could have been jettisoned in favour of more explicit general reflection on the study's broader implications. Are there more specific features of the Indonesian experience that have relevance in other situations?

More discussion and analysis of the historical features and the weaknesses of Indonesian capitalism and industrialisation could have enriched the analysis. Lane goes some of the way, noting that organised workers in large firms are only a small section of the working class. What emerges is a story of trade union leaders and political opportunism.

Some incorporation of Marxist insights on trade union bureaucracy and political opportunism would have been interesting. These are not and have never been the monopoly of the so-called "labour aristocracy" of the more developed capitalist countries.

Finally, how deep are the problems of Islamism and populism that Lane flags? Can they be redeemed in a more leftward direction, or is the ability of the dissident trade union activist layer to rekindle mass support for an independent socialist politics contingent on changes in mass struggle on a global scale?

www.ingramcontent.com/pod-product-compliance
Lightning Source LLC
Chambersburg PA
CBHW060035030426
42334CB00019B/2343